John Maynard Keynes:
Language and Method

ADVANCES IN ECONOMIC METHODOLOGY

General Editor: Warren J. Samuels

Michigan State University, US

This major new series presents original and innovative work in economic methodology, including all aspects of the philosophy, sociology and rhetoric of economics as well as the relationship of economics to other disciplines.

The series reflects the renewed interest in all aspects of economic methodology as well as the deepening sense both of conceptual and technical crisis plaguing the economics profession and that the crisis involves deep methodological considerations. It is also hoped that the series will contribute to the better understanding and solution of the economic problems of both mature and developing countries.

The series is open to all points of view and approaches.

Truth versus Precision in Economics
Thomas Mayer

John Maynard Keynes: Language and Method
Edited by Alessandra Marzola and Francesco Silva

Classical Economic Man
Human Agency and Methodology in the Political Economy
of Adam Smith and J.S. Mill
Allen Oakley

The Nature of Economic Thought
Essays in Economic Methodology
Johannes J. Klant

John Maynard Keynes: Language and Method

Edited by

Alessandra Marzola

Department of English Literature
University of Bergamo, Italy

and

Francesco Silva

Department of Economics
Università degli Studi di Torino, Italy

Translated by Richard Davies

Edward Elgar

Published by
Edward Elgar Publishing Limited
Gower House
Croft Road
Aldershot
Hants GU11 3HR
England

Edward Elgar Publishing Company
Old Post Road
Brookfield
Vermont 05036
USA

British Library Cataloguing in Publication Data
John Maynard Keynes: Language and Method. –
(Advances in Economic Methodology
Series)
   I. Marzola, Alessandra   II. Silva,
   Francesco   III. Series
   330.15

Library of Congress Cataloguing in Publication Data
John M. Keynes, linguaggio e metodo. English
   John Maynard Keynes: language and method/edited by Alessandra
   Marzola and Francesco Silva; with contributions by R. Bellofiore
   ... [et al.].
      p. cm. — (Advances in economic methodology)
   Includes bibliographical references and index.
   1. Keynes, John Maynard, 1883–1946—Language. 2. Economics–
  –Methodology—History—20th century. 3. Economics—Great Britain–
  –History—20th century. 4. Keynesian economics. I. Marzola,
  Alessandra. II. Silva, Francesco, 1942– . III. Bellofiore, R.
  (Riccardo) IV. Title. V. Series.
  HB103.K47J6313   1994
   330.15'6—dc20   93–33302
                                           CIP

ISBN 1 85278 923 9

Printed in Great Britain at the University Press, Cambridge

Contents

Contributors

Riccardo Bellofiore, Assistant Professor of Monetary Economics, Bergamo University.

Anna Carabelli, Professor of Monetary Economics, Padova University.

Maurizio Gotti, Assistant Professor of History of English Language, Bergamo University.

Rossana Bonadei, Researcher, English Literature, Bergamo University.

Alessandra Marzola, Professor of English Literature, Bergamo University.

Francesco Silva, Professor of Industrial Economics, Torino University.

Andrea Salanti, Assistant Professor of Economics, Bergamo University.

Foreword

Andrea Salanti

At first sight, the title of this collection might lead the reader to believe that it is meant to deal with themes such as the 'rhetoric of economics' and 'economics as a discourse' which have recently become more and more popular among economic methodologists, or with the equally recent upsurge of the 'new Keynesian fundamentalism'. Although a number of references and allusions to these issues may be found in some chapters, both their readings would be none the less somewhat partial and in some cases decidedly misleading if they are taken as the common concern hidden behind the whole collection.

In fact, the discussion which has resulted in the present volume originated from a different point of view, one which can be depicted as an attempt to challenge the rhetorical approach to economic methodology on its own grounds. As is well known, this methodological (or, if you prefer, anti-methodological) position hails from the observation that economists systematically infringe all the methodological prescriptions to which they appear to be committed, in deference to the philosophy of science. From what is nowadays a rather uncontroversial observation, the rhetorical approach jumps to a twofold conclusion. First, contrary to what more traditional methodological approaches would suggest, the really interesting object of methodological enquiry is the body of rhetorical devices actually employed by economists (and by scientists and other writers, for that matter). Second, prospective critics may be reassured that such an interest does not lead to throwing away all standards of good scientific practice, because every scientific community is already organized to encourage a sort of natural selection of the best arguments used in scientific 'conversations'.

All the contributors, as well as the author of this preface (who first suggested to the General Editor the appropriateness of publishing the English translation of this collection and who, therefore, feels some responsibility for the present outcome) share some dissatisfaction about both conclusions drawn by many who take the rhetorical approach. As to the first conclusion, we think that it would be clearly senseless to try to deny that 'rhetoric matters'. This is a perfectly innocuous statement, if not a triviality, so long as it is not spelt out more exactly. The real problem is to understand in what respect and to what extent such an acknowledgement really matters.

To the latter conclusion it can be objected that, fascinating as it may be, to approach the problem of the growth of knowledge and its inner rationality with the characteristic tools of economics is to run into a piece of circular reasoning. It would be pretty amazing if a discipline whose main methodological puzzle is the methodological status of the rationality hypothesis, were to rescue epistemology from the difficulties encountered in dealing with the rationality of scientists and/or science itself. The metaphor of the invisible hand is surely appealing; but it is doomed to remain what it is, a mere metaphor. In order to convert it into a convincing explanation, we should have to grasp both the difference between practical and scientific rationality, as well as the economics of the institutional setting in which science is currently practised. These are issues which are not best suited to making economists comfortable.

It is precisely in order to see what relevant consequences are likely to follow from a simple acknowledgement of the importance of rhetoric, without any presuppositions about its role in the growth of knowledge, that the editors of this collection have invited some linguists to try the strength of their specific competence against the issues of Keynes's language and method: the author of *Essays in Persuasion*, written well before the present hermeneutic fashion, is an obvious candidate for the role of case study in this field.

Ultimately, of course, it is the reader who will have to judge the quality of the achieved results. More details on the several concerns that have prompted this intellectual experiment may be found in the Introduction which follows; for my part I wish only to point out that, instead of simply claiming that 'rhetoric matters', all the authors have carefully investigated Keynes's language and its relations with its many-sided referents. In that way, they have surely arrived at a number of very interesting insights, but the whole picture is likely to appear somewhat less comprehensive than might have been expected at the beginning.

The conclusion to be drawn, in my opinion, is that rhetoric matters in a way rather different from that which McCloskey and others would have us believe. Indeed, to acknowledge that hermeneutic approaches may yield valuable services to the history of ideas does not necessarily imply that we must regard it as an anti-methodology or as the only historiographic approach to be followed.

Living in one of the few countries where rhetoric, by hook or by crook, has never ceased to be uncritically held in high esteem, we find such a conclusion not at all surprising. We know, as it were from daily experience, the unpleasant consequences of assigning to rhetoric tasks that it cannot perform satisfactorily. This does not prevent us, however, from recognizing its usefulness when employed to answer questions that can be properly dealt with by a rhetorical approach.

Andrea Salanti
Bergamo, Italy

Acknowledgements

The writings gathered in this volume arise from a programme of joint research among the Faculty of Foreign Languages and Literatures of the University of Bergamo, and the Faculties of Economics and Commerce of the Universities of Bergamo and Pavia.

The interdisciplinary project, making use of the skills of economists, linguists and literary scholars, and presented by the Department of Language Science of the University of Bergamo under the direction of Professor Alberto Castoldi, was approved by the Economic Science Committee of the Italian Ministry of Education, from which it received financial support.

During the four years in which the work was in progress, two seminars were held (6 February 1988 at the University of Pavia, and 23 June 1989 at the University of Bergamo) during which the participants presented their interim conclusions and discussed them with economists, linguists and literary scholars.

The authors would like to thank all those who took part in the two study days for their constructive interventions which helped to increase understanding of the matters under discussion.

Finally, particular thanks are due to professor Niccolò de Vecchi of the University of Pavia who offered invaluable advice, closely followed all stages of the research and discussed the individual parts of it with the various authors.

Editorial Note

All references to the works of John Maynard Keynes are to the *Collected Writings*, under the general editorship of Donald Moggridge and others, and published for the Royal Economic Society by Macmillan, London from 1973.

The abbreviation *CW* refers to this edition.

1. Introduction

Riccardo Bellofiore and Francesco Silva

This volume is the outcome of an intellectual experiment made possible by the physical arrangement of the University of Bergamo where
the Departments of Economics and of Literary Studies are situated side
by side. Although the distance between the concerns of the two groups
of scholars might at first seem to be unbridgeable, they live together in
the same 'grove'.

For several decades, perhaps since Robbins's classic definition in
1932, economists have been accustomed to regarding individuals as
endowed with a certain inherent rationality. Frequently, this boils down
to the logical procedure of choice among available options, in accordance with a criterion of efficiency in order to make the best use of
scarce resources capable of alternative application. In this way, human
behaviour is viewed from a very special perspective. Such an approach
applies to *any* human behaviour: it can have to do with activities which
produce or distribute wealth, with marriage, or even with criminality,
all considered as modes of behaviour involving choice. The perspective
in play is that of 'rational' decision-making, which takes notice only of
the most 'economical' way of getting from the givens of the situation
to the desired goal.

> We do not say that the production of potatoes is an economic activity and
> the production of philosophy is not. We say rather that in so far as either
> kind of activity involves the relinquishment of other desired alternatives it
> has an economic aspect. There are no limitations to the object of economic
> enquiry save this.[1]

What is in question is a mind-set which might be thought of as
second nature to economists. They are trained into it from the first year
of their studies in the subject. Of course, there are other definitions of
economic 'science', which, after all, began as the study of the ways that
wealth is made and which was therefore an aid to good government;

economic science as 'political economy' is suggested by the very title of Smith's *The Wealth of Nations*. Of course, it is increasingly widely recognized that the assumptions underlying that sort of 'rationality' are very, and perhaps too, strong, so much so that it has become necessary to rethink almost the whole of the definition, from the indifference towards the processes of the production of goods, to the reductive treatment of choice as calculation, and to the neutrality as regards ends.

The worries which are in play have, however, not yet much influenced the procedures of the 'normal' economist. Both in the way that it is taught and in the way it is practised today, economics is still picked out not so much by the objects of its study as by the method in accordance with which that study is conducted. No one would claim that the assumption that individuals act in accordance with the directives of a rational calculus is really a description of how they do behave; but such a calculus is nevertheless regarded as the proper starting point for giving an account of how they should act if they wish to be rational (and who would want to be irrational?).

Thus, economics can present herself imperialistically as the queen of the social sciences, claiming to be able to discuss everything and to be universal in space and time. Economics has therefore crystallized a language which is suited to the expression of her universalizing and reductivist aims. This is an analytic language with increasingly formalized inflexibility. It is a language that is meant to be neutral in rendering hypotheses as determinate propositions, and in translating ideas into scientific proposals. It has, therefore, become not just one among many means for expressing, sometimes appropriately and sometimes not, what we know about society; it has become the sole 'style' that is regarded as scientific. As Robert Kuttner has pointed out, Economics Departments are turning out a generation of *idiots savants*, brilliant at the higher reaches of mathematics, yet out of touch with real economic life.

For literary scholars, on the other hand, the privileged object of study is ordinary language, and the variety and complexity of meanings which can be expressed within a single communicative system. This is a language presupposing a notion of the subject and of reality which is composite, unstable and governed by contradictory logics. We cannot imagine anything further from what economic theory likes to take for granted; it is like a negative (or positive?) in which light and shade are reversed, and value judgements are turned upside down. In this picture, the neatness of the calculus can seem like a tactic for repressing what is of the essence, and the unequivocalness of the formalized language can be seen as a straitjacket obstructing the growth of knowledge, rather than aiding it.

Working thus at close quarters with literary scholars, the economist is challenged to raise deep and sometimes disquieting questions about what is being stated and what is passed over in silence. It would be easy to reply by retreating into an office and continuing with economic pursuits, to set aside basic questions as uncomfortable, questions which seem too deep and the answers to which are uncertain and perhaps inconclusive. But it was not merely curiosity that provided the spur to face these questions. We may distinguish two phases of the positive motivation.

First, there was a psychological motivation offered by a certain sort of experience. For it sometimes happens, that in addition to writing books and papers in the technical and analytic language of the profession, the economist is called on to address a wider public in a 'freer' style. In the former case, the economist can feel confident, as a neutral purveyor of arguments, protected by method; although perhaps he or she also feels a bit hemmed in by the narrow space which the technical language offers. In the latter case, the economist is embarked on a wilder sea: language and method seem less dependable, and the results are less predictable. All the same, it sometimes seems that it is in this sort of writing that one has the feeling not only of enlarging the circle of communication but actually of getting further forward with the business of gathering knowledge.

Second, there is a more radical question which fleshes out the foregoing psychological observation. We have said that the attention which literary scholars give to language and to communicative strategies calls for more than a bland recognition of the importance of 'form' in economists' writing. Nor should we stop short at emphasizing the intersubjective nature of the scientific procedure in economics, as in any other discipline. If that were all that was at issue, it would be enough to say cheerfully that hitherto economists have disregarded the norms of the ethics of discussion, that mathematical talent had made them forget the importance of writing well, that demonstrative logic has to go hand in hand with rhetoric, and that you have to persuade if you want to convince. In short, it would have been enough to be prepared to dress up the same contents in clothes which are a bit more colourful than the usual scientific grey.

The more radical question concerns what Alessandra Marzola describes in Chapter 6 as a doubt about whether language is inextricable from the object of analysis. In the light of this hypothesis, the issue of the primacy of ordinary as against formalized language would be a symptom of an epistemological dispute which, in turn, raises questions about the features of the matters under investigation. Paradoxically, the status of economics as a science would be in question. Alternative, heterodox approaches expressed in a less rigid and artificial language, more indefinite and fluid approaches, might be better suited than the received view to fit onto an object which is organic and structurally unstable, such as the economic system itself.

Inasmuch as this sort of attitude is tending in the same direction as the most critical thoughts of contemporary economists themselves, we are invited to wonder whether, in a world of uncertainty and change, instrumental rationality is not an impoverished instrument of thought, and whether, by limiting our studies only to those behaviours which fit it snugly, we are not betraying a deeper irrationality. And whether what economists like to call 'imperfections' are not, after all, the norm.

The challenge about language presented by literary scholars has seemed fruitful and has potentially wide-ranging implications. The problem was not so much to decide whether the First General Theorem of Welfare was richer in ideas or more persuasive than *The Merchant of Venice*, whether the language of science was more or less useful for describing human situations than a symbolic, metaphorical or poetic language would be. Rather, the problem was to adopt a new perspective, a new way of reading which did not depend on a rigid separation of the allegedly rational language of economics and more creative language, but which was prepared to allow 'contamination' between the two. From this perspective, economic discussions could and should be the objects of linguistic investigation. For the use of a formalized language is anything but neutral, and the rhetoric and persuasiveness of arguments are not mere ornaments but constitutive elements of meaning.

After all, Adam Smith, the founder of political economy, was a teacher of Rhetoric, and saw in 'a certain propensity in human nature ... to truck, barter and exchange one thing for another', one 'necessary consequence of the faculties of reason and speech'[2] and used it to explain the innate tendency to engage in trade which was the underpinning of the invisible hand.

Anyone who opens the first sections of the first book of Marx's *Capital* will run into pretty seriously obstacles. Even though the secondary literature has little to say about it, we find a striking literary richness, which runs from image-spinning to irony, from metaphysical metaphors to religious analogies. Nor is this a tacked-on style, a touch of 'mere' bellettrism. As Marx wrote to Engels, when he thought he had almost finished the theoretical part of the work, the final writing up was not an easy task:

> I cannot bring myself to send off any thing before the whole lies before me. *Whatever shortcomings they may have* [phrase originally in English], the merit of my writings is that they are an artistic whole, and that is only attainable by my method, never to allow them to be printed before they lie before me whole.[3]

That was in 1865. Two more years were to pass before Marx decided to publish only a part of the complete work.

The hypothesis that there is a link between the way in which a text is written and the analytic contents which it can express – between language, method and theory – seemed to us to be a hypothesis which held good also in the case of Keynes. Indeed, his seemed to be a paradigm case for testing the range of porisms picked out by the group whose efforts are collected in this volume. In particular, we have gained much from the contribution of Anna Carabelli, then at the University of Pavia and now at Padova, who has been studying Keynes's method for many years.

Without doubt, *The General Theory* marked a turning point in economic theory, a break with the classical tradition; it has been subjected to interpretation and reinterpretation, and is the focus of a debate which is still far from running out of steam. The novelty of its theoretical contribution would alone be enough to justify the attention which it has been given as a case study. But the interest which it has attracted has been added to by its language, which is complex and obscure, frequently being referred to as opaque.

Curiously, while the criticisms it has attracted have, over time, done an about-turn, what has remained fixed is a certain dissatisfaction with the way in which Keynes presented his views. In the years immediately following the publication of *The General Theory*, the objections tended to focus on its excessive formalization and on its inaccessibility to the general public. On the other hand, Keynes has more recently been accused of a vagueness in his assumptions and of an ambiguousness in his arguments, which, it is said, are the price to be paid for insufficient 'formalization' and for the texts' 'literariness'. This is explained –

when it is explained – in historical terms by reference to the underde-velopment of analytic tools and to Keynes's intercourse with the Bloomsbury Group.

We are directed to the main question that literary scholars raise, albeit from another angle, by the phenomenon of antithetical causes for complaint about Keynes's use of language – sometimes that it is too abstract and formalized, sometimes that it is too literary and metaphori-cal. It is not so much a matter of criticizing either formal or ordinary language as such, as of considering the use which is made of them, their appropriateness to their object, the relation – the balance one might say – which is set up between them and what they are used for. It is a matter of considering what is revealed by the overriding obsession with formal language which generations of economists have shared, considering what it has been for and what forfeits it has led to. A telling instance is to be found in the normalization of Keynes's language which took place ever more quickly during and after the years of the 'neoclassical synthesis'. What got the upper hand were reductive inter-pretations of *The General Theory*, surgical readings which were set to amputate everything that could not be fitted into the linear patterns of the 'normal' economic reader. A different text was invented, a different way of seeing things, a different way of acting and changing reality – thus demonstrating that choice of language and communicative strat-egy is not neutral and that the problem could not be reduced to a false dilemma of 'empty' formalization against 'mere' rhetoric. In the end, the question is still 'What economics?' and 'For what purpose?'

Setting out from the case of Keynes, it seemed possible for us to put forward the hypothesis that the imbalances and ruptures in his writing could and should be recovered by a different kind of investigation. It might be no surprise that the readings given by those 'innocent' of economics should have led to a less stifling vision.

It is for the reader to evaluate the results of this interdisciplinary en-quiry, in which literary scholars (Rossana Bonadei, Maurizio Gotti and Alessandra Marzola) and economists (Riccardo Bellofiore, Anna Carabelli and Francesco Silva) took part. We wish here only to preview the general thesis of the contributions and to pick up some points of intersection, convergence and divergence – some of the loose ends to be tied up.

Keynes's education as an economist and his subsequent theoretical work took place against a cultural background which was to an extraordinary extent preoccupied with epistemological problems and with lively debates on language and the relation between writing and the subject. In Chapter 2, Rossana Bonadei discusses this confluence of cultural streams. Keynes was the heir to his father's ideal of a non-specialized education, and his mother's social commitment. In his youth he participated in the Victorian and puritan inheritance: the search for commonly accepted foundations of discussion in which to express the intersubjectivity of knowledge and the broadcasting of a call for action, which was both a sermon and a prophecy. Through his intense contacts first with the Apostles and later with the Bloomsbury Group, as well as through his attachments to Russell, Ramsey and Wittgenstein, Keynes developed his own method of observation and rational objectification which does not exist outside a theory but which is imbricated within language and full of persuasive power. It is at this point that the Keynes who sees economics as one of the 'moral sciences' comes into contact with the modernist literary experiments of Virginia Woolf, and with the psychoanalysis of Freud. His identity as a virtually unique humanist economist is built on what are still innovative lines out of experiences and thoughts at the meeting-place of different disciplines.

The central role which language and rhetoric play for Keynes set him up as a forerunner of more recent epistemological debates. He had already taken account of the untenability of a Cartesian model of reason based on unassailable self-evidence; but attempts to replace the ideal of certain knowledge as representation with an equally certain demarcation between science and non-science also come to grief. The search for a universal and prescriptive method unites views which are as far apart as those of the logical positivists and Popper. In the last few decades, the sustained and effective attacks which have been made on the search for such a method, have also made space for a more attentive reading of Keynes's views in *A Treatise on Probability*. But once we have seen that Keynes's outlook is close to the main line of post-positivist thought, there is the further question of how exactly we are to understand his method.

In Chapter 3, Riccardo Bellofiore points to alternative ways out of the mind-set of traditional epistemology, which had been fixated on the metaphor of 'representation' and on the setting up of 'guarantees' for the truth of knowledge. On the one hand, there is the overall reduction of the process of knowledge-gathering to its linguistic aspects. In economics, this move has its most extreme proponents in those who cultivate the Rhetoric of economics. Knowledge is treated as a sort of 'speech', as a sort of 'story-telling', in which the scholar's knowledge collapses into the creativity of the poet. The assault on the claims of absolute foundations for knowledge results in a thoroughgoing relativism which denies any objectivity in the process of knowledge-gathering. On the other hand, there is the view which sees knowledge as a sort of 'practice' and which links theory to use. This is a minority view, but one for which Bellofiore sees hopeful prospects, in so far as its recognition of the way that truth-claims have to be contextualized does not destroy the part played by extra-textual elements. In short, it is a view that admits the importance of theoretical work, but at the same times holds on to a sense, still to be worked out in detail, of the importance of external reality. Keynes is here presented as a forerunner of some of the themes of this latter view: in the terms which Ian Hacking has recently popularized, it can be described as the abandonment of 'realism about theories' while accepting 'realism about entities'. From this point of view, the 'truth' of a theory may be accounted for in terms of its 'ultimate goodness of fit' with its object and its capacity to transform reality.

In Chapter 4, Anna Carabelli offers a close reconstruction of the distinctive characteristics of Keynes's method. In her view, Keynes's critique of the classical theory is not at bottom a critique of its contents, but of its method. By detailed examination of *The General Theory* and of Keynes's preparatory writings for it, Carabelli shows why he thought that previous criticisms of the classical theory were doomed to failure by their naive empiricism which aimed to set 'facts' up against the dominant theory. Worse, the critics of the classical theory wished to attack its conclusions even though they accepted its premises. But, just as the classical theory could not be attacked merely by observation of facts in conflict with it, so too was it a coherent system of premises from which conclusions has been validly drawn.

So, Keynes's attack takes another direction. This involves making the tacit premises of the classical theory explicit, showing how they all grow out of the hypothesis that given variables are logically independent of variation, and then demonstrating that the claim to universality in time and space is altogether deceptive. The justification which Carabelli supplies for this last move arises from the continuity of Keynes's thought about the theory of knowledge from the time of *A Treatise on Probability* up to and beyond *The General Theory*. The hypotheses of logical independence which had been smuggled in by the classical theory could be regarded as acceptable so long as the matters to be studied could be interpreted as atomic, and not as organically interdependent. For Keynes, it is with organic interdependence that we arrive at the genuinely 'general' theory, relative to which the classical theory can claim only localized validity.

Keynes was led by the open and complex character of the economic system, which is marked by change and organic functional relations among the variables, to prefer ordinary language to the artificial language of mathematics. Nevertheless he does not spurn this latter as long as the relevant hypotheses of logical independence have been established and fully defined. Unlike the 'pseudo-mathematical symbolic methods', ordinary language allows us always to know 'what we are doing and what the words mean', it allows us 'to keep "at the back of our heads" the necessary reserves and qualifications and the adjustments which we shall have to make later on'.

Taking up the linguistic angle, Maurizio Gotti (Chapter 5) shows how strange and inconsistent was the reception of *The General Theory*. While what were taken to be its main claims were apparently widely successful, there was also a generalized discontent with the way the book was written. It was thought to show signs of rushed composition, and its argumentation seemed to lack cogency and to be unsystematic. In Gotti's view, it is no accident that the book is ambiguous, that the language which Keynes employs is not univocal; rather, these features were part of the author's aim.

Gotti's thesis is certainly confirmed by Keynes's epistemological predilection for a non-demonstrative logic. This can be seen as at the root of his preference for non-specialized language and the strongly literary style of his writing, as well as his polemical tone and persuasive intentions. But that is not all. In Gotti's view, *The General Theory* turns out to be a genuinely open-ended work, as a consequence of the polyvalent and metaphorical language it employs. And, as open-ended, it not merely allows, but requires, that the reader intervene actively in it. That is, its intended recipient ought not to restrict himself or herself to decoding the text; she is incited, in some measure, to build it for him/herself, specifying the meanings of the words and filling in the gaps in the argument in different ways according to context.

The starting point for Alessandra Marzola (Chapter 6), is the observation, shared by the other contributors, that argument, understood as a 'rhetoric of persuasion', is a fundamental feature of Keynes's method and writing. Keynes's digressive and dissociative procedure is in evidence as much in the political writings, such as *The Economic Conse-*

quences of the Peace, as it is in the scientific writings, such as *The General Theory*. In both cases, it is a symptom of an argument which aims to unveil an alternative reality, one which is different from and which goes beyond the commonly accepted view. It is a reality that unveils itself to the author in the very process of writing. And the writing becomes the means for knowing relations and forces which, at the outset, were inconceivable.

On the basis of these premises, Marzola is able to give a fresh account of the metaphors that abound in Keynes's 1919 critique of the Treaty of Versailles. She is able to lay open the structural similarity between Keynes's analysis of the political and economic instability and the reconstruction he offers of the 'psychology of society'. In passages which are too often played down by economists reading the book, Keynes discusses the repression of the death instinct implied in the mechanisms of saving and compound interest, and so also through the blind drive to accumulation. These means of repression exorcise the fragile and chance nature of the progress which had been truncated by the First World War. The account that Keynes gives here is strikingly similar in some respects to the interpretation of the meaning of history which Freud was offering at about the same time, and it raises the question of the nature of psychoanalysis.

The theme is taken up by Bellofiore in Chapter 7. As he shows, it is a problem which Keynes never deserted: in Chapter XII of *The General Theory*, the dialectic between individual and collective investment follows a path of far-sighted and wakeful interaction between repression and what is repressed, between the force of convention and the prevalence of speculation.

Even if a participant in a research project is not the best judge of the resultant work, he or she may, nevertheless, have a better idea than anyone else of how he or she has been changed by it. The economists who took part in this experiment may have noticed how much – much more than they might have predicted at the outset – they have learnt from alternative readings of economic texts, from a more attentive look at their linguistic component. Some of the conclusions probably could not have been arrived at with the fixed focus of an economist's special interests. Perhaps it has been useful to the literary scholars to see how much closer were areas which had seemed far from their usual stamping ground, and how their interpretative tools could be applied to the most quantitative of the social sciences.

The following chapters certainly display different ways of accentuating the issues raised, and the reader may not always find it easy to draw a neat line, with the economists on one side and the literary scholars on the other. By way of a single example, there is a distinction between on the one hand, those who think that method is a linguistic matter, who take a word to be a sort of action, and who give priority to propositional knowledge, and those on the other hand, who see the text as something which must in its turn be set in context, who see language as the site at which appearances and superficial knowledge are overturned, and who take knowledge to be both the end and the beginning of interpersonal practices to transform 'reality'.

This distinction is a reprise, in a new and we hope, more fruitful context, of the conflict between conventionalism and objectivism about knowledge. It may not be accidental that the conflict is at its most pointed exactly where the various contributions most closely converge. Thus, where the conjunction between Keynes and Freud is raised, we find a very different Freud for each of the contributors to the volume. Likewise, while all the contributors reject the sort of realism that reduces knowledge to faithful mirroring of an already given reality, there is the widest divergence on the question of the extent to which economics is an experimental science.

It must also remain an open question whether the approach and the interdisciplinary techniques adopted here can be extended to other areas. It might be worth seeing how far attention to economists' language can illuminate thinkers other than Keynes, who might seem an untypical case in respect both of his high degree of methodological self-consciousness and the variety of cultural forces that were at work in him. And one may well wonder whether the dialogue between economists and literary scholars should stop short at putting their various writings together in a single volume, at summing their special talents with some sort of balance across an unstable border, or whether we could not take the opportunity to criticize the very separation which consigns to the 'dismal science' knowledge about the world of things (which is what even the individual is, when considered merely as a subject of calculation), and to the literati qualitative knowledge about the world of human beings.

NOTES

1. Lord Robbins (1935) *An Essay on the Nature and Significance of Economic Science* 2nd edn, London: Macmillan, p. 17.
2. Adam Smith (1776)*Wealth of Nations*, Book I, Ch. ii.
3. Letter 31 July 1865, in (1942) *Marx and Engels: Selected Correspondence 1846–95*, translated by Dona Torr, New York: International Publishers, p. 204.

2. John Maynard Keynes: Contexts and Methods

Rossana Bonadei

The master-economist must possess a rare *combination* of gifts. ... He must be mathematician, historian, statesman, philosopher – in some degree. He must understand symbols and speak in words. He must contemplate the particular in terms of the general, and touch abstract and concrete in the same flight of thought. He must study the present in the light of the past for the purposes of the future. (J.M. Keynes)

AUTOBIOGRAPHY THROUGH THE BIOGRAPHIES

The English tradition of biographical writing had been raised to an 'art' by the Victorians and Edwardians. Keynes also practised this art assiduously. The tradition demands that every history of an individual begins with an account of a father and a mother, of the family background and where there turn out to be noteworthy characters, of the ancestors. At a very early age, while at Eton, Keynes had begun to study the family's genealogy. He had got as far back as a certain John Keynes, who was a Jesuit priest keenly interested in rhetoric and the author, in 1684, of a *Rational Compendious Way to Convince All Persons, Whatsoever, Dissenting from the True Religion*.[1] This return to his origins, and the specific discovery of a family 'passion' for arguing and convincing others, could have been the inspiration for a first chapter of the autobiography which Keynes never wrote. Perhaps he never wrote one for the simple reason that he did not have the time, unlike many of his friends who outlived him and who recall him in their own autobiographies (for example, Moore 1942, Bell 1956, Woolf 1960, Russell 1967).

We have only two short and narrowly focused pieces of autobiographical memoir from Keynes, who was so inexhaustible an author, biographer and letter-writer. One concerns his undergraduate years in Cambridge: 'My Early Beliefs'; the other concerns the period of his involvement in the negotiations after the First World War: 'Melchior: a defeated enemy'. Both were originally undertaken as 'discussion papers' for his friends in the Bloomsbury Group and were only later included in Volume X of the *Collected Writings*, which is given over to the *Essays in Biography*.[2] Nevertheless, by rereading the biographical and historical writings which he produced from the first decade of the century in praise, memory or criticism of personalities from the scientific and cultural world of the more or less recent past, up to and including his contemporaries, we can make out through the interstices an indirect and fragmentary line of autobiographical thought which can be set against the 'official' reconstructions of Keynes's life and thought (see especially Harrod 1951, and Skidelsky 1983).

Thus, in writing about others, Keynes tells us indirectly and by fragments something about himself, about the unwritten spiritual autobiography which could have thrown so much light on the driving forces within him, on the contexts and progressive construction of a style of life and thought, of a destiny. The *Essays in Biography* are thus, at once, the site of an archaeological and phylogenetic reconstruction, and a subjective self-recognition. What the writing renders to its author and to the reader is the trace of an ideal subject, of an ideal economist, springing from the Great National Family, from the 'High Intelligentsia of England, who have built up the foundations of our thought in the two and a half centuries since Locke, in his *Essay concerning Human Understanding*, wrote the first modern English book' (*CW*, X, p. xix), among whom the author aspires, for reasons of 'solidarity and historical continuity', to locate himself.

In the light of this, Keynes's reconsideration of the lives of Newton and Malthus, of Jevons and Marshall, of the Paleys and the Edgeworths is also an investigation of family models. He gives himself away by insisting, whether knowingly or not does not ultimately matter, on questions of education, background and character which by their presence or absence describe a cultural identity and account for a personality. Indeed, it is matters of family standing and education that determine the typologies of the portraits he gives of Malthus and Marshall, the 'fellow economists' with whom it was most pressing to set up similarities and differences. And it is on this basis that we can see a first reason for his great affinity with Malthus, 'the first of the Cambridge Economists', and for the fatal diversity from Marshall, for all that he was Keynes's first 'master'. Thus the reader learns, from the author's cheerful enthusiasm that the family of Malthus, like those of Jevons and Keynes, were firmly in the Nonconformist liberal tradition, which is recognized as the vanguard of British intellectual and civil progress,

'the tradition which is suggested by the names of Locke, Hume, Adam Smith, Paley, Bentham, Darwin, and Mill, a tradition marked by love of the truth and a most noble lucidity, by a prosaic sanity free from sentiment or metaphysic, and by an immense disinterestedness and public spirit' (*CW*, X, p. 86).

The phylogenetic method is doing all the work here. From it there issues a set of attitudes and ways of behaving selected and handed down by the group to the man who proudly describes it: lucidity, rational clarity and service to society.

The importance of models and educational choices is not discharged in a short note, but continuously recurs in the whole portrait. Keynes observes how Malthus was favoured with the exceptional boon of having as his teacher Gilbert Wakefield, who was a pupil of Rousseau and inspired by principles which seemed to be sufficiently important as to call for lengthy quotation in Keynes's essay (*CW*, X, p. 78). His biographers tell us that Keynes too, was the object of a pedagogical eagerness which was probably resonant with Enlightenment echoes, and which was, in any case, proof against the distinctively Victorian educational fanaticism. It was his father, John Neville Keynes, who had the leading role in the education and instruction of the son. It was he who set out the curriculum of 'combined' studies, covering both the Classics and mathematics, which had such a strong influence on the son's choices at each stage in his early career. His father writes that at the age of ten, Maynard knew the First Book of Euclid, could solve complex algebraic equations, and read Ovid and the Latin prose writers fluently. At Eton, which had remained uninfluenced by the recent pro-positivist reforms, the Classics and mathematics continued to be the two basic studies. Keynes completed his education at King's College, Cambridge, which he chose in preference to Trinity on account of its less rigid curriculum, and which was therefore in closer accordance with his versatile personality. There arose a sort of complicity between the father's notion of a non-specialized, combined course of studies and the son's intellectual precocity, which was already branching out into diverse subjects, especially antiquarian and philological. Vicari-ously for the former and directly for the latter, this complicity became the mutual pursuit of an 'open', intellectual journey, often twisting but responsive to the most heterogeneous demands. On the one hand, for the father as an 'eminent Victorian', this journey of complexity and compromise represented an unresolvable fluctuation of interests between logical studies, 'morals', and a cause of a partial academic failure.[3] On the other hand, for the young Keynes, it had a structural and theoretical significance which underlay the original and deep distinction between himself and the 'fellow economists' who had been trained by Marshall. It is probably with this happy complicity in mind, which we have already noted in his account of Malthus, that Keynes takes up Marshall's primal unhappiness. For Marshall had been subjected to a severe and limiting education and 'had painful recollections in later days of his tyrant father keeping him awake into the night for the better study of Hebrew, whilst at the same time forbidding him the fascinating paths of mathematics' (*CW*, X, pp. 163–4). Thus, by setting out from marginal details, and by putting together psychological notes and historical evidence, Keynes assembles a picture of Marshall as deeply disturbed by internal conflicts, shut in by narrow horizons of division and ghettoization of knowledge, just as the family circle in which he grew up was closed and narrow. The biographer intermingles eulogistic writing with the impulse to criticize: indeed, Keynes recognizes Marshall's achievement in having made the study of economics socially useful, 'to get into closer contact with practical business and with the life of the working classes' (*CW*, X, p. 187); moreover he celebrates him as 'the first great economist *pur sang* ... who devoted his life to building up the subject as a separate science, standing on its own foundations' (*CW*, X, p. 222); however he still notes that, with Marshall and his Economic Tripos, 'economics could never again be one ... moral science of several, as Mill, Jevons, and Sidgwick took it' (*CW*, X, p. 222). This, then, was the end of a grand tradition of which Adam Smith, Professor of Logic and of Moral Philosophy at Glasgow, was the revered founder.

Indeed, with the foundation, in 1903, of the Economic and Political Tripos, sought by Marshall and opposed by Sidgwick and John Neville Keynes, the budding economist acquired a status distinct from that of the student of Moral Science, and was liberated from the study of philosophy and metaphysics. The reform of the Tripos followed a tendency towards a pro-positivist organization of knowledge which seemed in many ways to be accepted by official culture. Sidgwick's metaphysics and Marshall's economics were the emblems of an opposition which

had by then become unbridgeable, underwriting the forthcoming de-
mise of the dominant Victorian conception of intellectual activity as
organic and 'compromising'.[4] Under divisive pressures, that were in
any case part of the utilitarian world-view which was a historical product of Victorian consciousness, the Two Cultures were each specifying
more and more rigidly their own methodological and operational back-
grounds. Caught between metaphysics and Benthamism and overrun
by idealisms both old and new, the problem for the intellectual of
Victorian England was that of putting knowledge to social use and of
fitting action into a broadly accepted ethical scheme. This was the main
point of the so-called 'Victorian compromise'. In Sidgwick and Marshall,
prominent and influential figures in Cambridge, Keynes encountered
the pursuers of that ideal and potent compromise in its two possible
radicalized outcomes: the 'abstract' and the 'practical'.

Indeed, by means of a non-traditional distribution of roles and an
unusual hybridization of the male–female structure, the Keynes family
had taken on board and dealt with the double requirement for both
self-determination and social obligation which the Victorian conscience imposed. On the one hand, there was the father's learning producing logico-mathematical theories as well as 'useful' textbooks. On the
other, there was the pragmatism of the mother, who was engaged in
politics and civil rights, 'a pioneer of Women's Rights', and the first
woman to be elected Lord Mayor of an English city. Away from the
unusual parental arrangements and the family, the conflict and struggle
of conscience raged on. In this way, Sidgwick and Marshall, standing
as an alternative pair of models to those supplied by his parents, were
important reference-points for the young Keynes's subsequent self-
location.

When, in 1905, after reading for the Mathematical Tripos, Keynes
began to take an interest in economics and to attend Marshall's lectures, his own formation could not have been further from what his
'master' had set out. Keynes was deeply influenced by his Classical
background and at that time much attracted by the grand metaphysical
tradition of, especially, Leibniz and Kant. Marshall in his turn was
engaged in producing a model of a 'diagrammatic economics' which
would save economics from the complexity of vision and method which
ill-fitted the idea of a new science thought to be rigorous in its procedures and 'positive' in its results. It was Marshall who chose Keynes,
rather than vice versa, and who waited patiently for his young pupil to
find his place in the nascent community of Cambridge economists.

Keynes responded to the overtures of Marshall who, from 1906, invited him not to underestimate what seemed to him a noteworthy proficiency in economics,[5] by opting, less than reassuringly, for philosophy. Keynes continued to prefer the study of human knowledge and behaviour over the Cambridge notion of mathematical and neo-mechanistic economics as a 'new and powerful machine for thinking, rigorously and patiently constructed'. And, consistently with this preference, he followed the line of economic thought which kept a place for the human factor and which seemed temporarily to have been lost from modern economic science.

The *Essays in Biography* constituted an important opportunity for the young economist to review the tradition of English economic thought, with its theoretic and ideological polarity, and to adopt a position relative to it. For the Cambridge economic school and for Marshall, the tradition culminated in the line Ricardo–Bentham–Mill. For Keynes, the principal reference-points were different. First, there was Malthus, the 'pioneer of the application of a frame of formal thinking to the complex confusion of the world of daily events' (*CW*, X, p. 107). Second, the Mill of *The Principles of Political Economy* and the *Autobiography*, in which we find a theoretical recovery of the role of the imagination against the background of the harsh vision of Benthamism. And third, the eclectic Jevons, the nineteenth century economist who, more clearly than any other, had accepted the irreducible complexity of the object of economic study, and who, in his methodological choices 'had almost as few successors as predecessors' (*CW*, X, p. 127).

The extent to which these two lines of thought were alternatives, as the fundamental principles which were at stake in the vision of the object and procedure of economics, is clearly brought out by the correspondence of 1817 between Malthus and Ricardo which Keynes picks up and discusses.[6] For both of the pre-Victorian economists, the object of study was contemporary society considered under the aspect of its economic and political functioning. The aim was to make knowledge of the present useful to predict future possible changes. At stake was the relation between experience and analytic models, between particular events and general laws. There was an obvious friction between the two worlds of objects and ideas, between the transitory condition of phenomena and the alleged necessary permanence of description and theory, between irregularity and order. But for Malthus, the periods and methods of Ricardo's analysis seemed too reductive. Ricardo's generalizations stamped on reality an unnatural immobility, 'the most distant from the truth', which unacceptably falsified 'the state of things'. The task was rather to make the gaps between observations shorter and so to make them richer in information, in such a way that what is particular, transitory and irregular should not disappear in the face of an excessive desire for formalization. 'The artifical groove' into which Ricardo had forced English economic studies strongly affected its future development. It made it into a sophisticated and up-to-date 'intellectual construction', principally concerned to reduce reality to numbers, symbols and diagrams. Overall, Keynes stresses that we can find in the inaugural clash between Malthus and Ricardo, and in the latter's victory, the key to understanding a methodological schizophrenia which had hampered the subject's harmonious progress. Keynes was busy with the essay on Malthus at various times in the period 1914–16; but the decisiveness of its themes and arguments was so great in relation to the economic thought which he was developing that, nearly twenty years later, he felt it necessary to return to the matter in the premises of *The General Theory*.

Indeed, as Marshall had predicted, Keynes did not abandon economics, but nor did he abandon philosophy. He spent his student years dividing his attention between the Mathematical Tripos and the courses of Moral Science which were co-ordinated by Sidgwick and recommended by the curriculum of his college.

Alongside Sidgwick, old and new figures dedicated themselves to canonical instruction which Keynes followed industriously: history with Maitland, political economy with Lord Acton, ethics with the young Moore, metaphysics with McTaggart.[7] King's itself tended towards metaphysics and idealism under the sway of the educational and tutorial patterns of Oscar Browning and Goldsworthy Lowes Dickinson. The contours of intellectual influences and of personal attraction could hardly be anything but composite and overlapping. Nevertheless, it was in the many well-attended clubs, public and private, often associated with college structures, that the vibrant Cambridge philosophy, which was to mark the future of debate even outside England, was forged. Among these were the clubs of greatest prestige and tradition in King's and Trinity which Keynes duly attended: the King's College Society, the Trinity Essay Society, Browning's Political Society, Dickinson's Discussion Society, and most exclusive of all, the Cambridge Conversazione Society, also known as The Apostles.[8] Less elite, but very prestigious, especially in the 1920s and 1930s, were the Heretics and the Midnight Society which were open to women and a non-

university public and to which Russell and Virginia Woolf gave important papers.

We know that the tradition on which the societies' debates were founded
was above all philosophical, with an increasing emphasis on problems of
aesthetics, art and contemporary literature. Founded in 1820 by a group
of friends 'who wanted to work out a philosophy of life', the Apostles
added to the activity of debating a strong commitment to ethico-moral
clarification. Sidgwick, who was a very active member in the second half
of the nineteenth century, had infused into the debate the typical Victorian ethical fervour, directing it on questions and doubts which were
characteristic of the contemporary collective conscience, such as the
definition of the good, both in the abstract and in practical cases, the
ethical conflict between the 'public' and the 'private', between the 'good'
and the 'useful'. He was also among the first to emphasize the distinction
between religious and ethical issues, thus making of himself, along with
Leslie Stephen, Marshall and John Neville Keynes, a spokesman of the
religious dilemma of the Victorian dons, which would later culminate for
many in the choice of agnosticism and in the doctrinal shift to 'social
obligation'. The advent of Lowes Dickinson and McTaggart among the
Apostles had meanwhile precipitated a decided turn toward idealism
which, among other things, had added a neo-Platonic tinge to the bond of
friendship which was fundamental to the association of the group. Likewise, in the spirit of the Platonic revival, McTaggart had reformed the
debate on the model of the ancient Symposium, which, as Moore recalls,
demanded the active participation of the contributors, a continual effort
of conceptual clarification and a 'constant insistence on clearness' (Moore
1942, p. 18). As supporters of the anti-Hegelian reaction were enrolled in
the Society, rational–argumentative discussion turned into a rigorous
method. Moore bewildered his interlocutors with the fateful, 'What do
you *really* mean?', Lytton Strachey with his dizzying linguistic and
conceptual distinctions, Keynes with his insatiable cross-checking. Later
this method, grown into something more stringent and corrosive, was to
be exported by the Apostles Keynes, Woolf, Strachey and Fry to the first
core of the Bloomsbury Group. The method was to function as a standard
of selection for members of the group, for whom 'anyone who held
views that could not be justified rationally was regarded as a wilful
cultivator of illusions and therefore as a person who could not be taken
seriously (Brenan 1974, p. 15).

Therefore, membership of the Apostles brought the young Keynes
into relationships of vital intellectual importance and contributed to the

distillation of a set of problems and procedures which set the scene for his later intellectual work. Above all, it established for him an elevated idea of interpersonal relationships and of dialectical exchange. At the same time, it made him see the need for a continual and unremitting testing of ideas within the process of exposition, from which emerged the corruscating style of commentary and judgement which even his friends were to come sometimes to deprecate.[9]

His experience of the Apostles was such as to move Keynes to write one of his two autobiographical memoirs, which he explicitly entitled 'My Early Beliefs', referring to his student days. In what follows, we shall make use of those memories, and of many others which are quietly at work in Keynes's early writings, in order to analyse the soundness of those 'beliefs' in terms of their derivation from the puritan and Victorian tradition, and of their operation within the historical context of Keynes's thought and method.

THE PURITAN AND VICTORIAN INHERITANCE. THE 'WEIGHT OF LANGUAGE' AND SURPLUS ARGUMENTATION

> What should we say if someone asks us, 'do you have the thought before you have the expression?' and how should we answer the question, 'what did the thought consist in which was in us before the expression?' (L. Wittgenstein.)

With the spread of Darwin's thought and the growing trend to agnosticism, the moral, intellectual and scientific debate had undergone deep changes and was moving towards massive reassessment both of traditional premises and conclusions. Despite the many reservations which were entered concerning the scientific legitimacy of the Darwinian method, the new theory on the origin and transformation of life was overthrowing the story given in Genesis and producing immediate responses in science and ethics. Creationism and Theology, the sites at which tradition, faith and convention had rallied and survived the onslaughts of philosophical and scientific rationalism, sold the pass to new constructions which showed themselves no less powerful instruments for imaginative and conceptual invention. At Cambridge, evolutionary theories and agnosticism together made up the daily subjects of the debate of the dons who began to discuss Morality in non-doctrinaire but still religious terms. The religious problems, once removed from the realm of dogma, were applied in the more properly human realm of ethical conduct: the 'applied ethics' of Sidgwick, Marshall and Leslie Stephen. Nevertheless, some weak concession was made to the transcendental with respect to the existence and salvation of the soul. This was clearly a left-over of puritanism which, among other things, kept at bay the temptations of a materialistic conception, which would have been alien to the troubled consciousness of the Victorian dons. Even Leslie Stephen, the severest and most systematic of the Victorian agnostics, in his well-known *Agnostic's Apology*, doubts that life could really be nothing but an uncomfortable and fleeting 'flicker of consciousness between the womb and the tomb' (Stephen cited in *Charleston Papers* letter from Sir A. Lunn to Clive Bell, 18 January 1937). But likewise, the problems of the existence of God and of the salvation of the soul could go ahead along different lines, developing 'religious' options which had not been sanctioned by the official religions.

However, Victorian agnosticism was not merely a result of recent changes in the significance of the natural sciences. The spiritual search centred fundamentally on a premise proprietary to the Nonconformist tradition from which sprang a large number of the English intelligentsia in which Keynes too wished to locate himself. As he remarked, in reconsidering the 'religious' premises of his early beliefs, the new agnostic consciousness drew on and fed into features specific to the earlier puritan consciousness: 'our religion closely followed the English puritan tradition of being chiefly concerned with the salvation of our own souls' (*CW*, X, p. 347). By replacing dogma with the social imperative, agnosticism removed the question of works from the theological context which had been given to it by the Reformation. Agnosticism turned the old dilemma of faith into a moral dilemma: 'works' have no relation to God; they are of and for men; salvation of the soul is not determined in isolation by reference to God, but in relation to other men. From this arises the spiritual and intellectual overvaluation of individualism, in souls and consciences, which was taken to be the foundation of the new 'religious' and social project.

We can push our investigation of the historical continuity of puritanism with agnosticism further by reference to Keynes's forebears. We may think of the attitudes and practical choices which were fairly widespread among evangelical puritans, especially in the churches of Clapham and of Bunyan to which, respectively, the Stephens and the Keynes's had traditionally belonged (Rosenbaum 1987).

For the English evangelical puritans, who were often committed also to social and political dissent, the privileged means for evangelical clarification and propaganda were public preaching and writing. For the dissenters, 'action' was the spreading of the word from one reflective conscience to other consciences equally given to action, and the word was structured in an argumentative, polemical language aimed at persuasion. In the spoken homily or the written pamphlet, the puritan word was made 'to bear interest' in a cause held to be of public utility, and was exploited to 'throw light' on experience, to dissolve ambiguities, and thus it was saved from suspicions of sophistry and hedonism. And the argumentative style which informed it did not follow the twisted and complacent routes of occult persuasion, but those of the 'plain and positive' of rational understanding. Conceived and nurtured by individual 'sanity' and social obligation, and taken from the start in terms of the imperative of the authorial 'I' to reach out to the 'you' to which the communication was directed, this neo-rhetorical passion was afforded by the collective Victorian institutions a broad-based historical and literary legitimation in all areas of expository practice.

Even the centres of lay learning and cultural debate were affected by the vigorous mobilization of rhetorical activity which marked the upsurge of religious activity in the nineteenth century, from the High Church resumption of theological speculation in the Oxford Movement to the spread of Methodism and Baptism. The 'eminent Victorians' were distinguished as great preachers of their own knowledge and as orators and prose-writers of undoubted ability. Keynes even conceded as much about Marshall, describing him as belonging to 'the tribe of sages and pastors; yet, like them also, endowed with a double nature, he was a scientist too' (*CW*, X, p. 173).

As more detailed studies have revealed (see Levine and Madden 1968, Miller 1968, Landow 1989), the written and spoken word of the Victorian period are outstanding in the English cultural setting for their extraordinary rhetorical richness and for their unrelenting drive to communicate every possible branch of specialized knowledge. Malthus, Macauley, Mill, Dickens and Darwin had all wrought their works, in science, history and fiction, with the Victorian public in mind, among whom literacy and reading were growing at a much faster rate than in the past. The Victorian intellectual or scientist shared his knowledge with that public: the 'consciousness of the consciousness of the other' (Miller 1968). In its sometimes neurotic pursuit of a common ground for discourse the Victorian neo-rhetoric overthrew the artful and balanced neo-classical rhetoric. In its place, it took as the hallmark of its argumentative style the procedure of accumulation, by amplification or digression, of its material. In thus opening himself to the other's point of view, the writing subject reopened his own debate with language and with knowledge itself. And language became the true site of the imagination, of the impulse to speculate, of the gradual focusing on what had been left over from, or submerged in the discourse, but which had been included in, without being expressed explicitly by, conventional syntax. The point of concrete determination was reached ahead of thought for 'swerves' which followed the writing and were unpredictable by the author himself. This also gives rise to the sensation of an argumentative process with prophetic implications, one which is rich in information that has grown up along the way, which seems to outweigh and outstrip its premises. At the turn of the century, with its great preachers of agnosticism and with the Apostles, the privileged environment for debates and discussions aimed at clarification and non-technical explanation, Cambridge resounded with this verbal and rhetorical passion.

By cultural background and natural inclination, Keynes fully shared and further developed the puritan-Victorian passion for rhetorical exercises and writing. He made a method of it and went so far as to theorize about it, melding it with logic. From *A Treatise on Probability*, through *The Economic Consequence of the Peace* and the *Essays in Persuasion*, to the long argument of *The General Theory*, what is very clearly set out is a theory and practice of 'the word as action', which, once uttered or written, has already of itself changed its context. This attitude was crucial in setting the manner and style of Keynes's writing; it hardened *pari passu* with the development of a method which treats the weight of language and 'public' utterance as the fulcrum of his operation. We shall have occasion to return several times and from different points of view to this hypothesis, which is, among other things, at the centre of a recent book on Keynes (Carabelli 1989) and is discussed in various ways in all the contributions to this book.

Keynes's non-specialist writings call for some comment in the terms of the historical and cultural perspective which we have hitherto been sketching, and which is our direct concern. In particular, we ought to consider *The Economic Consequences of the Peace*, an indignant critique of the Treaty of Versailles, and the *Essays in Persuasion*, which discuss matters of current affairs and are aimed at the broad public of the newspapers, of the BBC and of the pamphlets put out by the Hogarth Press. For these two works are exemplary cases of the double rhetoric, appealing at once to reason and to the emotions, which was so much a part of the puritan oral tradition and of Victorian prose writing. On the one hand, we hear the voice of the preacher, determined to intervene in the face of a social emergency by setting out detailed information and explicit accusations 'in a spirit of persuasion', 'in an attempt to influence' (*CW*, IX, p. 17): against the 'Big Four' in Paris, for or against Lloyd George, according to circumstances, and against Churchill over monetary policy. On the other hand, we also hear the accents of the prophet, taking his stand, more passionate than convincing, and giving away the knowledge of a vision which resists a 'plain and simple' explanation. As our author himself was willing to recognize, these writings were too full of intuitions which remained undeveloped, of unclarified allusions, and of literary and learned references to be capable of really providing an objective picture of a situation or of convincing us of an idea ('the volume might have been entitled *Essays in Prophecy and Persuasion*, for the Prophecy, unfortunately, has been more successful than the Persuasion' (*CW*, IX, p. xvi)). In short, many of these writings were failed arguments which yielded precise prophecy. To return to the Victorian frame, they were arguments that 'went too far' and which clearly precipitated a crisis both for the conventions of observation and expression, and for reader expectations; rather, they called in aid the imagination and poetic or prophetic intuition.

As Keynes well knew, the rhetorical model of balancing rational excursus with intuition has a specific foundation beneath what was retained in puritan preaching. This was the scientific and communicative method from which the nineteenth century had set off in reforming its own knowledge.

Even in the absence of autobiographical declarations of his influences and tastes, we can feel, in the web of quotations which runs through Keynes's writings and notes, the weight of contemporary culture and of the particular seduction of certain Victorian thinkers and writers. This is evident in the *Essays in Biography*, where the generation of the 'eminent Victorians' is prominent in the memoirs of such as Marshall, Paley and Edgeworth. Again, in the long essay 'The End of *Laissez-faire*' (1924–6), Keynes offers a detailed history of English-speaking economic thought, against the background of a markedly nineteenth-century ethical and political debate. But it is above all in *A Treatise on Probability* that Keynes most explicitly weighs up his debt to, and his distance from, the Victorian debate and its methods. In the *Treatise*, Keynes makes use of the conceptual issue of probability to settle his account with the styles and theories of traditional epistemology (from Leibniz to Mill, as we read in the Preface). He does this in a framework of critical and theoretical ideas which was strongly influenced by the thought of the new Cambridge philosophers. But the fundamental questions on which Keynes's theory of probability focuses were the central topics also for nineteenth-century epistemology: the choice of ordinary language, 'the weight of argument', the scientific recovery of a role for intuition and imagination, the legitimation of the use of analogy within a logical structure, and the place of 'rational belief' in a world of probability and uncertainty. We find an exact historical response to just these topics in the work of two important contributors to the Victorian scientific and philosophical debate who made a great impact on Keynes: Charles Darwin and Leslie Stephen.

The hypothesis of a strong connection between Keynes and his two predecessors, for all that it goes beyond Keynes's own, mostly bibliographical, testimony and beyond the marginal comments of his biographers, is a hypothesis with a close bearing on what he had to say about method. Keynes showed that he was thoroughly acquainted with *The Origin of Species* and the ethical and social debate to which the Darwinian theory gave rise. The close connection between Darwin and Keynes is not so much in the content of the theory of natural selection as in the procedure which produced it. In the *Treatise on Probability* Keynes spells out his interest in Darwin, and identifies the Darwinian method as a crucial scientific and analytic step forward in terms of an epistemological problem that is wider than the future of any one discipline. For what was in play was not, as for every genuinely scientific proposition, the ultimate 'truth' of the theory, which was neither more nor less verifiable than many theories in physics or in astronomy; rather, it was the value of the theory considered in terms of its ability to hold both empirically and as fruitful in further discussion, and therefore, in terms of its epistemological implications.

Darwin was happy to describe the *Origin of Species* by saying that 'this whole volume is one long argument' (Darwin 1950, p. 359), thus emphasizing that the method underlying it was non-scientistic and non-demonstrative. By that, he did not mean to offer yet another catalogue of facts, nor a reduction of them to a mere formula. Instead, what he offers is a constructive hypothesis based on an increment of evidence, on an accumulation of small indicators, 'vestiges', traces of the past, clues. Within the structure of analogy and metaphor, he had worked out his vision of nature, equally suspicious of a priori and of empiricist methods. But, as Keynes stresses, it was exactly that method, based on ordinary language, which allowed Darwin to proceed without apparent scientific contradiction:

> Not only in the main argument, but in many of the subsidiary discussions an elaborate combination of induction and analogy is superimposed upon a narrow and limited knowledge of statistical frequency. And this is equally the case in almost all everyday arguments of any degree of complexity. (*CW*, VIII, pp. 118–9)

Mobilizing a mixture of intuition and empirical non-contradiction, science is returned to its original home with probability and uncertainty, with 'some reasons for believing'. Science is again methodologically open to the imagination of things which are not immediately observable and open to interpretation. From this point of view, the two basic forms of knowledge are not related to each other as mutually irreducible methods, nor are they divided one from the other by distinct zones of applicability. Rather, as Keynes pointed out in a youthful essay discussing the continuity of the methods of Newton, Leibniz and Darwin, the procedures of 'Science or Art' are not so dissimilar.

From the time of that early essay to that of the final version of the *Treatise on Probability*, 'intuition' and 'analogical argument' are for Keynes the cornerstones that hold for knowledge which is less than conclusive but not on that account irrational: 'given the body of direct knowledge which constitutes our ultimate premisses, this theory tells us what further beliefs, certain or probable, can be derived by valid argument' (*CW*, VIII, p. 4). Here, by 'valid argument' he does not mean the abstract constructions of 'academic logic, such as the theory of the syllogism or the geometry of ideal space' (*CW*, VIII, p. 3); rather, he means arguments like Darwin's, elaborated from the point of view of 'a plain man with an obvious argument for all to see' (Levine and Madden (eds), 1968, p. 162): from this point of view, the empirical evidence will function as a check on, rather than as a justification of, the argument as a whole. And, paradoxically, by referring to that evidence, Darwin was enabled to launch an attack on traditional knowledge and on habits of thought and accepted authority which, until then, not even scientific rigour had been able to modify. From this there arose a rhetorically structured argument which opposed the accepted authorities of the old knowledge and the incontrovertible facts selected in the light of the new scheme and accumulated in accordance with a persuasive drive.[10]

Thus the Darwinian theory grew up and took shape within ordinary language, depending on an analogical process which, more than any other, spawned words and images. It is in just this way that scientific discourse, saturated with images and metaphors, projected itself beyond the systematized areas of knowledge towards still nebulous and uncodified zones, towards dizzying visions (such as that of the *Origin*) which were inconceivable in the 'habits of looking in a given way', and towards the rhetorics which made up the means for expressing them. The intuition which underlay the theory, that the natural world was unstable and in constant evolution, went beyond any empirical laboratory, beyond any descriptive-demonstrative logic; while the argument conducted in vivid ordinary language and 'full of imagination' would have allowed Darwin gradually to give it an expressive and rational guise; as Keynes would note:

> When we argue that Darwin gives valid grounds for our accepting his theory of natural selection we do not simply mean that we are psychologically inclined to agree with him; it is certain that we also intend to convey our belief that we are acting rationally in regarding his theory as probable. We believe that there is some real objective relation between Darwin's evidence and his conclusions, which is independent of the mere fact of our belief, and which is just as real and objective, though of a different degree, as that which would exist if the argument were as demonstrative as a syllogism. (*CW*, VIII, pp. 5–6)

Every branch of knowledge, including therefore, economics, could help itself to the margins of understanding which are implied by knowledge of language, in its implicit and explicit operation in favour of conceptual expression and clarification. All the same, as Keynes himself admitted, natural language picks up and becomes encrusted with 'habitual modes of thought' and their implications which are more insidious and tenacious than those implied in procedures guided by formalized methods. This accounts for the fact that Keynes's writing is thick with metalinguistic remarks and with logico-conceptual checking at every stage. It is not a matter of chance that Keynes gave space at the very beginning of *The General Theory* to consideration of the maieutic and scientific significance of working through language and writing:

> The composition of this book has been for the author a long struggle of escape, and so must be the reading of it for most readers if the author's assault on them is to be successful, – a struggle of escape from habitual modes of thought and expression ... The difficulty lies, not in the new

ideas, but in escaping from the old ones, which ramify, for those brought up as most of us have been, into every corner of our minds. (*CW*, VII, p. xxiii)

In *The General Theory* Keynes's important and widely discussed reflection on the relations between language and methods of knowledge-gathering is inextricably fused within the theoretical and discursive purpose of the book and this is one of the reasons given for its difficulty. Traces of this reflection can, however, be detected in *A Treatise on Money* and in the *Essays in Biography*, especially where he is discussing Malthus and Jevons, who also thought of economics as a 'very contracted science' and not at all as a branch of mathematics, pursuing thus their own analyses in non-formalized terms of 'suggestive remarks and careful analogies' (*CW*, X, p. 132).

After Darwin, the debate about knowledge, method and language went ahead also in non-scientific disciplines. Leslie Stephen was among those who took up and developed the historical and philosophical aspects of the epistemological issues which arose from the scientific debate of the nineteenth century. He applied them to the Humanities in general and to the disciplines which most closely touch on human conduct, such as ethics and economics. The biographical and intellectual relations between Stephen and Keynes are generally dealt with by the latter's biographers in slightly vague terms, with a reference to Stephen as the great father of Victorian agnosticism and the 'father' of Bloomsbury. Keynes's encounter with Stephen, in any case, preceded the formation of the Bloomsbury Group and belonged, rather, to the period of Keynes's intellectual growth, of his reading of university textbooks, and attendance at lectures and debates in the various Cambridge clubs.

Leaving aside the gaps in biography and autobiography, Leslie Stephen's personal history, his cultural and intellectual power and the theoretical positions he espoused, must have made him very much to Keynes's taste. As a historian of English thought, an exponent of moral, political and economic ideas, a man of letters and critic, Leslie Stephen seemed the complete Victorian intellectual, a bearer of eclectic knowledge, and proponent of a unified theory of that knowledge, balanced between theory and practice, between science and art.[11]

It was in the light of Stephen's highly influential and interdisciplinary reading of Locke, Hume and Adam Smith, of Rousseau, Malthus, Bentham and Mill, of Coleridge and Darwin that Keynes came to recapitulate the development of English thought. He was probably most familiar with Stephen's historical and theoretical writings, such as the study of Malthus, written when Stephen was a young fellow of Trinity Hall, the moral essays on 'agnosticism' and 'materialism', and *English Thought in the Eighteenth Century* (1876), which Keynes frequently cites.

Cutting across the range of kinds of knowledge and subjecting them anew to scrutiny in terms of the Moral Sciences, Stephen discussed methods and applications of complex knowledge and offered the starting-points for transforming the concepts of soul, consciousness, perception, rationality, and moral conduct. Following Darwin and prefiguring the Keynes of the *Treatise on Probability*, he stressed the importance of the adoption of analogies as a way for the human mind to respond to the complexity of reality. In 'What is Materialism?' (1886),[12] Stephen offers a reflective articulation of knowledge that runs from physics to theology and which is particularly noteworthy for its close methodological similarities to Darwin and Keynes. He picks up the substantial continuities among human knowledge-gathering procedures, which he reads as the product of a primordial rational drive in the species that is destined to perfect itself under evolutionary pressure. Thus, 'all scientific progress is a development and a more distinct articulation of the same procedure' (Stephen 1931, p. 87), which goes beyond the standing dualism of method and is independent of the context of any given discipline. The scientific and cognitive process advances therefore, in Lockean style, by the double capacity to perceive and to express judgements, that is, for the scientist to abstract and to project himself beyond the point of view of the 'direct observer' and to 'place himself in imagination at a different point of view' (Stephen 1931). From this follows the recovery of the mixed method of observation and intuition, the theoretical adoption of the rhetorical-argumentative method based on analogy and inference, and the unavoidable option of construction, the 'circle' to which the fragments of perception and judgement should ideally be referred back:

> What, then are we doing when we raise this vast structure of physical science, composed essentially of time and space formulae? We are filling up the gaps in our immediate perceptions. Each man's experience is *fragmentary, discontinuous and narrow*. He sees infinitesimal arcs, and connects them by *drawing the whole circle*. We are doing so somehow every instant of our lives, and when we reach the furthest limits of the physical sciences we are still doing the same. (Stephen 1931, p. 86, emphasis added)

In this way, Stephen confirms himself as an exponent of a characteristically post-Darwinian epistemological perspective and a distinctive voice of his age, with the exception of a few elements which point in uncommon directions for a nineteenth-century debate. We may think, in fact, about the extraordinary emphasis he gives to the problems of perspective and about the passing reference he makes to misty mental zones which are 'more or less conscious' and which is associated with the energizing awareness of the centrality of an individual 'current of consciousness'. Stephen recognizes that this mute current, operative in the gap between 'womb and tomb', is the ultimate 'basis of our knowledge', so offering a foretaste of a modernist approach to reality. Stephen reinterprets in terms of this vexed category the two adjacent categories of conscience and consciousness, and he conjectures the sketch of a philosophical theory of the mental, redefining subjective/objective knowledge and individual/general truth:

> Each of us is an absolute unit, cut off by an impassable abyss from a direct knowledge of other consciousness. But we weave the whole universe out of the senses, which somehow indicate the varying relations of bodies, and, through them, of other conscious beings to ourselves. Time and space are the warp and woof upon which is embroidered all the shifting scenery of consciousness. By means of it signals are thrown out to us from other centres: our isolation ceases, and our very thoughts are built up by the action and reaction of other minds. From the living body which I see and touch I infer unhesitatingly the existence of a mind analogous to my own, for only so can I explain its actions. The belief in the existence of others is part of my most fundamental convictions: and my whole system of thought is developed through the constant necessity of harmonising my thoughts with yours. The meaning of objective truth is, simply, that which is true both for you and me. (Stephen 1931, p. 94)

On the threshold of the twentieth century, the strong and demonstrative rationality of metaphysics and empirical relativism are simultaneously held in check by an already modernist subject which, having accepted that 'experience is fragmentary, discontinuous and narrow', looks for 'wider formulae in which his own experience is included, not formulae from which it is excluded' (Stephen 1931, p. 88). And it is in this way that the hypothesis of an 'omnipresent consciousness' (Stephen 1931, p. 88) takes shape. Such a hypothesis does not bring with it the abolition of the subject, but the mutual recognition of different subjects and the pooling of 'articulate and explicit' information and judgments (Stephen 1931, p. 84). Thus, subjective experience becomes objective, the commonly-held knowledge characteristic of science. What therefore emerges is the reality of a subject which is at once strong and incomplete and which, beyond its own individuality, is structured by the 'fundamental conviction' of the existence of others, of another consciousness which is not known directly but only by analogy. This sets off a chain reaction, a set of analogical mirrors which allot the subject to the realm of the discontinuous, the indirect and the propositional. The complex inheritance that Stephen left to his followers was a compound of reopened boundaries, uncertain constitutions, and conceptual paradoxes, such as the ideas of an intersubjective individuality, of objectivized subjectivity, or of a weak and intermittent rationality enclosed within 'the shifting scenery of consciousness'. We find in this inheritance a significant part of the modernist consciousness which would guide the twentieth century's far-reaching revision of epistemology in philosophy and in literature.

Moore, Russell, the Bloomsbury Group and certainly Keynes are all in some way the 'sons' of Stephen. It is reasonable to trace to his intellectual project the modernist notions of the subject, of reality, of representation, and the specifically Bloomsburyite developments of the individual experience as an irretrievably fragmentary one. With specific reference to Keynes, we may note the widespread sharing of subject-matters and procedures. If we look again at *A Treatise on Probability*, Stephen's influence is immediately detectable even in the work's overall structure. The book shares the major concerns which Stephen put forward in his more concentrated argumentation; the value of non-demonstrative reasoning (Part I); inferentialness (Part II); the relations between induction and analogy (Part III); the application of the theory to ethics (Part IV); and the possible extensions of the theory to statistical inference (Part V). Over and above the general similarities, it is worth using Stephen to consider the question of Keynes's so-called 'realism', in terms of the dialectic between the 'subjective' and the 'objective', between individual choice and rational behaviour, (see discussion set out by Hacking 1983, and taken up by Bellofiore, 1988 and this volume).[13]

The overall hypothesis is that Stephen might be the link between the scattered and unsystematized intuitions of Victorian thought about the theory of knowledge, and some of the completed epistemological theories that emerged from Cambridge. We shall consider in particular, a possible line of connection running from Stephen through Keynes to Wittgenstein, which is based on the shared intuition that language is central to the process of knowledge-gathering, both in its elementary phase and in its more complex manifestations: an intuition which follows from the axiom that private experience is unknowable except relationally or propositionally. Indeed, it was Stephen who first noted that,

> We thus obtain general statements of fact which bear no explicit reference to our own personal experience. We fancy that we thus get an 'objective' universe in the sense in which 'objective' means outside all consciousness, instead of meaning a formula common to all consciousness'. (Stephen 1931, p. 90)

Private experience finds a public dimension of general assent through the mediation of grammar; and, conversely, language *says* the world, *formulates* it in an already Wittgensteinian sense, and with that formula it also says what its conventions are, and what its illusions and fallacies.

The 'Fundamental Ideas' which Keynes discusses in the first part of *A Treatise on Probability* derive from these premises, as a general categorical and conceptual corollary of the theory. For Keynes also the non-propositional nature of knowledge and the transmission of sensations is at the centre of consideration. From it follows the observation of the relation between experience and linguistic convention, of the decisive, though ambiguous, role of memory, and of the hidden operation of habits, false premises and mistaken analogies.[14] Thus, the problem of 'intellectual illusions' proceeds from that of grammatical illusions. As Moore would note, the solution of a philosophical problem calls for a discussion of language; the solution of an ontological problem *tout court*, as Wittgenstein would add, calls for a discussion of language.

CAMBRIDGE EPISTEMOLOGY. KEYNES'S DIALOGUE WITH HIS CONTEMPORARIES

What *exactly* do you mean? (G.E. Moore)

What can be said at all can be said clearly, and what we cannot talk about we must pass over in silence. (L. Wittgenstein)

We are driven to philosophise because we do not know clearly what we mean; the question is always 'What do I mean by x?'. And only very occasionally can we settle this without reflecting on meaning. But it is not only an obstacle, this necessity of dealing with meaning; it is doubtless an essential clue to the truth. (F.P. Ramsey)

In the first decade of the twentieth century, charismatic presences dominated the intellectual debate in Cambridge. They had made and were making theoretical contributions of the highest importance. The characteristic feature of the debate was a generalized rejection of the dominant philosophical orthodoxies in the natural sciences and in logic, in social theory and moral attitudes and customs, as well as a passionate pursuit of new levels of clarity and speculative rigour. It falls neither within our aim nor within our competence to go too far into the detail of the content of this debate or into the particular contributions to it. We shall restrict ourselves to looking at it from the point of view which we may suppose was Keynes's; and we shall try to use memories and texts to bring out points of intersection, reciprocities of method and influences both direct and retarded.

For Keynes too, those were years of great activity and philosophical research, of debates, conferences, papers and writings which, in large part, were gathered into the *Treatise on Probability*. He recalls of those years and studies, 'I was writing under the joint influence of Moore's *Principia Ethica* and Russell's *Principia Mathematica*' (*CW*, X, p. 445). Thus, complying with his original fate, Keynes was again suspended between mathematics and philosophy, which at that time were the privileged areas of debate in Cambridge. The joint influence of Moore and Russell reformulated the problem of how to settle down in the face of the opposing pulls of intuitionism and of formal logic. This issue left Keynes's theory free-floating between the alternatives and, in different ways according to the occasion of or the level at which his intervention was pitched, alternating between the two analytic aspects. It is in terms of this split that we can make out the complicated and shifting set of alliances. Keynes was with Moore and Russel against the Hegelian metaphysicians, with the logicism of Russell and the early Wittgenstein against Moore's Common Sense, but with Moore and Ramsey in favour of a more 'human' logic and against the symbolic systems of the logicists, as well as with Ramsey's 'pragmatism' and the general tenor of the reassessment of experience and ordinary language by the later Wittgenstein.

With *Principia Ethica* (1903), Moore opened a route which undermined the dominant metaphysical philosophy of Bradley and McTaggart and which, at the same time, freed the native empiricism from some of its problems. For Moore, philosophy was to be understood as critical, as the site for the testing of analytic tools and for the clarification of the logico-linguistic apparatus that functions within various constructs of knowledge. As Leslie Stephen had already seen, the historical defeat of metaphysics was to come about by means of a new consciousness of language:

> Metaphysical arguments are apt to take the form of arguments about words. A system of classification is already implied in a nomenclature. ... Philosophers are constantly at cross-purposes over the misunderstandings which are thus introduced. (Stephen 1931, p. 81)

Keynes was probably among the first to pick up the novelty of Moore's thought and to offer a constructive critique of *Principia Ethica*, proposing additions to and amendments of the book. His active response to Moore comes out in his writing of a set of papers for the Apostles on ethics and aesthetics between 1903 and the time he took the Civil Service Examination, at which time he decided to leave the academic world.

Keynes takes on and discusses Moore's influence, from his university days until the time of writing the paper, in 'My Early Beliefs' (1938). And the piece remains a noteworthy resumé of *Principia Ethica*, or at least of Moore according to Keynes thirty years later. What becomes clear from Keynes's autobiographical account is that the novelty of Moore's thought was to be measured against the background of the philosophical orthodoxy. For Keynes, reading the *Principia Ethica* must have tasted of a shock of recognition, the cultural and scientific location of trends of thought which had been barely understood by traditional culture, even if not entirely alien to certain strands of the late-Victorian consciousness. The longstanding puritan–Victorian lineage of rational and argumentative clarification found in Moore an inspired and vigorous representative. His friends and colleagues recall his extraordinary argumentative tenacity, his obsessive 'insistence on clarity and preciseness, which was remorselessly turned on ambiguities and verbal and conceptual fallacies'. And in all this, Keynes recalls, there was great passion, and an indication of method:

> It was a method of discovery by the instrument of impeccable grammar and an unambiguous dictionary. 'What *exactly* do you mean?' was the phrase most frequently on our lips. If it appeared under cross-examination that you did not mean *exactly* anything, you lay under a strong suspicion of meaning nothing whatever. It was a stringent education in dialectic. (*CW*, X, p. 440)

What is at issue is a method of working, of education, of something to do with verbal spelling out in the public realm. Then, at the point at which ethical and aesthetic values meet the world, the clarification of reference must be articulated metalinguistically.

Metaphysics and the utilitarian calculus were not lacking in criteria for the identification and the reckoning of the Good and the Beautiful. However, Moore preferred axioms to probable fallacies, and he proposed that ethical and aesthetic predicates refer to notions which are objective, simple, unique, indefinable, unanalysable and equally divorced from the principles of absolute truth or empirical checking. Being undefinable and unanalysable, the Good became for Moore an intuitive category which as such, was not subject to measurement or mathematical decomposition. In other words, the Good was a paradigmatic instance of an 'organic unity', in the traditional acceptance of a complex whole whose value is not a function of the sum of values of the parts. Thus, for example, the universal Good is not equal to the sum of the particular Goods. And with this move, as if by a miracle, Moore eliminated the Benthamite fantasies and freed the concepts of happiness and social utility from the one-sided interpretation which conventional Victorian morality had given to them. It is at this point that the distinction between goodness and rightness is made out and matures, with its freight of ethical and social implications, as Keynes, too reports, 'It was an important object of Moore's book to distinguish between goodness as an attribute of states of mind and rightness as an attribute of actions' (*CW*, X, p. 445).

The future members of Bloomsbury – Strachey, Bell, Woolf and Keynes – all insisted on the liberating effect of Moore's philosophy (see for example, Bell 1956). For all that it was analysed within the overall intersubjective scheme of human relations, the Good retained its character as an intrinsic Good. Originally, this was located in the inscrutable logic of 'states of consciousness' – which Keynes and Strachey called 'states of mind' – the fleeting but deep experiences which it is given to the human consciousness to undergo in the contemplation of nature or art objects, or in 'the pleasures of human intercourse' such as love and friendship. Such was the scheme which Keynes described as a religion without a morality, 'meaning by "religion" one's attitude towards oneself and the ultimate and by "morality" one's attitude towards the outside world and the intermediate' (*CW*, X, p. 436).

The members of the Bloomsbury Group partly rejected Keynes's reading of Moore; they did not accept the image of themselves as 'immoral', calling in evidence the social and political commitment which many of Moore's followers, including notably Keynes himself, shared (Woolf 1960 pp. 90–94). After all, in 'My Early Beliefs', Keynes selects and comments on those parts of Moore's philosophy which had absorbed his own attention, and he leaves aside many others. In his effort to provide a rational reconstruction of Moore's thought, he does not give adequate weight, among other things, to his own influence on the revision of parts of the *Principia*, particularly Chapter 5, which discusses 'Ethics in relation to conduct'.

In 1904, Keynes had presented to the Apostles a paper contesting the practical ethics which Moore had proposed. In particular, Keynes could not accept the justification of 'commonly accepted norms', according to which, in the absence of objective forecasts of a greater good, every individual is required always to conform to those norms which are both generally useful and generally accepted. As Keynes notes, this conservative attitude was a return to Common Sense as an 'obligation so to act as to produce by causal connection the most probable maximum of eventual good throughout the whole procession of future ages' and 'the duty of the individual to obey general rules' (*CW*, X, p. 446). Morever, it was not consistent with the theory's basic logical and argumentative drive. The logical consequence ought rather to have been the promotion of rational conduct, the mobilization of a fully autonomous 'right to judge' and an encouragement of civilization, understood in the utopian sense of a community of 'reliable, rational, decent people influenced by truth and objective standards' (*CW*, X, p. 447). It was certainly with this dichotomy in mind that Keynes went ahead and changed his own behaviour and judgements in the direction of heresy, taking the accusation of 'immorality' as the inevitable price to be paid for the moral conformity that had spread through the England of Common Sense and Queen Victoria:

> We had no respect for traditional wisdom or the restraints of custom. We lacked reverence, as Lawrence observed. (*CW*, X, pp. 447–8)

> Before heaven we claimed to be our own judge in our own case. I have come to think that this is, perhaps, rather a Russian characteristic. It is certainly not an English one. It resulted in a general, widespread, though partly covert, suspicion affecting ourselves, our motives and our behaviour. … It is, I now think, a justifiable suspicion. Yet so far as I am concerned, it is too late to change, I remain, and always will remain, an immoralist. (*CW*, X, pp. 446–7)

Setting aside biographical and autobiographical considerations, these *petitiones principii* had at the same time produced innovative theoretical stances about rational belief and moral behaviour. For Keynes, probability, judgement and action all formed part of a single project which was simultaneously logical and ethical, and which sought out reasons, contexts and hypotheses that are in fact probabilistic judgements expressed in ordinary language and based on action-oriented beliefs (cf. Carabelli 1988, p. 160). It was this double link between theory and action, whose roots are in the complex heritage that we tried to sketch in the preceding sections, that inspired Keynes to include in his *Treatise on Probability* a chapter devoted to practical ethics. Later, it would also be at work in the methodological orientation of his historical and economic analyses.

We shall return in the next section to consider at length the development and radicalization of Moore's ethical theory in Keynes's economic theory. For the time being, it is worthwhile to recall that Keynes built up the theoretical hypothesis of the 'immediate good' as an alternative to Moore's 'universal good' on logicist grounds, out of premises, choices and expectations appraised with logico-rational instruments in conditions of limited knowledge.

To distance himself from some traditional fallacies in moral philosophy, Keynes makes use of more sophisticated analytical tools, in part borrowed from Russell's formal logical schematism which was as influential as Moore on the background of the philosophical renewal. But Russell's influence on the theory of probability was limited to a procedural starting-point which was quickly set aside. The idea of systematically carrying out an analysis of ethical choice in logico-mathematical terms led to rigid and absolutely general formalizations, to schematic descriptions that said little about the complexity of experience or human behaviour. In fact in his book Keynes gave over a whole chapter, as controversial as it is full of methodological implications, to the idea of a 'complex and manifold' reality. What would be the status of issues of the 'individual' and the 'particular', which had been hard-fought gains from the metaphysical Absolute and from the Benthamite 'collective', in a world of general propositions that were indefinitely manipulable in accordance with a logical calculus? What, indeed, would be the status of reality *tout court*? After all, Keynes had found Moore's ethical thought wanting in its handling of the problem of the ontological and philosophical justification of the 'particular' (cf. the sacrifice of the 'individual case' to 'general rules'). For similar reasons, Russell was doomed at that point to fall by the wayside, as the mirror image, even though working separately, of the school of thought which, in order to make progress, had ended by being unable to distinguish 'propositions from tables'. It was nevertheless, through Russell, and more generally through the discussions of mathematicians and logicians, that Keynes encountered non-philosophical theories and analytic methods and learned to make use of 'mixed descriptions and norms', thus launching himself on the wider testing-ground of the growing Cambridge epistemology. From his experiences in that testing-ground, Russell himself had emerged profoundly changed, no longer a mathematician, but a theorist of knowledge and of representation, gripped by disputes about the particular and the general, experience and observation, and thus, as we shall see later, again an interlocutor for Keynes.

After the natural sciences, it was the logico-mathematical sciences which began to re-lay the foundations of their own knowledge. By the turn of the century Frege had proposed techniques for defending the logical status of thought as something universal and objective. To underwrite the well-formedness of the propositions of logic and mathematics, Frege developed a logically 'perfect' formalism, relieved of the weight of emotive significance of ordinary language, by which to discipline inferential and mathematical procedures. Partly independently of Frege, Russell had arrived at similar conclusions and likewise thought that artificial languages could afford an effective means for reducing ambiguity and fallacy to a minimum. Thus, the logico-mathematical sciences had found, in considering the role of language in the transmission of knowledge, common ground from which, indirectly, to attack the imprecise language of metaphysics. But in venturing onto ground which had traditionally been philosophy's private property, these disciplines were making themselves philosophical, as Keynes notes, 'in the year 1903 ... Bertrand Russell's *Principles of Mathematics* was published, giving a new life to formal logic and seeming to bring new kingdoms within its scope' (*CW*, X, p. 337).

The crisis for one model, and the consequent urgency of redefining working methods and instruments, had opened up the boundaries of the discipline and pushed it towards others, transmitting also to these others the symptoms of its unease, of fundamental inadequacy. In the face of this collapsing of barriers and of the possible compromising of contexts and tools, epistemology set itself up as an Ur-discipline, liberated from the distinct heritages of specialized branches of knowledge. Briefly, mathematics, logic, philosophy and history worked laterally with each other under the umbrella of Cambridge epistemology on the metalinguistic and metascientific cutting-edge questions, before they broke up and returned to the confines of their own specializations. It is against the background of this slippage and mixing of disciplines that the philosophy of language and the philosophy of science came into their own, setting the terms of the new debate on knowledge; without that background Keynes's economic method is not conceivable or would have been rendered barely intelligible by its complexity.

Along with Keynes, F.P. Ramsey and Ludwig Wittgenstein were paradigmatic products of the interaction of logic, mathematics and philosophy in those years. There is no precise biographical information, and there have been no systematic studies which would support a strong claim of their mutual influence; but there is evidence of their relations, which were intermittent because of the well-known historical and biographical vicissitudes of those years.

On Frege's advice, Wittgenstein arrived in Cambridge in 1911 to meet Russell. He established a useful relationship with Moore in particular; it was in part through Moore's intervention that the *Tractatus Logico-Philosophicus* was published in English. Wittengstein's *Tractatus* followed Keynes's *Treatise* by a few months. The first translation of the former was by C.K. Ogden and F.P. Ramsey. Ramsey was then a promising nineteen-year old undergraduate; and his involvement with the book continued with a critical notice of it printed in *Mind* for 1923; likewise, he reviewed Keynes's book for the *Cambridge Magazine* in 1922 and further discussed it in his essay 'Truth and Probability' (1926, reprinted in Ramsey 1978). Between 1923 and 1928, Ramsey went to visit Wittgenstein in Austria on several occasions; and the criticisms that he mounted against the theory of language which the *Tractatus* expounds were among Wittgenstein's motives for starting his self-criticism. At Ramsey's insistence and with Keynes's support, Wittgenstein returned to Cambridge in 1929 and was made a Fellow of Trinity. In 1931, Ramsey died prematurely, and Keynes wrote several essays, printed together in *Essays in Biography*, about his brief but very intense intellectual activity, which extended also to problems of economic theory. As usual for Keynes, the biographical fragment was an occasion for rethinking and for reconstituting a thinker's connections and influences; for us, it is a useful key for the progressive focusing of his method.

In the *Tractatus* Wittgenstein went further along the road of clarification of the logico-analytic apparatus which had been opened up by Russell and Moore. He concluded by putting in check the foundations, the very *raison d'être* of philosophy, consigning its predicates to the realm of nonsense. The *destructio destructionis philosophiae* which the text contains sets out from the demonstration Wittgenstein offers of the fundamental absurdity of 'saying' in philosophy. This is allowed to spread to all matters in which there is no system of verification and in which there is metaphysics and false analogies. Philosophy ought not to found anything, but only concern itself with the refinement of appropriate instruments of 'showing', not of interpretation or argument or demonstration. Only when it is wholly free from the trammels of essence and causality can the analytic language be thought to have achieved a rigorous and scientific standing. Hence, Wittgenstein is envisaging the bare bones of a 'pictographic' language which operates on combinations of propositions which serve merely to present autonomous, independent and immediately verifiable representations of states of affairs which are neither related one to another nor permit the deduction of the existence or non-existence of other facts or states of affairs. This move of prohibiting philosophical 'saying' has a noteworthy *abime* towards the end of the *Tractatus*:

> My propositions serve as elucidations in the following way: anyone who understands me eventually recognizes them as nonsensical, when he has used them – as steps – to climb up beyond them. (He must, so to speak, throw away the ladder after he has climbed up it.) (Wittgenstein 1921, English trans. 1961, 6.54)

One underlying thought here might be that every piece of everyday language, since it is affected by conventions and habits, must be capable of continual reassessments. But over and above any issue of a scientific or philosophical metalanguage, the *Tractatus* picks out with great precision 'saying' *tout court* as the site of possible misunderstanding and of the possible solution of the problem of ontology, thus bringing about the complete dissolution of the traditional problems of philosophy. And, in line with the solutions proposed by Russell's thoughts about logic and mathematics, Wittgenstein in the end agrees with the need to construct an artificial analytic language, untainted by the ambiguities of the grammar of natural languages.

For all that they were working in the same theoretical atmosphere, Keynes and Wittgenstein found themselves in very different positions in terms of their conclusions and working choices at this stage of theorizing. They diverged, for instance, on the role to be assigned to causality, which in revised form was for Keynes fundamental to the building up of logico-rational thought; on the scientific legitimacy of argumentation, and on the cultural and social necessity of 'saying' in philosophy and ethics. And where Wittgenstein aimed at 'showing' more or less aseptically, Keynes chose to employ a representative method which was narrative and anti-mimetic. Where Wittgenstein sought a stripped-down means of expression, and spurned all non-deductive connections among propositions, Keynes chose a 'controlled' verbal proliferation and exercised himself to find connections which could be rigorously underpinned by a 'rational' calculus of probabilities. Against the background of this picture of disparity, the one thing which unites Wittgenstein and Keynes is the search for a theory that aims to put the fragment of experience, the 'particular', back into the verbal and ana- lytic framework with the least possible distortion.

The attraction which experience exercised on Keynes was internal to the scientific project from the very outset, and, as we have seen, had priority. On the other hand, for Wittgenstein, it took shape with the process of revising the views expressed in the *Tractatus*, with the aban- donment of the distribution of possibilities in truth-tables and the build- ing up of the concepts of 'range' and 'field'.[15] But the new logicism ran into ever more radical prohibition on 'systematizing' ideas, and into the preference for aphoristic writing. Keynes was right, from his standpoint, to observe that 'Wittgenstein's solution was to regard everything else as a sort of inspired nonsense, having great value indeed for the individual, but incapable of being exactly discussed' (*CW*, X, p. 338).

It was Ramsey's thinking which filled the gap between the *Treatise* and the *Tractatus*, and also helped to reinforce the small amount of common purpose between them. As Keynes notes, with Ramsey, the project of logic returns to fill itself with experience and humanity. The problem was not so much the gathering and evaluation of 'facts' as the context of experience, 'not things, but *life* in general'. Ramsey's gen- eral outlook is cited by Keynes in the 'Anthology' appended to his memoirs of the young philosopher:

> My picture of the world is drawn in perspective and not like a model to scale. The foreground is occupied by human beings and the stars are as small as threepenny bits. I don't really believe in astronomy, except as a complicated description of part of the course of human and possibly animal sensation. I apply my perspective not merely to space but also to time. In time the world will cool and everything will die; but that is a long time off still and its present value at compound discount is almost nothing. Nor is the present less valuable because the future will be blank. Humanity, which fills the foreground of my picture, I find interesting and on the whole

admirable ... You may find it depressing; I am sorry for you. (*CW*, X, p. 345)

Ramsey's humanistic bent returns analytic speculation to topics which were for Keynes more reassuring and attractive – 'comfortable to the human intellect' (*CW*, X, p. 335). The human scale of a limited and perspectival rationality, of the time-span of experience and of the short-term, is operative, free of anguish, within the unstable phenomenal world. Moreover, Ramsey proposed important new ideas in the philosophy of language, moving ever more rapidly towards a pragmatic conception of speech as linguistic act, as an act endowed with ethical and social significance. In Keynes's words:

> Ramsey's reaction was towards what he himself described as a sort of pragmatism, not unsympathetic to Russell but repugnant to Wittgenstein. 'The essence of pragmatism', he says, 'I take to be this, that the meaning of a sentence is to be defined by reference to the actions to which asserting it would lead, or, more vaguely still, by its possible causes and effects. Of this I feel certain, but of nothing more definite'. (*CW*, X, p. 338)

or again:

> Yet in attempting to distinguish a more 'human' logic from formal logic on the one hand and descriptive psychology on the other, Ramsey may have been pointing the way to the next field of study when formal logic has been put into good order and its highly limited scope properly defined. (*CW*, X, p. 339)

Indeed, in two essays, 'Facts and Propositions', published in 1927, and 'General Propositions and Causality', written in 1929 as the second part of 'Law and Causality' and published only posthumously, Ramsey asserted the pragmatic significance of linguistic expressions. He emphasized the operative force with which propositions are freighted, and the power of language to direct human behaviour. Ramsey re-established an analytic technique which moreover, rejected the closed and artificial procedures of analysis in terms of the equivalence and substitutability of alternative forms of the same proposition. Rather, he aimed to refer propositions to the real context from which they arise, to the habits and accidents of actual beliefs, which men create by connecting verbal propositions with behaviour patterns of varying degrees of utility. Thus, philosophical enquiry was returned to a space altogether more in tune with the British tradition, and extraordinarily close to the

outlines supplied by Leslie Stephen and longed for by Keynes. This
was a realm of relations, in which we see at work the conjunction of
consciousnesses, facts, judgements, verbal and social behaviour and
'rational' prediction about them. Thus stripped of the task of providing
a foundation or prescriptions, logic found a no less dignified *raison
d'être* in the more modest programme of making 'fragmentary progress',
and finding 'provisional solutions', a programme which is always subject to modification and correction.

Under these theoretical provocations, Wittgenstein returned to Cambridge and to philosophical work in 1929. The *Philosophical Investigations* (written from 1941 onwards, and published incomplete and posthumously in 1953) begins with the abandonment of the notion of a
formal language and endorses the good standing of the meaning and
usefulness of ordinary language. Once the theory of the double use of
language has been eliminated, and the general validity of ordinary
language has been accepted, understanding no longer seems to be a
sophisticated process; it is rather, 'operating with language'. It was
with the lectures on private experience delivered in 1934–6 (Wittgenstein
1968), that Wittgenstein began to face the matter, by analysing the
representation of sensations in relation to the grammar of the categories
of ordinary language, and by studying the formation of the systems of
expectations which ordinary language includes and activates.

At this point, Keynes and Wittgenstein come back into contact on
more solid ground. With Ramsey and Wittgenstein in mind, we propose
rereading the well-known *petitio principii* which, in order to clarify and
justify his own approach to economic analysis, Keynes places in *The
General Theory* in favour of ordinary language and against formal
languages:

> The object of our analysis is not to provide a machine or method of blind
> manipulation, which will furnish an infallible answer, but to provide our-
> selves with an organised and orderly method of thinking out particular
> problems; and after we have reached a provisional conclusion by isolating
> the complicating factors one by one, we then have to go back on ourselves
> and allow, as well as we can, for the probable interactions of the factors
> amongst themselves ... it is a great fault of symbolic pseudo-mathematical
> methods of formalising a system of economic analysis ... that they ex-
> pressly assume strict independence between the factors involved ... whereas,
> in ordinary discourse, ... we can keep 'at the back of our heads' the
> necessary reserves and qualifications and the adjustments which we shall
> have to make later on. ... Too large a portion of recent 'mathematical'
> economics are merely concoctions, as imprecise as the initial assumptions

they rest on, which allow the author to lose sight of the real world in a maze of pretentious and unhelpful symbols. (*CW*, VII, pp. 297–8)

Earlier in probability theory, now in economic analysis, the central plank of the method is argumentation in ordinary language. This follows from the idea of the complexity of the object of study and of the 'organic interdependence' which no formal language can cope with; and it satisfies the need for a procedure that is subject to rational control but not rigid. It is a method at once rigorous and flexible, capable of sustaining subsequent additions, subtractions, adjustments and, if occasion demands, restarts. With *The General Theory*, Keynes confirmed his interest in 'high theory' which had already been a feature of his intense work on the *Treatise on Money* (1930), and which now followed the long suspension in which he was engaged in practical affairs, as Government economic expert at the Treasury, and teaching in the Economic Tripos. From the point of view and the experience of social and political commitment he returns with an articulated theoretical project, and it is at this point that the paths of Keynes and Wittgenstein parted once and for all. In fact, Wittgenstein's faithfulness to the fragments of experience cannot be brought into line with any project of systematic observation and theoretical construction. For Wittgenstein, philosophy was to be solely a 'practice' made up of 'long and involved journeyings' (Wittgenstein 1953, Preface) in which all the pleasures of theory-building were to be denied. As he would say of the *Investigations*, the book brings together 'a number of sketches of landscapes' which could not and ought not to be anything else: 'the book is really only an album' (Wittgenstein 1953, Preface). Or again:

The fundamental fact here is that we lay down rules, a technique, for a game, and that then when we follow the rules things do not turn out as we had assumed. That we are therefore as it were entangled in our own rules. This entanglement in our own rules is what we want to understand. ... The civil status of a contradiction, or its status in civil life: there is the philosophical problem. (Wittgenstein 1953, sec 125)

The untangling, and the learning which follows from this process is for Wittgenstein, a tacit return to 'mythology', in so far as it is founded within the powerful image of persuasion. In this respect, Wittgenstein's thought ceases to connect with Keynes's. By contrast, the latter was searching for an overall design, and was building models for the gradual harnessing of expectations and predictions, in order to be able to give interpretations. In the process of relaunching the project of pursuing and offering interpretations, Keynes came into contact with rather different theoretical undertakings: first, the theory of representation which inspired the modernist experimentation in the visual arts and literature of the Bloomsbury Group, and second, the Freud of the narrative 'method' and of analytic construction – the very same Freud whom Wittgenstein had included among the modern bearers of 'mythology' (Wittgenstein 1978, p. 52).

FROM CAMBRIDGE TO BLOOMSBURY: CONVERGENCES IN METHOD

> Whoever wishes to become a philosopher must learn not to be frightened by absurdities. (B. Russell)

Away from Cambridge and academic debate, Moore's *Principia* and Russell's *Principles* kept all their meaningfulness in the London context. After passing the Civil Service Examination and having been accepted by the India Office, Keynes arrived in London in 1906. He seemed still to be occupied with philosophical issues, like the old and new friends who at that time made up his London 'family' around Bloomsbury: Lytton Strachey, Roger Fry, Clive Bell, Leonard Woolf, Desmond MacCarthy, Leslie Stephen's three children Adrian, Vanessa and Virginia – in short, the Bloomsbury Group.[16] In moving from Cambridge to Bloomsbury, the new ethical and philosophical thought had found its way into everyday life, into behaviour and talk; it was reflected in private choices, in social, political and creative activity, and became a lifestyle.

Bearing in mind the variety of interests represented, there was an underlying intellectual and moral unity in the group which went beyond the sometimes acerbic disagreements (such as the disapproval in the case of Keynes of his work at the Treasury and his governmental commitments). This unity was made up in the first place by shared influences and, in the second, by a genuine convergence of interests and aspirations.

As Keynes clearly states in 'My Early Beliefs', we ought to look for the grounds of the homogeneousness of the group in the historical process of its formation. First of all, the members shared a common family and cultural background, that of the Great Family, to which we referred earlier. And then there was the youthful acceptance of the 'religion' inspired by Moore's *Principia Ethica*, the reading of which was 'overwhelming ... exciting, exhilarating, the beginning of a renaissance' (*CW*, X, p. 435). It was thus the analytic 'method' of the new Cambridge philosophers which provided a rallying-point for the future Bloomsburyites. This led to the choice of a clear-headed and unflagging practice 'on the basis of a firm desperation' (Russell 1967) by means of which to make new sense of the various fields of human experience, of knowledge and of art. And from it there arose that characteristic view of the world which was unfettered by 'habit' but which also strove to put together rigorous but flexible tools with which to confront a reality whose complexity and multiplicity had been taken on board. And it is to this that we may also trace the consciousness of the centrality of language as the primary site of the conservation and refraction of 'habits' and 'conventions of thought', and therefore, also as the site at which they could be changed.

'What is reality?' was the question which every Bloomsburyite had to face. Fry faced it by proposing new critical approaches to understanding the difficult art of the avant-garde in painting. Strachey and Virginia Woolf faced it in their pursuit of a way of writing biography and narrative which was capable of representing human experience according to a modern consciousness. And Keynes did so in redefining the realm of economic reality, and in constructing an analytic method which could embrace the current situation, which classical economics had shown itself hardly able to understand at all. In these projects, the widest variety of experiences grew up in some sort of concord to produce the Post-Impressionist Exhibition set up by Fry and Clive Bell (1910), Strachey's *Eminent Victorians*, Woolf's *To the Lighthouse* and Keynes's *The Economic Consequences of the Peace* and *The General Theory*.

As we said, in terms of the question of influence we may pick out the initial core of the Bloomsbury Group in terms of a particular reading of Moore's *Principia*, or, a particular misunderstanding of it, according to Keynes's report, anxious to specify the changes which had taken place in his and the group's intellectual life since their early outings in Cambridge. Moore's contribution was decisive both in terms of method and with respect to the contents of the analysis. In the *Principia* Moore had set out new bases for philosophical reasoning, and built on those bases in order to put the whole edifice of Victorian ethics in check. Where traditional ethical theories had admitted, so to speak, only one possibility, Moore showed that there were other possibilities and a variety of alternatives for practical conduct, all of which were compat-

ible with the ethical predicates (Gargani 1979, p. 80). Thus Moore's
writing licensed a new analytic scrutiny which was attentive to multiplicity and to possibility, and which could therefore be hoped to be free
from 'crude obstacles to vision', from encumbering left-overs of habits
and conventions. This was a scrutiny which, in accepting the multiplicity of practical choices available to humans, at the same time ques-
tioned itself about the criteria and procedures of the analysis, about
method. In Moore's *Principia*, the discussion of method is carried on
pari passu with the conceptual clarification and precedes the declara-
tion of general principles. In the text 'method' is a word which recurs
frequently. We hear of 'ethical method' and of 'a reason of method', of
a procedural rigour which is nevertheless subject to checking and to
further adjustments, and thus distinct from the neat, but costricting,
alternatives presented by the choice between a priori and inductive
reasoning.

This discussion of method also fired the enthusiasm of Moore's
young followers. Lytton Strachey was among the first to praise, 'that
Method which shines like a sword between the lines. It is the scientific
method deliberately applied, for the first time, to Reasoning'; while
Russell picked up its specific features: 'it strikes me as a triumph of
lucidity ... the whole seems to me to be intelligible to any attentive and
candid reader ... I think the book all through is a model of exposition'.[17] Thus, lucidity, intelligibility and expository control were the
constitutive elements of a method which, as Russell had seen, found its
source in a new consciousness about, and a certain use of, language.

Moore's pupils, in Cambridge and Bloomsbury, made the debate
about method their own and enriched it with independent materials,
extending it from ethics to logic, aesthetics, criticism and literature. In
particular, Keynes had devoted ten years to the study of method. And
the book which discusses it, and which was to be before his mind in
considering economics and politics, was brought to its final form in the
years in which he was associated with Bloomsbury.

Virgina Woolf, too, took up and worried about matters of 'method' in
her essays of criticism and of refoundation of the narrative form ('methods of writing and describing life'). More specifically, she sought in
'method', as a variant on 'design' and 'pattern', a means, between
perception and observation, of giving a controlled exposition of reality.[18] She notes that it is from the method that we can deduce the
observer's perspective. If it is immediately clear – she argues – that the
method that is meant to transmit something in a mute consciousness is

not up to the task, is incrusted with conventions, expectations and emphases which can no longer be taken to be true, then it is the method that must be changed. It must be changed in such a way as to bring the representation into line with the new consciousness, to allow the new vision to emerge freely. Without doubt, Fry's *Vision and Design* (1920) had a more direct influence than did Moore on Woolf's pursuit of modern solutions to the problem of the relation between experience and art. But, in his turn, Fry justifies his critical method in that book's preface with thoughts which are full of echoes of Moore:

> A certain scientific curiosity and a desire for comprehension have impelled me at every stage to make generalisations, to attempt some kind of logical co-ordination of my impressions. But, on the other hand, I have never worked out for myself a complete system such as the meta-physicians deduce from *a priori* principles. ... My æsthetic ... has been held merely until such time as fresh experiences might confirm or modify it. Moreover, I have always looked on my system with a certain suspicion. I have recognised that if it ever formed too solid a crust it might stop the inlets of fresh experience, ... So that even in its latest form I do not put forward my system as more than a provisional induction from my own æsthetic experiences.[19]

Fry's self-revelation could be very well applied to Keynes. Whether we are talking about pictures, about literary figures or about economic facts, however strange it may seem, the questions to be asked seem much the same and the answers show a surprising similarity. What is the relation between reality and representation, between particular and general? What method, model or design permits us to bring together experience and theory, object and pattern? How are we to represent the complex scene of instances and human behaviours without the scrutiny, the method which we superimpose, rendering a version which is too simplified or too generic?

Seeking a way between the a priori and empirical experience, Moore had ended up outlining a casuistry of the Good, which sought to cut across the divide between the particular and the general, but, in cases of ethical doubt, 'general rules' were to have sway over individual judgement. At this point in the argument, he was vitriolically attacked by Keynes and, in some measure, lost his hold on the Bloomsbury writers. They, by contrast, made the precariousness and provisionalness of the context and method into one of their philosophical values and a criterion of the firm foundation of their theoretical programme. And in line with this, the programme was marked by constant experimentation, provisional solutions, ever-shifting syntheses and tensions of genre.

The trajectory of Virginia Woolf's developing narrative technique is, in this regard, paradigmatic, balanced between 'moment' and 'pattern', between the minimal and the symbolic. Keynes's case is equally paradigmatic, inasmuch as, after the limbering up of the *Treatise on Probability*, he conceives of economic analysis as the result of a constant interaction between experience and idea, between practice and theory, and reappraising the individuals in the English-speaking economic tradition who had operated with a similar consciousness. Also for Keynes the problem from the very start, was to find measures, to find the relation between vision (observation) and design (theory). In other words, he sought sufficiently complex and flexible means for representation and descriptive models to enable him to open up new vistas on reality which had been passed over by superficial and conventional observation. *The Economic Consequences of the Peace* and *The General Theory* are the two texts in which, albeit at different times and in different contexts, Keynes most explicitly confronts the problem. In the one case, he deploys a mode of writing which privileges the 'fragment' and which operates on the apparently 'minor' in order to restore to the official story a lost or suppressed wholeness. In the other, he takes on the dizzying challenge of providing a general theory which nevertheless will be able to 'take account of a more detailed complex of facts than can be treated on general principles' (*CW*, VII, p. 249).

What Keynes learnt from Moore's choice of ordinary language, against the background of their shared puritan–Victorian consciousness of the 'weight' of language, and from the way that the exposition itself is a crucial stage of conceptual clarification, he immediately put to work. Keynes made use of the experience as a theorist of probability and he gradually extended what he had learnt to economic analysis until, in *The General Theory*, he reaches a meta-discursive level which Moore had not foreseen. Kahn provides an indirect comment on Keynes's original impulse to employ ordinary language, when he discusses the case of two writings which are nearly consecutive and flatly in conflict: *A Tract on Monetary Reform* and *A Treatise on Money* (cf. Kahn quoted in Keynes, M. (ed), 1983, pp. 47–85). At a distance of three years, Keynes reconsiders the matter of currency, and, with a methodological justification reminiscent of Moore, he warns his reader of his intention 'to analyse and arrange our material in what will turn out to be a useful way for tracing cause and effect, when we have vitalised them by the introduction of extraneous facts from the actual world' (*CW*, V, p. 125).

The new treatment rises from the ashes of the old in the light of events and new perspectives – cf. the 'precious light' shed by the appearance of Robertson's theories (Preface, *Treatise on Money*). Using techniques that would be used again in *The General Theory*, and the use of which he explicitly admits in the Preface, Keynes arrived at a definitive version of the new treatise after 'a long struggle', which, then as later, involved 'the process of getting rid of the ideas which I used to have and of finding my way to those which I now have ... I feel like someone who has been forcing his way through a confused jungle' (*CW*, V, p. xvii). In short, what he proposes is to metabolize the classical theory, taken to its logical conclusion, in such a way that the old theory is enveloped in the new and makes up the material of it, although it is transformed by the work which language does.

In *The General Theory*, the 'long struggle', the process of laborious, stepwise readjustment of thought within writing, would achieve its greatest radicalization, producing among other things, the well-known problems of 'obscurity' and of rhetorical excess. Here, at the macroscopic level, the discussion continually reflects on itself and the writing turns itself into a fertile site for the generation of thoughts which do not pre-exist it, but which are sown within the language and within the non-linear, infectious, branching logic of ordinary discourse, that embraces temporary contradictions and tolerates disgressions and restarts. This, then, is a handling which has little in common with the formulaic process of 'symbolic pseudo-mathematical methods of formalising' (*CW*, VII, p. 297). Rather, it gradually settles into the opaque material of common language, which is thick with margins and fragments of meaning, and is unique in allowing us to 'keep "at the back of our heads" the necessary reserves and qualifications and the adjustments which we shall have to make later on' (*CW*, VII, p. 297).

We may return to the underlying hypothesis around which all the contributions to this volume gather: that, in *The General Theory*, the method is markedly a matter of language. For Keynes, the theory is distilled out of the contexts of ordinary talk, which shares the rhythms of conversation, of story-telling and of literary representation. As Marzola points out in Chapter 6, this aspect of Keynes's experience can be plausibly inserted in the framework of the theoretical and literary debates of Modernism. And we can likewise make out, in terms of the primacy of the 'narrative' over the 'descriptive', a claim in favour of a convergence between Keynes and Freud. But Keynes's thought was absorbing novel discourses even before the totalizing experiment of

The General Theory which, for chronological reasons, is the highpoint of his intellectual voyage and reflects the whole range of his influences and connections. The wellsprings of his method were growing stronger and others were coming to fruition. Perhaps the most important among these was connected with the development of the concepts of multiciplicity, particularity and intrinsicality which were implied in taking up radically Moore's methodological option. That option carried with it a reassessment charged with philosophical implications, which required an important correction to the temporal framework to which the analysis was to be applied: from the absolute time of metaphysical reality to the phenomenological time of experience.

It was by an argumentative route, by picking out the context in which ethical choices are rationally made, that Moore had reached the analytic and conceptual reassessment of the time of experience. Given that there is no logico-rational plausibility in the idea of a certain or absolute 'list of duties', and before his proposing his cautious recourse to Common Sense ('though we may be sure that there are cases where the rule should be broken, we can never know which those cases are, and ought, therefore, never to break it' Moore 1966, pp. 162–3), what Moore arrived at was a programmatic recommendation of ethical doubt, and of probability as the sole epistemological measure which was rationally ascertainable. Hence,

> we never have any reason to suppose that an action is our duty: we can never be sure that any action will produce the greatest value possible. … An ethical law has not the nature of a scientific law but of a scientific *prediction*: and the latter is always merely probable, although the probability may be very great. (Moore 1966, pp. 149 and 155, emphasis original)

The overall picture of great precariousness and instability issued in the need for an analytic and rhetorical strategy which was as refined as it was exhausting, shot through with distinctions of prepositions and adverbs, and sustained by postulates which seem almost parodic ('A less good that is more likely to be attained, is to be preferred to a greater that is less probable' Moore 1966, p. 166). The cutting edge of Victorian consciousness – those heretics who, as we saw in Leslie Stephen, favoured analysis and agnosticism – culminated with Moore in the fully modernist vision of the consciousness as powerful and alone in the face of the dizziness and the limits of the perceptual and mental constructs which constitute it. The only rationally and scientifically practicable solution was to be found outside the impractical metaphysical measure of the Absolute or the mathematical measure of the Infinite. Instead, it had to be found in predictions of the short term, referred to the 'relatively short' time interval which stretches from the present context to the 'immediate future'. Indeed, the longer the period selected for the evaluation of an effect, the greater the margins for possible modification of the picture which had made it plausible, and, therefore, the greater the margin of error in the calculation. Thus, there was no avoiding the conclusion that 'Goods, which can be secured in a future so near as to be called "the present", are in general to be preferred to those which, being in a further future, are, for that reason, far less certain of attainment' (Moore 1966, p. 167). This was a conclusion which fitted perfectly with the Bloomsburyite valorization of the 'intrinsic good' of states of consciousness without reference to a before or an after. Actually, the 'religion' of the Bloomsburyites was born as the radicalization of the 'intrinsic good' understood in individualistic terms, and it grew up into the practice of human and intellectual experience lived 'in the present'. From this arose the double-edged injunction, which they all accepted, both to 'undisturbed individualism' and to social commitment. The former led to their well-known psychological radicalism, and the latter to a whirl of activity in commenting on public affairs, in book-publishing and in politics.[20]

Virginia Woolf's theory of narrative, which was much influenced by the philosophical and conceptual reassessment of the present, also takes the 'instant', the contingent 'moment of being', as the point at which the subject reveals and diffuses itself within the story.

As for Keynes, we find the idea of the centrality of 'the specious present' cropping up in pretty well all his writings. Its influence is felt in his intellectual choices: to be active, decisive, 'in the maelstrom', always in the front line of the cultural and political affairs of his times. And it decisively affects his political and economic thought. The urgency for Moore's young follower of being and acting 'in the present', in a moment that recalls and reinforces his Victorian sense of activism, translated itself into a set of choices of work which were pragmatic, and into an entirely business-like way of being an economist. A very young employee at the India Office, a functionary of the Treasury, a government economic adviser during the First World War and in the reconstruction after it, and at the same time an academic, committed to various prestigious schools and periodicals, Keynes stands out as one of the most extraordinary examples of a man who is at once a scholar and an economist working in the field, involved in an astonishing range of 'activities', as is testified by the large number of volumes of the *Collected Works* which bear that sub-title. As one of his colleagues put it, Keynes was a 'do-gooder', an economist concerned to 'do good deeds', 'essentially an applied economist, a man of action, seeking the best possible solution of a practical applied economic problem' (A. Robinson in Worswick and Trevithick 1983, p. 256). Skidelsky interprets Keynes's doing of good deeds and the economic revolution that followed from it in the light of the 'revolt against Victorianism' which was widely shared by the Edwardian generation and which had clustered around the rejection of the 'means-ends' ethic characteristic of Benthamite rationalism. Keynes's 'good deeds', performed with the immediate future in view, are to be understood as the negation of the 'life aimed at a goal', originally Calvinist and then specifically puritan–Victorian, which was an ethic of deferral, of saving and of abstinence. Keynes took on the characteristic inclination of that ethic to exploit words in their being 'speech acts', developing the 'non-abstinence' – one is not to abstain from acting, speaking, writing – as a theme of a new ethic, in 'the absolute conviction that life is for living in the present and not in the shadow of the past or the future' (cf. Skidelsky 1977, p. 2). Speaking, writing, protesting are rather the chosen means by which man in society declares himself, imposes himself on reality, to change the opinions of others and to affect the course of events. The writing of *The Economic Consequences of the Peace* was an action, of international importance, which opposed the inaction of the politicians, 'levity, blindness, insolence, confused cries from without' (*CW*, II, p. 3), which sought to understand and to explain 'the great historic drama of modern times' (*CW*, II, p. 4) and to set 'in motion those forces of instruction and imagination which can change *opinion*' (*CW*, II, p. 188).

What a man can do, he should do in a relatively short space of time, given that, as Keynes was fond of saying, 'in the long run we are all dead'; in this agreeing with Ramsey for whom 'the present is no less valuable because the future will be blank'. On the contrary, destiny and the present come together in a flux which is made and remade by the actions and decisions of those who have been able to live in the present without reservations. Doing good deeds means being proactive subjects in that 'flux', even while bearing in mind that every action takes its place in a world of probability and is acted out on a reality which has meanwhile changed and is no longer the context for that action:

No one can be certain of anything in this age of flux and change. ... We shall do well not to fear the future too much. Preserving all due caution in our activities, the job for us is to get through the next five years. ... We shall run more risk of jeopardising the future if we are influenced by indefinite fears based on trying to look ahead further than anyone can see. (*CW*, XXVII, pp. 445–6)

Thus, for Keynes, the present corresponds more exactly to what is actually existing, concrete and verifiable, but flowing in perpetual change and so, unstable. The past and the future are functions of precipitates of the present and participate in the same instability by being its cause and effect. They are the 'consequences' brought about by the whole range of actions of men and groups (the Versailles Treaty, the currency fluctuations at the hands of bankers, Mr Churchill) which the attentive observer of the political scene picks up and puts in context; or the 'proposals', 'suggestions', 'possibilities' that are argued for with vigour and lucidity; or the expectations the economist passes in review, guided by 'short-term' projections that can be verified and continually adjusted rather than by 'long-term' predictions, calculated on a statistical basis or in terms of a rigid schematism. In this case too we find the influence of Moore working at a distance: but where Moore was thinking of *prediction*, which at bottom betrayed the Victorian worries about 'justification', Keynes accepts instability as the norm and not an exception, and reinstates non-demonstrative logico-rational probability within politics and economics. For this reason, also for the economic agent, the theoretical and operational principle of '*some* reasons for believing' is in force relative to a reality that is always changing, even if imperceptibly and for reasons that *can* be changed. Expectation will therefore not be rigid, but likewise linked to '*some* reasons', it does not seek a guarantee of a future good, but the actuality of a shaping action which is already itself a change. It will be based on 'practical intuition' and will seek support from the 'observational data' of factual evidence and of hidden implication. In *The Economic Consequences*, Keynes hints at 'hidden currents' which make the political and economic scene 'unstable, complicated and unreliable'; in *The General Theory*, there is explicit reference to the 'psychology of the market and of business'.

From the time of *The Economic Consequences of the Peace*, the first book of the Bloomsbury years, other pressures are at work in Keynes's formal and intellectual scheme, that are not at all separate from the debate about the contents and time-frame of experience and which help the development of the idea of a radically unstable reality, in continual

flight, complex and many sided. As a consequence of this new awareness and in order to deal with the unstability and complexity, a new
flexibility of perspective was required to catch the wrinkles, the hidden
currents and therefore ready to accept even a multiplication of points of
view.

The 'immediate future' which had already been pointed out by Moore
as the focus of analytic and ethical projection, treated the reality which
the analysing subject had to deal with as less absolute and less remote
from experience. The Bloomsbury intellectuals work to radicalize that
foreshortening, to bring the subject and reality both within the
phenomenological and experiential 'present'. In this, they were possibly swayed by the sense-datum theory of knowledge which Russell had
outlined in *The Problems of Philosophy*, which in turn was indebted to
the unpublished writings of Moore and Keynes (Preface to Russell,
1988 (1912)). If we look at some texts of Russell, Keynes, Strachey
and Woolf, there are startling similarities among the views which they
express in various passages and notes about the contents of reality. As
Gargani (1979) has usefully noted, one of Russell's precisifications
seems to act as the crucial starting-point for a whole set of theoretical
and poetic attitudes:

> We shall find it convenient to speak of things *existing* when they are in
> time, that is to say, when we can point to some time *at* which they exist (not
> excluding the possibility of their existing at all times). Thus thoughts and
> feelings, minds and physical objects *exist*. But universals do not exist in
> this sense; we shall say that they *subsist* or *have being*, where 'being' is
> opposed to 'existence' in being timeless ... . The world of being is un-
> changeable, rigid, exact, delightful to the mathematician, the logician, the
> builder of metaphysical systems, and all who love perfection more than
> life. *The world of existence is fleeting, vague, without sharp boundaries,*
> *without any clear plan or arrangement*, but it contains all thoughts and
> feelings, all the data of sense, and all physical objects, everything that can
> do either good or harm, everything that makes any difference to the value
> of the world. (Russell 1967, p. 57, last emphasis added, others original)

Considering the issue of direct and indirect knowledge, Russell distinguishes between a thing which 'exists' and a thing which subsists or
has 'being'. The former come to us by means of sense-data, while the
latter are the proper objects of universals. An 'existing' thing, therefore, belongs to the realm of the immediate, the local, the 'human
neighbourhood', which the pragmatic philosopher likes and seizes for
an appreciation which is more aesthetic than epistemological.

Apart from Keynes, the writers of Bloomsbury were neither mathematicians nor logicians, but their intellectual experience was nevertheless affected by the 'tincture of philosophy', of the discourse on method inherited from Moore and of echoes of the epistemological thoughts which Russell and Keynes himself had voiced. Russell's specification was crucial in classifying the content of experience that, once for all, located in the world of fragmentary and phenomenological contingency while definitively installing the subject in those perplexing and 'uneasy flickerings of consciousness' that so much express the modernist epistemology. But new methods of analysis and of representation were then needed: methods capable of coping with experience that was at one time 'existence', namely the fleeting vision of consciousness, and with the forms that bring it to expressions, namely the 'universal' cage of sensory perception and of language.

As Strachey acutely noted 'the really interesting question is always the particular one; but it's only the general one that it's possible to discuss' (Strachey 1972, p. 123). Thus, in thinking about a modern mode of writing biography, he proposed 'to come close to life ... when it happens with its minuteness, and its multiplicity and its intensity' (Strachey 1980, p. 21); none the less, as he ruefully admits, writing must operate selectively on an 'infinite succession' of fragments, and art especially 'depends on a process of selection' so that only some of the phenomena of life would be fixed and expressed. Writing at roughly the same time, Virginia Woolf found herself reflecting on the multiple and fleeting essence of experience, as 'an incessant shower of innumerable atoms' and on the constant struggle of representation and art when confronted with life that inexorably 'passes' (Woolf 1919, repr. Woolf 1967). What then, does have value for representation? What is 'the proper stuff of fiction'? Woolf's response was precise, and was the announcement of a new poetics:

> Look within and life, it seems, is very far from being 'like this'. Examine for a moment an ordinary mind on an ordinary day. The mind receives a myriad of impressions – trivial, fantastic, evanescent, or engraved with the sharpness of steel. From all sides they come, *an incessant shower of innumerable atoms*, and as they fall, as they shape themselves into the life of Monday or Tuesday, the accent falls differently from of old ... . *Life is not a series of gig lamps symmetrically arranged*; life is a luminous halo, a semi-transparent envelope surrounding us from the beginning of consciousness to the end. Is it not the task of the novelist to convey this varying, this unknown and uncircumscribed spirit, whatever aberration or complexity it

may display, with as little mixture of the alien and external as possible?
(Woolf 1919, repr. Woolf 1967, p. 189, emphases added)

Thus, turning the look within, the reality perceived by habit and convention as 'symmetrically arranged', explodes into a 'shower of
atoms', into a halo, a spreading mark. For the philosopher, as for the
biographer or the novelist, the problem is then to bring about the move
from 'the colloquial to the lyrical, from the particular to the general'
(Woolf 1919 repr. Woolf 1967, p. 214) without oversimplifying or
selecting 'with placid perfection', without reducing the mark to too
'symmetrical' a pattern.[21] A large part of the aesthetic project of Strachey
and Woolf would be given over to the complex representation of the
phenomenological and everyday, of the life of 'Monday or Tuesday'
which make up existence. This project culminates in the seizure of the
'moments of being', the brief shocks of consciousness in which the
subject comes together and reveals itself, and in the emphasis on apparently 'unimportant' details which are nevertheless revealing of the
whole complex of being. In literature this was a conscious feature of
Modernism, in opposition to the 'materialist' line laid down by bourgeois realism. This was a particular way of understanding and representing human experience, which rather followed the lessons learnt
from James, Proust, Tolstoy and Dostoevsky – all writers appreciated
and loved by the intellectuals of Bloomsbury.

Keynes was neither a novelist nor a poet, but he was equally affected
by the 'tincture of philosophy' as he was by a taste for literature. A
mathematician, logician and economist, he was not unsympathetic to
the challenge of representation which his writer friends took up, and
was equally aware of the shortcomings of the models of representation
which had been accepted by traditional learning. In this way, we ought
to take seriously the idea that *The Economic Consequences of the
Peace* and *The General Theory* were also challenges which the author
issued to himself, albeit at different times and with different purposes,
to test his own ability to represent with 'truthfulness' and in its essence,
an event, a personality, or the whole of the economic world from the
Modernist point of view of the new compromise between the particular
and the general, the detail and the whole. Indeed, *The Economic Consequences of the Peace* (1919) makes use of techniques of the construction of history and personality on which Strachey and Woolf were
already at work. The products of their common labours issued in *Emi-*

nent Victorians (1918) and *Jacob's Room* (1921) which, as we can see, appeared soon before and soon after the *Economic Consequences*.

Keynes's book was inspired by the conclusion of the Treaty of Versailles, which he had attended as a government official. In terms of its genre, it is a historical and political witness, a chronicle which was in large measure made up from the notes which Keynes took down in Paris from day to day. But with hindsight, the multiplicity and complexity of the scene was such that the effort to pick out and understand the origins, motivations and influences broke the bounds of the normal layout of a historical essay:

> Paris was a nightmare, and everyone there was morbid ... . Seated indeed amid the theatrical trappings of the French saloons of state, one could wonder if the extraordinary visages of Wilson and Clemenceau, with their fixed hue and unchanging characterisation, were really faces at all and not the tragic-comic masks of some strange drama or puppet-show.
>
> The proceedings of Paris all had this air of extraordinary importance and unimportance at the same time. The decisions seemed charged with consequences to the future of human society; yet the air whispered that the word was not flesh, that it was futile, insignificant, of no effect, dissociated from events. (*CW*, II, pp. 2–3)

'Proceedings', 'decisions', 'words dissociated from events': the political and diplomatic occasion seems to be plunged from the outset into a chaotic 'human comedy', a recital dominated by the personalities of the main characters, by 'certain personal factors', rather than by the genuine desire to discharge with a sense of responsibility and justice the dramatic situation which had led to the Treaty. Dissociated from past and future facts, the story of the negotiations seemed and probably was rather the story of personal feelings and ambitions, of meannesses, of neuroses and idiosyncrasies. Not unlike the trials which Dostoevsky obsessively proposed as a metaphor of human reality, the process 'in the name of Justice' had its unofficial side, which was hidden and 'minor' but nevertheless indispensable in building up a rigorous and 'truthful' picture. Keynes's observations and accounts would also refer to this side of things: and the picture is, in the end, bifurcated between official history and everyday banality, between tragedy and farce, between portrait and caricature, as a result of a method of portrayal which we find also in the biting pen-portraits of Strachey and in the ironic counterpoint which Woolf employs in *Jacob's Room*. In order to proceed to representation Keynes, in the manner of Strachey,

> will attack his subject in unexpected places; he will fall upon the flank, or
> the rear ... he will row out over that great ocean of material, and lower
> down into it, here and there, a little bucket, which will bring up to the light
> of day some characterisitic specimen. (Strachey 1986, p. 9)

So the writer goes ahead obliquely, apparently aiming at no conclusion,
in a series of divagations of marginal episodes, incidental conversations, verbal and personal tics, little clues. What comes of it is a long
digressive argument where, however, digression makes up the substance of the argument, where the particularities tell of the essence, like
Sterne's un-novel, or like some 'minimalist' realism supremely found
in Tolstoy or Dostoevsky.[22] Over and above his well-known affinities
with Strachey and with modernist painting (Garnett 1975, Skidelsky
1983), it is in terms of a composite literary and intertextual context that
we can make best sense of the digressive discursiveness and the oblique psychology which shape Keynes's account of the Treaty of Versailles and his masterly and provocatively private portraits of the three
great 'puppets': Clemenceau, Lloyd George and Wilson, respectively
'an old man of the world, a *femme fatale* and a non-conformist clergy-
man' (*CW*, X, p. 22).

A clearer picture of Keynes's style of analysis and representation
emerges from looking at his connection with Freud, the last of the
contexts of his method which we have picked out. Keynes encountered
Freud in the context of the intellectual experience of Bloomsbury.
There was a reciprocal and explicit recognition of influence as between
Freud and Bloomsbury. In a letter to the *Nation* in 1925, Keynes evalu-
ated Freud with singular warmth: Freud 'presents himself as one of the
great disturbing innovating geniuses of our age, that is to say as a sort
of devil' (*CW*, XXVIII, p. 393). For his part, Freud would praise
Strachey's *Elizabeth and Essex* and in general, his historical and biographical method, which he thought was 'impreganted with the spirit of
psychoanalysis'.

The story of the connection goes back to the very first years of the
publication of Freud's works in English. It continues with the production
of a fresh edition of his writings by the Hogarth Press under the direction
of the Woolfs. As Leonard Woolf records, the initiative took shape around
1924, in an idea of James Strachey and Ernest Jones, but his was the
crowning of a familiarity which the Group had been showing for at least
ten years.[23] Thus, the links between Bloomsbury and Freud, as a matter
of cultural curiosity and of research commitment, belonged in a way, and

perhaps more than commentators have hitherto recognized, to the very life, the common intellectual property of the Group.[24]

'On or about December 1910 human character changed', observed V. Woolf to the Cambridge Heretics in 1924. Even if it was not the sole cause of the change which Woolf so brusquely announces, Freudian analysis, with its range and radicalism, invaded the whole field of being and knowing. Covering biology, neurology, ethics and aesthetics, it redefined previously held concepts of the subject and of reality. As Virginia Woolf was to explain, on reading Freud 'one immediately becomes aware of certain facts, or at least of certain hypotheses of others' ambitions and reasons that the previous generation could hardly imagine' (Woolf 1924).

The facts and hypotheses which Freud's analysis had gradually built up would have an immediate impact on Bloomsbury thought and writing. In her diaries, letters and critical essays, Woolf makes use, albeit unsystematically, of Freudian tools. Freud's 'Introductory Lectures on Psychoanalysis' would inspire Fry's *The Artist and Psycho-analysis*. And Freudian influence on Keynes is particularly noteworthy. It pointed the way to using psychological motivations and the theory of mass behaviour into one of the central planks of his historical and economic analysis.[25] But, for Bloomsbury and above all for Keynes, the origin and development of the relationship with Freud seemed to have quite different roots. Underlying the content of the Freudian theory, for all that it is controversial and controverted, there was a novelty of vision and indications of a method which interacted much more deeply with the theoretical and methodological preoccupations that were already characteristic of the group. It is not for nothing that Leonard Woolf, in reconstructing the beginnings of the connection with Freud, turns his mind back to a review of *The Psychopathology of Everyday Life* which had appeared in 1914 and had been read with great attention. This review insisted, not so much on the substance of Freud's theory as on

> his great subtlety of mind, a broad and sweeping imagination more characteristic of the poet, than the scientist or medical practitioner ... his power of grasping in the midst of intricate analysis of details the bearing of those details on a much wider field of details. (Woolf 1960, p. 120)

Freud's credentials could not have been more impressive: a scientist who made human behaviour and verbal experience the privileged object of his analysis, who therefore knew how to use both facts and his imagination, both numbers and metaphors. Moreover, thinking back over the characteristic theoretical preoccupations of Modernism in philosophy and literature, there is a certain family resemblance between what we have been thinking of as the new 'consciousness of multiplicity and complexity' and the 'intricate' world of relations and interdependencies which is picked out in Freudian analysis. For Freudian psychoanalysis the central object of observation and study was 'life' or 'experience' as they were understood by Bloomsbury, looked at from an oblique point of view and specified by an unconventional logic, in terms of the left-overs of the phenomenal world, or, as Freud defined them 'the inconsiderable events which have been put aside by the other sciences as being too unimportant' (Freud 1915–17, Lecture 2).

The seeds of psychoanalysis were actually sown in medical practice and clinical research and reinforced the already accepted need to pay attention to the microscopic level. They found a home, albeit with significant differences, within the literature of the 'clinical case'. Indeed, the beginnings of psychoanalysis, and of Freud's writings, had set off from the presentation of 'cases' – biographical fragments which are reconstructed with minute precision and insist on the inclusion of the smallest, most insignificant-seeming pieces of evidence, such as certain details of behaviour, of dress or speech patterns, of words said or left unsaid, of fleeting glances, of coughing fits. At this stage of the method, the analyst appears, from behind his writing, to be a great 'reader', highly observant and attentive to the smallest wrinkles and to hidden relations. Or he is a wonderful investigator, coming to grips with cases and mysteries which are otherwise insoluble. His business is to bring together facts which may be distant one from another, to follow clues that have been side-lined, to patiently draw out from evidence their context and then to widen the context further. Like Morelli, the great art critic who had learnt to recognize a painter's hand from single strokes which were involuntary and often inappropriate,[26] Freud proceeds from the particular to its context and then to larger contexts, and investigates the appearances in order to arrive at the essence of a character, at the core of the disease.

But it quickly became apparent that psychoanalysis did not offer certainties, resolutions and cures. Rather, cures were rare. Moreover, the presentation of a case was the opposite of a description, and gave way rather to the rhythms of story-telling. The analyst's unravelling of the tangle of separate details was also a patient unravelling of words and 'stories', which had first been shared with the analyst and later shared afresh by means of the act of writing. What emerges is an oblique, digressive 'novel', a minute portrait full of details, but no less oblique and digressive for that. As Freud more or less explicitly recognizes, those stories are indeed written and readable like proper novels and their verbal and narrative style is made up of reminiscences of texts and writers in the great literary tradition, that of Shakespeare, Sterne, Goethe and Dostoevsky. After all, it was to these among others that he owed the inspiration for his method of writing and describing life.

In this way, the lesson Freud taught spilled over into a critical choice in favour of certain ways of representing which, for similar reasons and at much the same time, had been at the bottom of the new-born Modernist approach to literary representation, and which had close ties, as we have partly seen, with the theories and writings coming out of Bloomsbury.

With reference to Keynes as a biographer and recalling in particular the context of *The Economic Consequences of the Peace*, we can say that the text was a product of a 'Freudian' modernist attitude which had taken on board the point of view and the techniques of psychoanalysis. The book was, so to speak, the presentation 'based on facts' of a dramatic and mysterious 'case', whose substance and 'consequences' had been fatally misunderstood by even the best informed and influential public opinion. It was a case which Keynes was committed to reinvestigate in all its complexity, beginning with a revision of those aspects of personalities and situations to which no historian would have given serious consideration. Perhaps with Freud and Morelli in mind, Keynes found himself in a Paris full of confused events and unintelligible words, resembling more than anything a theatrical stage or a nightmare, rather than a chapter of history. Even so,

> He looked into faces ... he listened. He looked in particular at hands. From his earliest days he had learned that no hands are alike. They can resemble a claw or a paw; they can be elegant, they can be brutal, they can make one shudder at their brutality. They clasp and unclasp in nervous fidget: fingers drum on a table or on the arm of a chair; they can be fussy reaching, gesturing – a whole nervous system. They *express* as eyes express, as the straightness or droop of a back expresses, as the way a person sits expresses. M. Keynes instinctively learned to read messages in hands. ... Eternal scoffers at selective and 'significant detail' would not understand, but to those who know how much men and women express in the smallest things they do, M. Keynes' game of private recognitions added a wide margin of certainty – if not infallibility. (Edel 1981, pp. 55–6)

But, of course, *The Economic Consequences of the Peace* aimed to do something more than merely log the glances and the slight but 'significant' gestures. It aimed at providing a global account which would refer to 'the future destiny of Europe'. By conquering the 'particular', he could supply a 'general' vision, to which his writing and passionate argument gives form and substance. Following working methods and rhythms which Freud was building up for use in psychoanalysis, Keynes would dedicate his future efforts to the consolidation of the passage from the particular to the general, to create a vision of the whole which, nevertheless, tries not to simplify the picture.

Even though he was working in a context of scientific isolation and controversy, Freud's discourse was rapidly growing and acquiring scientific credit, moving from his accumulation of particular case histories towards a theoretical and conceptual project: indeed, in the space of a few years, he would publish some of the explanatory and definitional essays which would determine the course of the discipline, such as 'On Narcissism: an Introduction' (1914), 'Drives and their Destiny' (1915), 'Beyond the Pleasure Principle' (1920), 'Group Psychology and the Analysis of the Ego' (1922), 'Inhibitions, Symptoms and Anxiety' (1925). In this move, Freud was clearly aware of the new opportunities opened up by the ninteenth-century debate in epistemology, in which Darwin was so important also to him. At the same time, he yearned to establish the scientific basis of his own work in the eyes of the medical and scientific community, which was conservative and resistant to methodological adventures and miscegenation. Psychoanalysis, originally organized by its own 'father' as an empirical science, was nevertheless operating with and within language and the diegetic structures of everyday usage. Its analyses cut across the boundaries and conventions of official learning, but aimed at providing a legitimation in terms of its procedural rigour, which even if it appeared heretical, could be clearly seen to be such. In 'On Narcissism', Freud makes a claim in favour of the scientific standing of the discipline, though in terms of a novel theoretical background:

> Philosophical speculation can be based on precise and logically unassailable foundations while science must content itself ... with *a few fleeting and nebulous basic principles* of which it can hardly form a clear idea, hoping that they will become clearer as the work progresses and promising itself to replace them in due course with others. (Freud 1914)

For Freud, therefore, 'old theories can persist alongside new ones', with a continuous mutual clarification and rational objectivization which also serves as an equally constant empirical control. What emerges is an operational rationalism in which evidences and ideas are ever more closely connected until, after successive modifications, the latter are purified of all incoherence and become more 'generally' usable. From the 'fleeting and nebulous basic principles', the scientist will eventually arrive at 'definitions' which will never themselves be rigid, and which are not the 'foundations' of the whole edifice, but can be replaced or removed without damaging it.

The trajectory of Freud's declarations about the discipline's status reaches its climax at the end of an article on psychoanalysis for a Lexicon of Sexology which sums up much of what we have already said, but with a firmer emphasis on the interdisciplinary nature of psychoanalysis and on its future:

> Psycho-analysis is not, like philosophies, a system starting out from a few sharply defined basic concepts, seeking to grasp the whole universe with the help of these and, once it is completed, having no room for fresh discoveries or better understanding. On the contrary, it keeps close to the facts in its field of study, seeks to solve the immediate problems of observation, gropes its way forward by the help of experience, is always incomplete and always ready to correct or modify its theories. There is no incongruity (any more than in the case of physics or chemistry) if its most general concepts lack clarity and if its postulates are provisional; it leaves their more precise definition to the results of future work. (Freud, 1922)

In this 'open' theoretic attitude towards the sharing and the extending of the method, Freud is at the interface of no less radical revisions and redefinitions. We may think again about the great intellectual upheavals in the arts and sciences which, after 1910, as Virginia Woolf dated it, had literally overthrown the consciousness and the map of collective knowledge; we think of the Modernism of Bloomsbury and its new methods of representation, together with some well-known aesthetic developments which accepted more complex and stratified visions of the world and which carved out new mythical and symbolic syntheses for representing it.

Keynes and 'Keynesian' economics belong in some way within the context of this upheaval and new synthesis. For all that they appear distant from each other, the two disciplines, economics according to Keynes and psychoanalysis presented a number of similarities. They had the objects and aims of their study in common: the analysis of

66 John Maynard Keynes: Language and Method

human behaviour, from the motivations to the effects. As regards their history, each seemed to fall between the opposed statutes and programmes of the 'arts' and 'sciences', and yet to belong to both. The methods and chosen techniques of the two thinkers are ever more similar: empirical observation, objectivization and conceptualization, ordinary language, and diegetic and argumentative presentation. But it is above all in virtue of their common purpose to relaunch grand theoretical projects that, especially after the 1920s, it seems to us that the relations between Keynes and Freud are at their clearest.

Apart from anything else, it is not difficult to make out this affinity by returning to texts in which Keynes defines his theoretical and conceptual position. Thus, for example, his ideas about conceptual definition resound with Freudian echoes: 'A definition can often be *vague* within fairly wide limits and capable of several interpretations differing slightly from one another, and still be perfectly serviceable and free from serious risk ... provided that ... it is used consistently within a given context' (*CW*, XXIX, p. 36). We may also recall the discussion, to which we have already attended, on the need for ideas to be flexible, never fixed but always being tested by experience, which makes them live or die in a continuous and productive cycle of clarification.

> I am more attached to the comparatively simple fundamental ideas which underlie my theory than to the particular forms in which I have embodied them, and I have no desire that the latter should be crystallised at the present stage of the debate. If the simple basic ideas can become familiar and acceptable, time and experience and the collaboration of a number of minds will discover the best way of expressing them. (*CW*, XIV, p. 111)

Thus, for Keynes, as for Freud, there was value in the choice of a theory which was 'open' and interdisciplinary, in a systematic project which was, nevertheless in its very nature always 'under construction', never closed or definitively defined, always able to keep 'the necessary reserves and qualifications and the adjustments which we shall have to make later on' (*CW*, VII, p. 297), or which other minds will contribute to making. In particular, this controlled maintaining of 'vague ideas' (Freud's 'nebulous basic principles') which are successively tested against experience and rational objectivization, and the choice of a project which has foundations but no roof, is the essence of Keynes's *General Theory*. And it is, in any case, the essence of all theorizing, if it is true that every theory, especially scientific theories, venture into uncertain territory, fill gaps, build bridges, create images and metaphors which are capable of encapsulating visions which would be otherwise inaccessible to the collective imagination. This, as Freud would admit in a famous conversation with Einstein, is a 'form of mythology' (Freud 1932a). And at this point, which seems to us to be the Gordian Knot of our consideration of Keynes's method, we must refer again to Wittgenstein.

With his suspicions of systematic aspirations, and in opposition to bearers of theories, the post- 1929 Wittgenstein blamed Freud himself for a theory which was becoming the opposite of knowledge. It was a theory which, as a 'new mythology', settled on suspensions and on 'mental cramps' and exchanged clarification for persuasion ('at the end of reasons comes *persuasion*', Wittgenstein (1974a) sec. 612).[27] For Wittgenstein, to understand everything that makes a difference is already a theory,[28] and every linguistic adventure which 'exercises some attraction' 'turns the spade' of explanation. For Freud, as for Keynes, observation and rational objectivization do not exist outside some theory. In their cases, the theory is built into language and is full of persuasive force. For both of them, it was within the citadel of rhetoric that the demolition of the 'conventions and habitual modes of thought' would be performed and the 'new foundations' of the method would be laid. In this way, there could be no conflict between the nurturing of theoretical projects and persuasive seduction, because the issue in the end, was that of convincing the reader, of gaining the scientific community or 'fellow economists' to one's own view. Thus the intellectual paths of Keynes and Wittgenstein, some of whose crossing we have already seen, separate once and for all at this point. This separation is witnessed in the different ways in which *The General Theory* and the *Philosophical Investigations* were composed. Both derive from work done in the 1930s, but the former is a long digressive argument; the latter a series of disconnected aphorisms. All the same, there is a sort of paradoxical reconciliation between their methods. Keynes (with Freud) hangs on to the project of building a theory without giving up on the 'explanatory spade' to which, in the end, Wittgenstein trusted the advancement of knowledge.

Perhaps it is for this reason that the tangled mixture of persuasion and linguistic and theoretical metareflection which is *The General Theory* constitutes a challenge; a challenge so radical that the reader can even risk emerging defeated or unconvinced. Yet much more powerful than the ambiguous image of persuasion, the reader is left in command of a vision of the world which is capable of switching the most different and heterogeneous contexts.

Keynes's is an intricate vision, one which risks 'mental cramps', but which is conceived in scrupulous relation to experience, on the basis of cases which are not excessively 'particular' nor abstractly 'general'.

NOTES

1. H. Phillips 1951.
2. The two memoirs were written in 1938 and 1919 respectively and are introduced in the *Collected Writings* by David Garnett.
3. Both Harrod and Skidelsky devote considerable space in their biographies to the figure of John Neville Keynes. The latter especially focuses on the eclecticism of his interests and commitments.
4. The idea of a 'compromise' and the phrase 'Victorian compromise' recurs in many of the standard works on the history and culture of the period. These denote the widespread desire at the time to face the various questions posed by social life (ethical, political, religious, aesthetic, and so on) with a spirit which aimed at balance, dialectic, mediation. The consciousness and logic of 'compromise', which finds premises in a composite context of specifically British events and attitudes, was the expression of the dominant culture which reacted in this way to challenges to the establishment. Basic reading on the Victorian scene would be J.K. Buckley (1952); W.E. Houghton (1957); N.F. Cantor (1967); and, more recently, P. Gay (1984).
5. Keynes's and Marshall's explicit interest in each other dates from 1905, when Keynes took to reading the Victorian economists closely (particularly Jevons, Edgeworth and Marshall himself). It was at that time that Marshall, who had been favourably impressed by Keynes's work, insisted that he should sit the Economic Tripos and make his interest in the subject concrete. See the letters between the two cited in Skidelsky (1983), pp. 165–8.
6. Keynes uses a part of the correspondence to highlight what he took to be the modernity of Malthus's economic thought. With hindsight, we can see that Keynes's choice of passages is significant:

    > *Ricardo*: You always have your mind on the immediate and temporary effects of particular changes, whereas I put these immediate and temporary effects quite aside, and fix my whole attention on the permanent state of things ...

    > *Malthus*: I certainly am disposed to refer frequently to *things as they are*, as the only way of making one's writings practically useful to society, and I think also the only way of being secure from falling into the errors of the taylors of Laputa, and by a slight mistake at the outset arrive at conclusions the most distant from the truth. Besides I really think that the progress of society consists of irregular movements, and that to omit the consideration of causes which for eight or ten years will give a great *stimulus* to production and population, or a great *check* to them, is to omit the causes of the wealth and poverty of nations – the grand object of all enquiries in Political Economy (*CW*, X, pp. 95–6, first emphasis added).

7. On the courses and lectures provided in the Moral Sciences Tripos and on Keynes's preferences, see Harrod (1951), esp. the chapter 'Undergraduate at Cambridge' and F.C. Crews (1962).

8. In addition to Harrod and Skidelsky, information on the background of Cambridge, the clubs and colleges, is to be found in B. Williams (1931); Crews (1962); P. Levy (1981). Also useful is E. Heine's preface to the Arnold edition of Forster's *The Longest Journey* (1984) which is set against his experience of college life.

9. Many of Keynes's friends and acquaintances have left reports of the cuttingness of his words and judgements; cf. C. Bell (1956); L. Woolf (1960); and B. Russell (1967).

10. For rhetorical-linguistic readings of *The Origin of Species*, see A.D. Culler 'The Darwinian Revolution and Literary Form' and W.F. Cannon 'Darwin's Vision in "The Origin of Species"', in G. Levine and Madden (eds) (1968). A more recent detailed analysis of the argumentation of the *Origin* is to be found in M.K. Hallyday (1990). For the historical and social aspects of the debate which grew up around the *Origin*, see T. Cosslett (1984) with its detailed bibliography. More recently S. Finzi (1989) has devoted several essays to the *Origin* in discussing Darwin and Freud.

11. On Leslie Stephen, the standard work was Maitland (1903), superseded by Annan (1984). S.P. Rosenbaum (1983) underlines the intellectual affinity between Stephen and Keynes.

12. The essay 'What is Materialism?' was first published by the South Place Ethical Society and reprinted in *An Agnostic's Apology and Other Essays* in 1893.

13. Hacking's discussion is to be found in *Representing and Intervening*, 1983. It is taken up by Bellofiore to point out that Keynes denies that categories can be either true or false independent of what we know, but that he asserts that many theoretical entities really do exist, in so far as they enter into a practical relation with external reality. See Bellofiore (1988), pp. 454–5 and his contribution to the present volume.

14. See, in this connection, the passages in the *Treatise on Probability* in which Keynes discusses the problematic cases of indirect knowledge: the 'universal' of perception/definition of colour ('the sensation of yellow' versus 'the meaning of yellow') and the unverifiable memory function, such that 'at any given moment there is a great deal of our knowledge which we neither know directly nor by argument – we remember it (*CW*, VIII, p. 14). It might be worth recalling that some of Wittgenstein's later meditations come into contact with such thoughts about the indirect aspects of our knowledge of sensations, about 'private experience' and about the representation of them.

15. The hypothesis that there was a 'strong' connection between Keynes's theory of probability and that on which Wittgenstein was working after the *Tractatus* deserves further investigation. If it were vindicated, such a hypothesis would lead to a different evaluation, even by the specialists, of Keynes's theory and significant consequences. As Carabelli notes, the existence of an alternative to Russellian logicism would be a form of disobedience on Keynes's part towards Russell and not an idiosyncratic error; it would represent an original contribution to general thought resisting, and opposed to, neo-positivist models (cf. Carabelli (1989), p. 12). I am grateful to Claudio Pizzi for much useful discussion of these matters: by the way, he advances the hypothesis including the suggestion of a possible line of non-orthodox logicism running from W.E. Johnson, with whom both Keynes and Wittgenstein had close contacts.

16. The body of bibliographic and critical writing on Bloomsbury is now extremely rich and includes many monographic studies of the single members of the group. The most useful of the general studies include: J.K. Johnstone (1954); Q. Bell (1968); L. Edel (1981); S.P. Rosenbaum (1987). As to the relations of single figures to the group, see M. Holroyd (1971); E.D. Crabtree and A.P. Thirlwall (eds) (1980); J. Marcus (ed.) (1984).

17. Strachey's and Russell's notes, dated 11 October 1903 and September 1903 respectively, are cited in Levy (1981), pp. 234–5.
18. Discussions of 'method' are sprinkled pretty well throughout Virginia Woolf's writings, but especially in her letters to Roger Fry, whom she clearly considered to be a privileged interlocutor on the matter, and in her essays on the 'foundations' of narrative method. The longest and most important reflection on method is to be found in the essay 'Modern Fiction' (1919). More indirect, but equally pertinent are 'The Art of Biography' (1921); 'Mr. Bennett and Mrs. Brown' (1925); 'Life and the Novelist' (1926) and 'The Narrow Bridge of Art' (1936), all in *Collected Essays* (1967).
19. See R. Fry (1920), pp. 284–5.
20. In addition to the significant amount of public comment which almost all the members of Bloomsbury went in for (in the major national newspapers and, subsequently, with the BBC), the concrete militancy of some of them on behalf of their cultural values, of civil rights and of pacifism ought not to be forgotten. This ended up in further writings, such as Clive Bell's *Peace at Once* and *Civilisation*, Keynes's *Economic Consequences*, Virginia Woolf's *A Room of One's Own* and *Three Guineas* and Leonard Woolf's numerous pamphlets. But they also took part in running official organizations, associations and groups, as we have already seen in Keynes's case, or with Leonard Woolf's work for the League of Nations and the Labour Party, and Virginia Woolf's engagement in associations for emancipation and intellectual education of women.
21. For a discussion, both 'philosophical' and aesthetic, of this point, see in particular her short stories 'A Mark on the Wall' (1917) and 'Kew Gardens' (1919); a remarkable critical comment on what is defined as 'a new model of intellection' between the perceptual and the mental, which Woolf was working out in her writings, is to be found in R. Poole *The Unknown Virginia Woolf* (1982).
22. It is worth recalling that it was just at that time that the Hogarth Press was issuing a wide range of Russian novels, with particular attention to the works of Dostoevsky and Tolstoy, who, until Constance Garnett's translations, had been almost unknown to English readers. Woolf dedicated many of her essays to promoting these novelists. And in one of them ('The Russian Point of View' (1922)), she picked out their 'new realism' and their ability to traffic between the microscopic and the essential, and to link 'a coughing fit or a movement of the hands' to the wider dynamics of character and plot (Woolf (1945), p. 229 repr. in Woolf (1967)).
23. Indeed, by 1912, American editions of Freud were available in England alongside the English editions which were coming out under the editorship of Joan Rivière and of James and Alice Strachey, who in any case ensured contacts between Vienna and the London Institute of Psycho-Analysis. The revised English edition was originally designed to emend what were thought to be huge errors in the American translations. It was continued as new books appeared by Freud and should have culminated in two collections: the *Collected Papers* edited by Joan Rivière of the Institute of Psycho-Analysis (1924–50); and the *General Selection from the Works of Freud* edited by Rickman for the International Psychoanalysis Press (1937), which was the publishing section of the Institute under the control and ownership of Leonard and Virginia Woolf. These two publishing projects formed the basis of the Hogarth Press Standard Edition which began to appear in 1954.
24. The most useful and reliable source for the relations between Bloomsbury and Freud is Leonard Woolf's *Autobiography*. There are sidelights on the issue in the books listed in Note 16, especially in Edel (1981) and Marcus (1984). There is a brief specific account of the relations between Strachey and Freud in M. Spinella 1987.

25. It is above all in this direction that attention to themes and concepts has hitherto been moving in Keynesian criticism, picking up what seemed to be references to certain problematic psychological assumptions about motivation (cf. Sharrot, cited in Crabtree and Thirlwall (1980), and especially Winslow (1986)). The discussion of Freudian influence is thus confirmed not only by other contributions to this volume, but by the presence of Freudian 'arguments' within Keynes's thought, such as those which occur in the analysis of the 'psychology' of post-war Europe, in the studies of the meaning of the use of money, and in the attention given in *The General Theory* to the instability and fluctuations of the market.

26. Freud refers to Morelli and his method of attribution in the second chapter of *The Moses of Michelangelo* (1913), with in mind the critic's writings on Italian painting (1883). Freud recalls that, according to Morelli, speakers and writers (like painters), unknowingly expose themselves – they have verbal habits and use words and phrases involuntarily and sometimes inappropriately, with characteristics which escape them. There are many studies on psychoanalysis as a development of the investigative methods which had grown up in the nineteenth century.

27. Wittgenstein's criticism of Freud belong to a controversial chapter of the relation between the two thinkers, a relation which Wittgenstein himself described less than clearly and univocally. His hesitancy about the logical and scientific standing of psychoanalysis is made plain in his 'Conversations on Freud' (transcribed 1942–6, in Wittgenstein 1966) and in *On Certainty* (1974a). For a recent discussion, see G.F. Gabetta (1984).

28. Wittgenstein quotes Goethe with approval: 'Don't look for anything behind the phenomena: they themselves are the theory' in section 889 of Vol I of Wittgenstein (1980); the Goethe passage is in *Maximen und Reflexionen* ed. Max Hacker no. 575 (Weimar 1970).

REFERENCES

Annan, N. (1984) *Leslie Stephen, the Godless Victorian* (2nd edn), London: Weidenfeld and Nicholson.

Bell. A. (ed.) (1977) *Sir L. Stephen's Mausoleum Book*, Oxford: Clarendon Press.

Bell, C. (1915) *Peace at Once*, London: Hogarth Press.

Bell, C. (1928) *Civilisation*, London: Hogarth Press.

Bell, C. (1956) *Old Friends*, London: Hogarth Press.

Bell, Q. (1968) *Bloomsbury*, London: Cambridge University Press.

Bellofiore, R. (1988) 'Rhetorica ed Economia', *Economia Politica* **V**, (3), December.

Brenan, G. (1974) *Personal Record*, London: Hogarth Press.

Buckley, J.K. (1952) *The Victorian Temper: Studies in Literary Culture*, London: Macmillan.

Cantor, N.F. (ed.) (1967) *The English Tradition*, vol. II, London: Macmillan.

Carabelli, A. (1988) *On Keynes's Method*, London: Macmillan.

Charleston Papers (The correspondence of Clive and Vanessa Bell to friends and Bloomsbury Group), Brighton: unpublished holdings of Sussex University Library.

Clifford, W.K. (1918) *Lectures and Essays*, Stephen, L. and Pollock, F. (eds), London: Watts & Co.

Cosslett, T. (ed.) (1984) *Science and Religion in the Nineteenth Century*, Cambridge: Cambridge University Press.

Crabtree, E.D. and Thirlwall, A.P. (eds) (1980) *Keynes and the Bloomsbury Group*, Proceedings of the 4th Keynes Seminar (1978), London: Macmillan.

Crews, F.C. (1962) *E.M. Forster: The Perils of Humanism*, Princeton: Princeton University Press.

Darwin, C. (1859, repr. 1950) *The Origin of Species*, London: J. Murray.

Dowling, D. (1985) *Bloomsbury aesthetics and the novels of Forster*, London: Macmillan.

Edel, L. (1981) *Bloomsbury: A House of Lions*, Harmondsworth, London.

Ensor, R.K.C. (1960) *England 1870–1914*, Oxford: Oxford University Press.

Finzi, S. (1980) 'Silhouettes', *Il Piccolo Hans*, **27**, Bari: Dedalo.

Finzi, S. (1989) *Nevrosi di guerra in tempo di pace*, Bari: Edizioni Dedalo.

Freud, S. (1913) 'The Moses of Michelangelo', in Strachey, J. (ed.), Standard Edition, vol. 13.

Freud, S. (1914) *On Narcissism: an Introduction*, Standard Edition, vol. 14.

Freud, S. (1914) *The Psychopathology of Everyday Life*, Standard Edition, vol. 14.

Freud, S. (1915) *Drives and their Destiny*, Standard Edition, vol. 14.

Freud, S. (1915–17) *Introductory Lectures on Psychoanalysis*, Standard Editions, vols 15 and 16.

Freud, S. (1920) *Beyond the Pleasure Principle*, Standard Edition, vol, 18.

Freud, S. (1922) *Group Psychology and the Analysis of the Ego*, London: The International Psychoanalytical Press, Standard Edition, vol. 18.

Freud, S. (1925) *Inhibitions, Symptoms and Anxiety*, Standard Edition, vol. 20.

Freud, S. (1927, pub. 1928) *Dostoevsky and Parricide*, Introduction to German edition of *The Brothers Karamazov*, Munich.

Freud, S. (1928) Letter to Lytton Strachey 25 December 1928, in Freud, E. and L. (eds) and Stern, T. and J. (trs), *Letters 1873–1939*, London (1961).

Freud, S. (1932a) *Why War?*, Standard Edition, vol. 22.

Freud, S. (1932b) *Introduction to Psychoanalysis* (New Series), Standard Edition, vol. 22.

Fry, R. (1920) *Vision and Design*, London: Hogarth Press.

Fry, R. (1924) *The Artist and the Psychoanalysis*, London: Hogarth Press.

Gabetta, G.F. (1984) 'La seduzione della mitologia', *Il Piccolo Hans*, **42**, Bari: Dedalo.

Gargani, A. (1979) *Wittgenstein tra Austria e Inghilterra*, Turin: Stampatori.

Gargani (ed.) (1983) *Ludwig Wittgenstein e la cultura contemporanea*, Milan: Longo.

Garnett, D. (1975) *Mr. Keynes as a Biographer*, Cambridge: Cambridge University Press.

Gay, P. (1984) *The Bourgeois Experience. From Victoria to Freud*, Oxford: Oxford University Press.

Gay, P. (1986) *Freud for Historians*, Oxford: Oxford University Press.

Gotti, M. (1988) 'Il modello argomentativo di J.M. Keynes nella *General Theory*', *Quaderni del Dipartimento di Linguisitica e Letterature Comparate*, Bergamo: Università degli Studi.

Hacking, I. (1983) *Representing and Intervening*, Cambridge: Cambridge University Press.

Hallyday M.A.K. (1990) 'The Construction of Knowledge and value in the Grammar of Scientific Discourse; with reference to Charles Darwin's *The Origin of Species*', in De Stasio, C. (et al.) (eds), *La rappresentazione verbale e iconica*, Milan, Guerini.

Harrod, R. (1951) *The Life of John Maynard Keynes*, London: Macmillan.

Heine, E. (1984) Introduction to E.M. Forster, *The Longest Journey*, London: Arnold.

Hession, C.H. (1984) *John Maynard Keynes*, London: Macmillan.

Holroyd, M. (1971) *Lytton Strachey and the Bloomsbury Group*, London: Macmillan.

Holroyd, M. & Levy, P. (eds) (1980) *The Shorter Strachey*, Oxford: Oxford University Press.

Houghton, W.E. (1957) *The Victorian Frame of Mind 1830–1870*, New Haven: Yale University Press.

Johnstone, J.K. (1954) *The Bloomsbury Group*, London: Hogarth Press.

Kahn, R.F. (1975) 'Una rilettura di Keynes' in Caffé, F. (ed.), *Keynes: Riletture e Rievocazioni*, Turin: Einaudi.

Keynes, J.M. (1937) 'The General Theory of Employment' in *The Quarterly Journal of Economics*, February.

Keynes, J.N. (1884) *Exercises and Studies in Formal Logic*, London: Macmillan.

Keynes, J.N. (1891) *The Scope and Method of Political Economy* London: Macmillan.

Keynes, M. (ed.) (1983) *Essays on J.M. Keynes*, Cambridge: Cambridge University Press.

Landow, G.P. (1989) 'Elegant Jeremiahs: The Genre of the Victorian Sage', in Clubbe, J. (ed.), *Victorian Perspectives*, London: Macmillan.

Lawson, T. and Pesaran, H. (eds) (1985) *Keynes' Economics: Methodological Issues*, London: Croom Helm.

Levine, G. and Madden, W. (eds) (1968) *The Art of Victorian Prose*, Oxford: Oxford University Press.

Levy, P. (1981) *G.E. Moore and the Cambridge Apostles*, Oxford: Oxford University Press.

Maitland, F.W. (1903) *The Life and Letters of Sir Leslie Stephen*, London: Allen and Unwin.

Marcus, J. (ed.) (1984) *Virginia Woolf and Bloomsbury*, London: Macmillan.

Marcus, S. (1984) *Freud and the Culture of Psychoanalysis*, London: Allen and Unwin.

McGuinness, B.F. (1982) *Wittgenstein and his Times*, Oxford: Basil Blackwell.

Mellor, D.H. (ed.) (1980) *Prospects for Pragmatism: Essays in honour of Ramsey*, Cambridge: Cambridge University Press.

Miller, J.H. (1968) *The Form of Victorian Fiction*, Indiana: Notre Dame University Press.

Moore, G.E. (1966, reprint of 1903) *Principia Ethica*, Cambridge: Cambridge University Press.

Moore, G.E. (1942) 'An Autobiography' in Schilpp, P.A. (ed.), *The Philosophy of G.E. Moore*, Chicago: Chicago University Press.

74   *John Maynard Keynes: Language and Method*

Morelli, G. (1883) *Italian Painters: Critical Studies of the Works*, London: C. Bell & Son.
Patinkin, T. and Clark-Leith, J. (eds) (1977) *Keynes, Cambridge, and 'The General Theory'*, London: Macmillan.
Phillips, H. (1951) *J.M. Keynes: Vision and Technique*, Stanford: Stanford University Press.
Poole, R. (1982) *The Unknown Virginia Woolf*, Brighton: Harvester.
Ramsey, F.P. (1978) in D.H. Mellor (ed.), *Foundations*, London: RKP.
Roberts, J.H. (1946) 'Vision and Design in V. Woolf', Proceedings of the Modern Language Association.
Robinson, A. (1983) 'Impressions on J.M. Keynes' in Worswick, D. and Trevithick, J. (eds), *Keynes and the Modern World*, Cambridge: Cambridge University Press.
Rosenbaum, S.P. (1987) *Victorian Bloomsbury*, London: Macmillan.
Rossini-Favretti, R. (1987) 'Argomentazione nella communicazione e nella epistemologia keynesiana' *Collana del Dip. di Scienze Sociali* 33, Bologna.
Russell, B. (1903) *Principles of Mathematics*, London: Allen and Unwin.
Russell, B. (1912 repr. 1988) *The Problems of Philosophy*, Oxford: Oxford University Press.
Russell, B. (1914) *Our Knowledge of the External World*, New York: Open Court.
Russell, B. (1967) *Autobiography 1872-1914*, London: Allen and Unwin.
Shepard, M. (1985) *Sherlock Holmes and the case of Dr. Freud*, London: Tavistock Press.
Simili, R. (ed.) (1986) *L'epistemologia di Cambridge 1850-1950*, Bologna: Il Mulino.
Skidelsky, R. (ed.) (1977) *The End of the Keynesian Era: Essays on the Disintegration of the Keynesian Political Economy*, London: Macmillan.
Skidelsky, R. (1983) *John Maynard Keynes: Hopes Betrayed*, London: Macmillan.
Soffer, R. (1978) *Ethics and Society in England: the Revolution of the Social Sciences, 1870-1914*, Stanford: University of California Press.
Spinella, M. (1987) 'Due scorci su Lytton Strachey', *Il Piccolo Hans*, **54**, Bari: Dedalo.
Stephen L. (1893) *An Agnostic's Apology and Other Essays*, London, repr. 1931 for the Rationalist Press Association, London: C.A. Watts.
Strachey, L. (1918 repr. 1986) *Eminent Victorians*, London: Harmondsworth.
Strachey, L. (1924) *Elizabeth and Essex*, London: Hogarth Press.
Strachey, L. (1972) *The Really Important Question and Other Essays*, Levy, P. (ed.), London: Hogarth Press.
Williams, B. (1931) *G. Lowes Dickinson, J.E. McTaggart*, Cambridge: Cambridge University Press.
Winslow, E.G. (1986) 'Keynes and Freud: Psychoanalysis and Keynes's Account of the Animal Spirits of Capitalism', *Social Research*, **52**, (4).
Wittgenstein, L. (1921 trans. 1961) *Tractatus Logico-Philosophicus*, D. Pears & B. McGuinness (trs), London: RKP.
Wittgenstein, L. (1953) *Philosophical Investigations*, Oxford: Basil Blackwell.
Wittgenstein, L. (1967) *Zettel*, Oxford: Basil Blackwell.

Wittgenstein, L. (1968) 'Notes for Lectures on "Private Experience" and "Sense Data"' in Rhees, R. (ed.), *Philosophical Review*, vol. 77.
Wittgenstein, L. (1974a) *On Certainty*, Oxford: Basil Blackwell.
Wittgenstein, L. (1974b) *Letters to Russell, Keynes and Moore*, in von Wright, G.H. (ed.), Oxford: Basil Blackwell.
Wittgenstein, L. (1978) *Lectures and Conversations on Aesthetics, Psychology and Religious Belief*, Oxford: Basil Blackwell.
Wittgenstein, L. (1980) *Remarks on the Philosophy of Psychology* (2 vols), Oxford: Basil Blackwell.
Woolf, L. (1960) *Autobiography*, London: Hogarth Press.
Woolf, V. (1921) *Jacob's Room*, London: Hogarth Press.
Woolf, V. (1924) 'Character in Fiction' paper presented to Heretics 12 May 1924, Sussex University Library: Monkhouse Papers, repr. (1967) as 'Mr Bennett and Mrs Brown'.
Woolf, V. (1929) *A Room of One's Own*, London: Hogarth Press.
Woolf, V. (1934) *Three Guineas*, London: Hogarth Press.
Woolf, V. (1967) *Collected Essays*, L. Woolf (ed), London: Hogarth Press.
Woolf, V. (1976) *Moments of Being*, J. Schulkind (ed), London: Grafton Books.
Woolf, V. (1985) *A Writer's Diary*, L. Woolf (ed), London: Grafton.
Woolf, V. (1987) *Complete Shorter Fiction*, London: Triad Grafton.
Worswick, D. and Trevithick, J. (eds) (1983) *Keynes and the Modern World*, Cambridge: Cambridge University Press.

3.   The Poverty of Rhetoric: Keynes versus McCloskey[1]

Riccardo Bellofiore

INTRODUCTION

> I believe it might be of interest to a philosopher, one who can think for himself, to read my notes. For even if I have hit the mark only rarely, he would recognize what targets I had been ceaselessly aiming at. (Ludwig Wittgenstein)[2]

The methodological aspects of Keynes's thought have attracted attention only recently. Albeit slowly and cautiously, the situation seems to be changing. More books have been, or are about to be, published which are solely concerned with Keynes's epistemology or with the method implicit in his economic and other writings (Lawson and Pesaran 1985; Vercelli 1987; Carabelli 1988; O'Donnell 1989).

An explanation of this phenomenon would have to refer first, to the publication of Moggridge's *Collected Writings* (*CW*) and particularly the *Treatise on Probability*, and second, to the crisis which Keynesianism is undergoing, as are the 'strong' epistemological theories of neo-Positivism and Falsificationism. Each of these crises has aroused debate about the interpretation of Keynes's works, and has encouraged a more careful, and therefore more faithful, rereading of them. Moreover, each of these crises has prompted a flood of publications: a library could be filled with writings on the crisis of Keynesiamism as an economic theory and as a guide to economic policy. Likewise, though after some delay, the spread of post-Positivist philosophies of science has given rise to a new and growing research project in economic methodology (we need only recall, in English, Blaug 1980; Caldwell 1982; Boland 1982; in French, Schmidt 1985; Mingat, Salmon and Wolfelsperger 1985; Latouche 1984; and in Italian Zamagni 1982).

Thus, it is no surprise that this new way of viewing Keynes has produced as many problems as it has advances, and probably more than it is at present capable of solving. In particular, three issues seem to me to be the most urgent and unresolved:

1. How is Keynes's method, so to speak, 'embodied' in the content of his economic theory (which clearly presupposes an answer to the question of whether the two are separable)?
2. Apart from its known differences from Logical Empiricism and from Popperianism, how are we to account for Keynes's method relative to post-Positivist theories of knowledge?
3. How is Keynes's method related to his use of language, in other words, how far is the former moulded by the latter, and how far is Keynes's non-demonstrative argumentation moulded by his rhetoric?

Donald N. McCloskey's recent book, *The Rhetoric of Economics* (McCloskey 1985), offers a straw to the wind to help us orientate ourselves in the new landscape which is opening up before us. McCloskey's book does not deal with Keynes's method head on, but only fleetingly, with a few references. Nevertheless, I shall try to show that it gives an answer (to my mind a wholly mistaken one) to the question of the role of language in Economics. Though it is rather abstract, the answer is one which offers a challenge to anyone considering Keynes's language and method.

McCloskey's answer may be summarized with the following claims:

1. that Economics (and, indeed, any science, natural as well as social) is inherently rhetorical, given that the economist's aim is to persuade rather than to prove;
2. that, therefore, any 'modernist' philosophy of science (as he calls, not without reason, prescriptive methodologies) hinders rather than helps the day-to-day work of economists, who would do better to undertake a 'literary critique' of Economics, instead of worshipping methodological rules which should guarantee the certainty of knowledge, but in practice are routinely ignored; and
3. that the cognitive power of a theory is measured by its power to convince other scholars, the other participants in the economic 'conversation', and therefore that a theory's rhetorical 'form' is inseparable from its scientific 'content'.

It is rather peculiar that hitherto Keynes has not been used as a case study corroborating McCloskey's claims. The peculiarity can be seen from Keynes's view that Economics is a non-demonstrative moral science which aims to persuade by means of rational argument. And, at first glance, this view might seem to be close to the claims of McCloskey's *The Rhetoric of Economics*. Nevertheless, I shall here try to do the exact opposite and use Keynes as a case study *disconfirming* McCloskey's claims. If you like, mine is a sort of critique *avant la lettre*; taking up McCloskey's language and categories, it might be thought of as a straightforward argument *a fortiori*: 'if McCloskey's Rhetoric does not fit the case which seems most favourable to it, then it will not fit the others either'.

In fact, my aims are wider and more ambitious. I would like, if not to prove, at least to display convincingly that McCloskey's anti-epistemology is self-contradictory or banal, that Keynes's method cannot be delineated in the terms of McCloskey's Rhetoric, and that, nevertheless, Keynes's language and rhetoric were not merely important but crucial in bringing about a revolution in economic theory.

My account is divided into two parts. The first, made up of sections 2 to 5, describes and objects to McCloskey's claims as they stand; this will involve suggesting, at least in outline, not only the epistemological, but also the more purely philosophical background of McCloskey's position. While we can assume that the recent debates in the philosophy of science about the 'growth of knowledge' (from Popper to Lakatos, and from Kuhn to Feyerabend) are widely known, we may not be able to say the same about McCloskey's philosophical starting-point, which is the particular brand of pragmatist relativism whose leading and brightest light, much quoted by McCloskey, is Richard Rorty.

The second part of my account confronts Keynes and McCloskey. In this part, I shall try to show that Keynes's rhetoric has little to do with McCloskey's Rhetoric; and I shall put forward the view that, unlike McCloskey's post-Positivist position, Keynes's method points, perhaps diffidently but quite clearly, a way out of controversies about the presence or absence of guarantees of truth and about the certainty of knowledge, but points instead toward a non-foundationalist notion of the objectivity of knowledge. Again, in this second part, I shall have to refer to an author who is not part of an economist's normal equipment, and again it is a philosopher: Wittgenstein.[3]

THE RHETORIC OF ECONOMICS

> If we want things to stay as they are, things will have to change. (Giuseppe Tomasi di Lampedusa)[4]

In getting to grips with the meaning which McCloskey gives to his Rhetoric, one difficulty is with the welter of definitions to be found in his writings. I have picked out a few which seem to be worth pausing briefly over. In the book's 'Exordium', Rhetoric is given a variety of meanings. It is said to be 'the paying of attention to one's audience' (McCloskey (1985), p. xvii); but on the very same page, it is given the wider meaning 'the study of all the ways of accomplishing things with language'; and then its aim is specified as that of persuasion: the scholar who speaks rhetorically tries to persuade (ibid., p. xviii). But we ought to take note that, in its turn, persuasion is given a precise meaning when it is said that the scholar (whether he be a literary critic, a philosopher, an economist or a mathematical physicist) 'doesn't speak into the void, or to himself. He speaks to a community of voices. He desires to be heeded, praised, published, imitated, honoured, enNobeled. These are the desire. The devices of language are the means' (ibid.). Here, persuasion seems to be merely the pursuit of honours and of the agreement of one's peers. It is no surprise that McCloskey draws this conclusion: 'Rhetoric is the proportioning of means to desires in speech. Rhetoric is an economics of language, the study of how scarce means are allocated to the insatiable desires of people to be heard' (ibid.). Thus almost before it is off the ground, the Rhetoric of economics seems to have found in its principal supporter not its Protagoras or Gorgias, but its Plato; just as for Plato, rhetoric is subordinate to dialectic, so for McCloskey, Rhetoric seems to be a branch of economics, undoubtedly of the neoclassical variety.

In this case, one might ask why McCloskey as economist seeks the support of Rhetoric, given that he defines Rhetoric in the terms of neoclassical economics. The reply to such a puzzle is this: 'The subject [of McCloskey's book] is scholarship. It is not the economy, or the adequacy of economic theory as a description of the economy, or even mainly the economist's role in the economy. The subject is the conversation economists have among themselves for the purposes of persuading each other' (ibid.). If, therefore, economics is a rhetorical discipline, it is in terms of the 'conversation' that success or failure in it will be judged, and certainly not in terms of anything so crude as 'something outside it', outside the talk of economists, outside Senior Common Rooms, outside its academic setting. As a consequence, there is strictly no point in the 'internal' critiques, of the sort that passed in the 1960s between Cambridge, England and Cambridge, Mass., nor in 'external' critiques, and still less in in a 'critique of political economy'. On this point, McCloskey is utterly clear: 'economics is successful' (ibid., p. xix); and in a later chapter, he insists that 'one thing is clear: the absorption of rhetorical thinking in economics will not precipitate any revolution in the substance of economics' (ibid., p. 174). And again:

> Economics at present is, in fact, moderately well off. ... The criticisms of economics for being 'too mathematical' or 'too static' or 'too bourgeois' are not very persuasive, though articulated often enough. They are of the form 'you can't know the Truth using those wretched mathematical/static/bourgeois methodologies' (ibid.).

The set of quotations which we have been supplying is aimed at showing how McCloskey's Rhetoric offers a new lease of life to a conservative undertaking in economics (and perhaps in philosophy too). We now proceed to show by detailed examination of McCloskeys' arguments just what he is offering.

McCloskey's book is divided into two blocks of chapters. The rationale of his arranging the material in this way can be understood from the definitions which he gives of Rhetoric: 'Rhetoric is not a new methodology. It is an antimethodology' (McCloskey 1985, p. 51). This negative account can be set against his positive assertions: that the rhetorical scholar, 'used also the special topics of economic discourse' (ibid., p. 130) and that 'the common topic appeals to reasons that most people can appreciate' (ibid.). More generally, 'Linguistics is an appropriate model for economic science' (ibid., p. 62). Economics is not an exception to what goes not only for literary studies but also for the 'hard sciences': 'Science uses literary methods' (ibid., p. 54).

In the first block of chapters, which comprises the first three in the book, McCloskey sets out his position on the purely epistemological issues. The second block runs up to the penultimate chapter, before the summing-up and concluding chapter. The six chapters of the second block put forward a 'literary critique' of economics which is tested against four cases. The examples chosen are John Muth on rational expectations, Robert Fogel on economic history, econometrics and statistics. McCloskey's aim is to show that even authors who think of themselves as 'scientific' do not follow methodological rules and do not argue demonstratively; rather they engage in rhetorical exercises in persuasion.

McCloskey's argument against epistemology can be summed up as follows:

1. Economists' official Methodology asserts a demarcation between science and non-science; the former is picked out as being aimed at predicting and at controlled, repeatable experiments, objectivity, quantification; the latter concerns introspection, belief, morality and values.

2. What is at issue is a Received View which applies to all and every science a model deriving from seventeenth and eighteenth century physics. Because of its unhistoricalness and pretensions to objectivity, this Received View may be called 'positivist' when applied to the Philosophy of Science. In so far as it has become a commonplace of wider culture over the last four centuries under the influence of the Cartesian project of the refoundation of knowledge, it might be better to call it 'modernist'.

3. The positivist methodology must be rejected for a variety of reasons: because it has been abandoned by philosophers of science; because there is no chance of definitive refutation by means of a crucial experiment; because an historical science such as economics cannot provide predictions; but, above all, because it is a general and prescriptive Methodology which tries to set out in advance of actual scientific endeavours the criteria which they ought to meet, and because it is no more observed in practice by economists than it is by any other scientist.

4. The modernist philosophy, which chases the will-o'-the-wisp of 'certain' knowledge, can be replaced by a different mode of self-understanding by intellectuals, as enlightened thinkers involved in a conversation which proceeds along rhetorical lines; on this view, truth is to be found only within the linguistic realm, because it is not so much 'discovered' as 'produced' in and by the conversation itself and boils down to the fact of one person persuading another.

It would be easy but fruitless to pick on the inaccuracies and, in some cases, outright contradictions in which McCloskey is embroiled. It would be fruitless because it seems to me that his line of thought picks up some real and significant difficulties for traditional epistemology. Nevertheless, we shall restrict ourselves to pointing out three of the more prominent inaccuracies which seem to call for a closer examination.

The first is the vagueness of McCloskey's dismissal of all the methodologies which he wishes to criticize as 'positivist'. This blanket term covers logical empiricism as much as Popperian falsificationism, when it is well known that the latter was produced as a retort to the former. Popper himself, along with Lakatos, is sometimes classed with the modernists and sometimes with the antimodernists. The attack on falsificationism is an attack on one of the many kinds of 'positivist' epistemologies and is mixed in with them without appropriate discriminations. We could go on in this vein.

The second inaccuracy points to an incoherence of which McCloskey may not be aware. At some points in his book (for example, McCloskey 1985, pp. 24–8), and in many of his subsequent writings, he seems to conceive of Rhetoric as the sort of conversational norms (*Sprachethik*) discussed by Habermas; but he does not notice that Habermas himself is seeking to vindicate the very idea of a universalistic truth which McCloskey is wishing his Rhetoric to overcome.

The third inaccuracy might be better described as a sort of havering. At some points, McCloskey's appeal to Rhetoric seems to be directed merely, but powerfully, at undermining the epistemological foundations of economics. Taken in this role, it presents a radical opposition to pretensions to 'truth' in the economic, and more generally in any other sort of, conversation. At other points, however, we can see that Rhetoric is being called on as the art of conversation in a stronger sense. The 'conversation' offers an alternative and more 'faithful' model of scientific work, and makes space for its own theory of truth.

It seems to me that McCloskey's criticisms of 'positivist' methodologies can be accepted and even strengthened. This is so even if we take on board a more lifelike scheme of the Philosophy of Science in the twentieth century, which we shall briefly sketch in the next section. On the other hand, the incoherence as between the 'critical' and the 'reconstructive' senses of Rhetoric seems to point to a serious shortcoming. This is McCloskey's failure, shared with many other philosophers of Science who are 'against method'; first, to make a decisive break with the traditional project of epistemology and, as a result, to distinguish between anti-foundationalism and relativism. This is the failure which lies behind McCloskey's confusion about Habermas. For all that this may be unclear at the moment, we shall try to unpack it in the following sections.

CRITICISM OF RHETORIC

> We may imagine some sailors on the open sea who are re-building their clumsy ship from being round to a slimmer shape. They make use of stray pieces of wood brought by the current as well as parts of the old structure to change the hull and the keel of their boat. But they cannot put the boat into dry-dock to take her apart. They have to remain within the old structure while they work and struggle with occasional storms and high waves. In modifying the boat, they take care not to open any dangerous holes. Slowly a new ship emerges out of the old one and, while they continue to work, the sailors can already start thinking about a new structure and be in disagreement with one another. The whole affair will go ahead in ways which we cannot yet foresee. This is our fate. (Otto Neurath)[5]

Epistemological discussion has traditionally been divided into two camps. On the one hand, there is the view that a theory is true in virtue of corresponding in some respect to the way some extra-theoretical object is (the 'correspondence' theory of truth). On the other hand, there is the view that a theory is true in virtue of being constituted of statements which cohere with a body of true statements (the 'coherence' theory of truth). These two views have several features in common. Their initial premise is the distinction between the knowing subject and the object of that knowing (generally identified as the object of knowledge), each of which is independent of its opposite and antecedent to the mutual relation between them. Furthermore, the two theories of truth share in the project of 'justification'; that is to say, they both aim at offering a guarantee for claims to truth. Such a guarantee, if it is to perform its allotted role, must be external to the claims for which it provides the 'foundations' and must, therefore, be general so as to apply to any body of knowledge whatever.

Popper (1934) represents a watershed in the prevailing understanding in the philosophy of science. He got away from the idea that a theory 'mirrors' the facts and from the neo-Positivist idea that truth is guaranteed by the 'evidence' for it. He thus set rolling the approach to the philosophy of science which has gone under the label of 'the growth of knowledge'. But he nevertheless retained the standing dichotomy between subject and object as well as the justificationist project.

It is well known that the Popperian proposal involves the acceptance of a demarcation between science and non-science by means of the criterion of falsificationism. This, in summary, is the requirement that there be some empirical propositions which could falsify a given theory. This criterion appears in many guises in Popper's considerable output of reflections on methodology. But one distinctive feature remains invariant: the scientificness of knowledge does not depend on the discovery of evidence which corroborates a hypothesis, but rather on the clearest and most open subjection of it to experimentation aimed at uncovering facts which are *in*consistent with the hypothesis.

Popper asserts that in certain important respects he is giving up on the idea of science as absolutely certain and demonstrable knowledge, and therefore also on the pursuit of the impossible task of giving a foundation to knowledge. Nevertheless, his attempt to pick out the distinctive characteristic of scientific knowledge in terms of the critical method of the falsification of theories simply shifts the terms of the pretensions of the philosophy of science. Whereas previously, the aim had been to give a guarantee of the indubitability of knowledge, Popper offers the guarantee of the potential testing to destruction of the conjectures that scientists dreamt up. One of the presuppositions of this way of viewing the matter is the doctrine that scientific rationality's 'critical' function can be specified by abstract and ahistorical methodological reflection and that this can come about prior to, and independent of, the individual sciences. And this in turn presupposes a neutral, unified, and unchangeable standpoint from which to judge how scientific or otherwise a given theory is, and whether knowledge is progressing.

If these sketchy remarks can be allowed to pass, McCloskey's criticisms have a certain basis of their own. For after all, what Popper shares with logical empiricism – despite claiming to have murdered it – is the desire to construct a universal Method for Science, rather than for the individual sciences. The capitals, which McCloskey uses when referring to 'positivist' methodology, are an ironic reference to the pretentiousness of the enterprise: the desire to take a God's-eye view of things. Any Method of that sort cannot fail to be prescriptive: after all, the scientificness of a theory depends on its being susceptible to investigation by appropriate methods.

The rest of the discussion does nothing to alter these conclusions. Rather, they show that criticisms internal to Popperianism have dissolved it, without succeeding either in escaping from its *aporiai* nor in getting away from the traditional epistemological worries. Popper himself quickly realized that the 'facts' to which the method, both of neo-Positivism and of his own falsificationism, must refer are themselves theory-laden. The neutrality of the observational 'givens' is put into question in a way radicalized by Quine's revival of Duhemian thoughts about the holistic nature of experimental controls. That is, the falsification of a proposition may be due to the falsity of one of the auxiliary hypotheses which mediate between the hypothesis which is being tested and the experimental observation. Popper, however, finds a way out of this predicament only by appeal to the conventional decisions which scientists make to count a certain core of knowledge as not subject to test. It is this core that enables a novel hypothesis to be compared with the empirical base and thus exposes it to the possibility of criticism and falsification.[6]

Kuhn (1962 repr. 1970) moved the debate from one about the context of justification to one about the context of discovery. This seemed to make a place for history in epistemological debate, by introducing the notions of 'scientific revolution', 'paradigm' and 'normal science'. However, it has been rightly noted (for example, in some contributions to Lakatos and Musgrave (1970)) that Kuhn's innovation adds up more to a psychology of research than to a sociology. Moreover Kuhn, like Popper, tends towards what is a form of conventionalism, from which not even Lakatos' methodology of 'research programmes' escapes. Even the methodological anarchism which Feyerabend proposes (1975) seems like the inevitable upshot of epistemology after Popper. For Feyerabend, one of the heroes of McCloskey's book, because different theories are expressed in different languages, they refer to different 'facts', or can use one term to refer to different objects. Holism about theories entails their incommensurability. The positive message of the author of *Against Method* is then, the famous 'anything goes', which he offers as a way out of general and prescriptive Method.

But the 'anything goes' can, like McCloskey's Rhetoric, be understood in two opposed ways. It can be taken to be a tactical manoeuvre in the internal criticism of epistemology. In this sense it forms part of Feyerabend's ironizing attitude, which doesn't take itself, and therefore also its own 'anything goes', too seriously: a sort of jibe at his peers rather than an alternative methodology. In support of this account, one could cite the many places where Feyerabend, again like McCloskey, stresses that he is not wanting to abolish all rules but rather to expose the supposed generality of the rules that are doing the rounds, and to emphasize their limitations.

At the same time, the 'anything goes' cannot but appear as an epistemological proposal which is itself universal and prescriptive. It cannot but appear in this guise because the attack on Method needs to be launched from a general standpoint outside the sciences, even if it prescribes that we should not indulge in Methodology.

We are thus faced with a choice between two very different lines which we might take. On the one hand, there is a critique of epistemology which is purely destructive and claims to be devastating. On the other, there is an antimethodology, which is the mirror image of the reviled Methodology, whose every feature it retains and reproduces. If we end up choosing either of these lines, we have to pay the price of giving up on the idea that there is something objective in the scientific endeavour. Popper had already accepted the subjectivity of the process of conjecture-formation; but, within his critical rationalism, recourse to Method preserved the notion of the objectivity of knowledge, whose growth could be detected. By skipping the whole 'fairy story' of Method, Feyerabend blocks off this last move into a non-subjective dimension of scientific work.

It seems that Feyerabend's methodological anarchism carries to its logical conclusions the justificationist project in epistemology based on the radical independence of a subject from the object of knowledge. Given that the conclusion is negative for this project, we must conclude that a critical theory of knowledge will have to be built on very different foundations. The notion of objectivity will have to be redefined so as to square with the fact that subject and object are individuable only in terms of their interaction and not presupposing any antecedent separation between them. As a consequence, we shall have to give up the ambition of dictating rules from outside the actual practice of enquiry; instead, we may content ourselves with contextual or internal justifications of the conclusions of theories. As we shall see, this is not McCloskey's view; so we shall temporarily leave unworked-out the details of an alternative epistemology.

With what has already been said, we may begin to subject McCloskey to scrutiny. If, setting aside the inaccuracy of his account of twentieth-century philosophy of science, it is reasonable to follow him in the bulk of his criticisms of 'positivist' epistemology, he nevertheless runs into the same difficulties which beset Feyerabend, although he seeks a way out of them. Let us see how.

To begin with, it is clear that McCloskey's Rhetoric is subject to the same criticisms which he directs at 'positivist' Method. If his line of thought is correct, then it cannot but be applied also to itself: it is self-refuting. If, as a matter of fact, Method is prescriptive and universal, the same can be said of McCloskeys' Rhetoric – which is our reason for the capital 'R'. Sometimes the prescription is purely negative: do not do 'positivist' Methodology. Sometimes it is positive: scientific method is the method of the humanities; in this way it turns on its head the traditional appeal to the 'hard' sciences in the definition of scientific rationality. In either case, what we are faced with are general claims; and in the latter, with a new version of unitary Method, albeit a different one from that of the 'positivists'. The fact that sometimes the prescription is dressed up as a description ('this is what scientists do anyway') does not make much difference. Nor does it make much difference that what is at issue is not an ahistorical proposal. After all, allowing, for the sake of argument, that the Rhetoric of economics is meant to reflect the actual, rather than the official, methodology which economists follow, this attitude can be taken as a starting-point for a book like McCloskey's only if we think that acceptance of what the unofficial methodology consists in is a step forward, an improvement in the way that economics is actually done. And this is just what our author frequently claims. On the other hand, it is true that post-Popperian epistemology has introduced history into method. It is however, equally true that epistemology retains its status as an independent discipline claiming to analyse scientific Method, even when, as in the case of the Rhetoric of economics, it ends up denying that there is such a thing.

We are faced with a position which will not relinquish the claim to be able to talk, as from an external and neutral standpoint, about the actual procedures of the scientific enterprise. Rhetoric shares with Methodology the capacity to constitute a transcendental self-reflection from without on the actual work of scientists. Moreover, McCloskey's Rhetoric displays its own version of epistemological neutrality, which marks down as practically irrelevant and interchangeable the various options which competing theories offer: anything goes because nothing makes any difference.

McCloskey's position also tends to let go the idea of objectivity. He is led by his holism about theories and about experimental procedures to deny that truth makes any reference to an extra-linguistic realm. The social character of meaning is given by the agreement of researchers, and scientific revolutions boil down to the creation of an audience.

We thus arrive at the point at which McCloskey tries to uphold the plausibility of his position by showing the rhetorical nature of economics. And we witness his resourceful attempt to dodge the difficulty into which he and Feyerabend run. This is the difficulty presented by the fact that his reflections have brought him to a forking result, neither of whose prongs is comfortable. He seems to have to choose either an internal and purely negative critique of epistemology, or a positive but self-refuting anti-epistemology. Following in Richard Rorty's philosophical footsteps, McCloskey tries to find a way out by viewing economics as a discipline in which what is taking place is a fragment of the 'conversation of mankind'. The aim is not so much to solve the problems of the philosophy of science as to dissolve them, seeing them as the unavoidable and in some sense a necessary expression of our predicament as researchers and intellectuals.

It should be noted that what I have set out is meant as a rational reconstruction of McCloskey's position, an analysis of its logical structure which tries to improve, when possible or appropriate, on the arguments so as to be better able to criticize the whole in its essential core, and not its details. It is hard to tell how far McCloskey is aware of the incoherence of his position in the philosophy of science, or of the implications of his appeal to Rorty. But it seems to me that it is only by showing how essential the appeal to Rorty is for McCloskey's line of thought that we can avoid the impression that the whole of the second half of his book is merely banal. And this is what we shall try to do in the next section.

A PHILOSOPHY FOR THE SENIOR COMMON ROOM

The problem of why and by what right we accept a logical law can be answered within logic only by referring this law to other logical laws. Where that is not possible, logic owes us an answer. Going beyond the boundaries of logic, we can then say: we are forced by our nature and by external circumstances to make judgements, and if we make judgements, we cannot deny the said law (such as the law of identity); we are forced to accept it if we are not to upset all our thought and to give up all judgement. I do not wish either to attack or to defend this view, but only to note that it presents us with a logical line of reasoning. It does not explain why the law is true, but why we take it to be true. Moreover, the impossibility which we face of rejecting the law does not prevent us supposing that there are beings which reject it; but it does prevent us supposing that they are right in doing so. It prevents us having even the slightest doubt about whether they are right or we are right. (Gottlob Frege)[7]

There is something rather disappointing about the part of McCloskey's book in which he sets out the advantages of a 'literary criticism' for economics and then goes into detail so as to show that even the most devout economists argue by rhetorical means. This disappointment is due, in the first place to the startling regularity McCloskey finds against innovative ideas and in favour of orthodoxy. Some examples may help here: the criticism levelled at the concept of aggregate capital 'was equivalent to showing mathematically or statistically that a woman cannot be a summer's day' (McCloskey 1985, p. 80); likewise, Polanyi's views are dismissed as 'a fallacy of negating the antecedent' (ibid., p. 146); and, again, Keynes's *General Theory* is condemned, implicitly but nonetheless clearly, for being a theory of a closed economy. By contrast Becker, Muth and Fogel have praise heaped on them and are masters of rhetoric, whether they know it or not.

But, the source of the disappointment runs deeper. It resides in the fact that McCloskey thinks it sufficient to show that rhetorical elements are in play, for him to be able to assert that economics is a rhetorical science. We may again sum up in a few lines the main claims which McCloskey makes in the second half of his book:

1. Analogy and metaphor have a large role to play in economics and elsewhere, as do various rhetorical moves, either derived from classical rhetorical theory or borrowed from the particularities of the scientistic milieu.
2. This is because economics is one among the many conversations which take place in our civilization; hence new theories are submitted for critical scrutiny by the participants in that conversation, who alone decide the theory's 'truth'.
3. A theory's success is therefore dependent on its rhetorical effectiveness, and that is the sole standard by which to judge it; since the critique of epistemology has shown that any appeal to provide foundations or justification for a theory must be inconclusive, the sole measure of the greater or lesser 'goodness' of a theory is its capacity to persuade, and even to create, an audience.

Nowadays, no one would deny that analogy and metaphor have a role to play in science. But some extra argument is needed to get from there to the idea that the only standard by which to measure a theory is its success, considered in the reductive sense of the theory's ability to persuade the participants in a discussion. In other words, allowing room for rhetoric (lower case 'r') in economics is not, at first sight, incompatible with the adoption of methodological (lower case 'm') standards internal to a particular theory, nor even with hanging on to a criterion of demarcation.

One might reasonably ask why McCloskey did not go for this option in preference to his Rhetoric with all its commitments. We can pick out two reasons. One is that it is dictated to him by the critique of epistemology at which we have already looked and which pushes him to offer a straight alternative to Method. The other, which is closer to our present concerns, is the inner logic of the view that sees in the metaphor of 'conversation' the best way of representing scientific, and also other work. From this point of view, as before, McCloskey's position is stronger than his occasionally glib style of argument might lead us to suspect. Nevertheless, it is a position which must be rejected even in its improved variant.

As we indicated earlier (see p. 78), a proper understanding of McCloskey requires that we bear in mind the philosophical views of Richard Rorty, which we shall now summarize. This apparent digression perhaps ought to be explained, since it is rare to find references to Rorty in the literature on McCloskey's book and even when there are such they do not, to the best of my knowledge, go beyond mere quotation. Perhaps the reason for this is, as an unkind observer might think, the fact that if economists read little philosophy of science, they read less philosophy *tout court*. However that might be, Rorty's presence in McCloskey's text is beyond doubt (and even beyond the already large number of entries in the index). Rorty is invoked by name in the 'Acknowledgments' in round terms ('I was especially fortunate to overlap for a month with Richard Rorty. Talking to him, and reading his book *Philosophy and the Mirror of Nature*, made many things clear to me' (McCloskey 1985, p. xii). He is set up, in company with Feyerabend, as a critic of 'positivist' epistemology ('Paul Feyerabend's demolitions of the philosophy of science and Richard Rorty's deconstructions of philosophy have left methodologists apoplectic. Rorty views the history of epistemology since Plato as an intellectual bet that did not come off' (ibid., p. 23). And McCloskey's central metaphor of intellectual life as like a conversation itself comes from Rorty (though he borrowed it from Oakeshott, cf. ibid., p. xv).

The focus of Rorty's view lies in his transferral of the limitations of epistemology and, in a wider sense, of the tradition of English-speaking analytic philosophy, to the altogether vaster phenomenon of the working out of the Cartesian project in its various Kantian and neo-Positivist forms. Descartes added to the classical distinction between mind and body, as found in Plato, along with the image of the eye of the mind which perceives universal truths whereas the body's eyes perceive only singular facts. What Descartes added was the claim that the distinctive feature of the mental is its indubitability. Employing this feature, he was able to escape from the radical doubt with which a sceptical attitude threatened our knowledge of every other thing, starting with the existence and nature of an external world. Philosophy thus comes to be coterminous with the epistemological task of finding a guarantee for the certainty of knowledge, beginning with the indubitability of the 'inner world'.

It is from this position that there arises Kant's effort to see the whole of philosophy as a fully realized 'theory of knowledge' employing the recognition of the *a priori* certainties from the mental world to secure non-mental knowledge. And it is likewise from this position that there develops the neo-Positivist understanding of concepts as determined by the givens of sensation. With these moves, there is established a hierarchical bond between philosophy and science. This latter is regarded as supplying the sole 'true' knowledge, in the sense of a faithful reflection of external reality, independent of the observation or intervention of the scientist. Nevertheless it is on the 'guarantee' given by philosophy that we rely for the correctness of the image of the mind as a 'mirror of nature'. Thus, philosophy comes to occupy the role of the 'foundation' of science.

Rorty mobilizes the self-critical work of some analytical philosophers, in particular Sellars, Quine and Davidson, the details of which need not detain us, and the recent developments in the philosophy of science, as sketched in the preceding section. What he employs these materials to show, is that it is impossible for philosophy to fulfil the role in which, since Descartes at the dawn of the modern era, it has been cast. No foundation is possible because every reference to the external world is mediated by a theory and therefore, every justification carries with it the reference of one proposition to another. But if knowledge is nothing but language, Rorty continues, there is no compelling theoretical reason why one proposition should be more indubitable than any other.

All philosophical utterance – and indeed any other sort of utterance – cannot be anything but a 'voice in the conversation of mankind'. This metaphor has to be understood in a strong sense. No critique of philosophy or anything else is possible which says that things are otherwise, in terms of a notion of truth which makes reference to an external reality. So far as knowledge is concerned, the world of objects has, so to speak, evaporated. On the other hand, we cannot perform any translation from any other language; all we can do is familiarize ourselves with it by getting inside the aliens' skin. In this way, the critique of one theory from the point of view of another is hobbled from the start by the objection that incommensurability implies that we may have misunderstood or misapplied 'other' ways of reasoning. The pragmatic understanding of truth is the only one which remains operable. According to it, only what is true 'for us', or is defensible in terms of a theory we accept, is true. This slides into the thought that only what is 'more desirable' or 'better' from our point of view, is true. Consequently, just as in a conversation, the aim is not so much to arrive at 'a' conclusion, but to perform 'poetically' making up new meanings and new interpretations. And this is not a matter, as Rorty himself says of 'expressing a view about a subject' but merely of '*saying something*' (Rorty 1980, p. 371, emphasis original).

I wish to locate the three essential elements of my account relative to this brief sketch of Rorty's views. The first task to be performed is an underlining of the parallelism between McCloskey's attitude towards neoclassical theory in economics and Rorty's towards systematic philosophy and normal science. McCloskey's 'conservative' analysis thus turns out to be not merely an option, but a necessary part of his 'conversational' approach. Our second aim is to demonstrate how McCloskey's reference to Rorty explains why he also calls positivist epistemology 'modernist' and even why he prefers the latter label. The background against which the issue of the Rhetoric of economics is situated is, thus, the *querelle* between the modern and the post-modern. The third element in our account is to explain why the appeal to the conversational model, hitched up to Feyerabend's epistemological anarchism, seems, at least on the surface, to offer an escape route from the stalemate into which the first part of McCloskey's book plays itself.

As to the first matter, we may restrict ourselves to the following points. Rorty's progress through the three separate stages of anti-foundationalism, anti-realism and relativism results in a dissolution of truth. This in turn leads him to allot to philosophy the task of edification: the 'project of finding new, better, more fruitful ways of speaking' (Rorty 1980, p. 360). However, edification is not offered as an alternative to the sort of systematic philosophy which 'single[s] out one area, one set of practices, and see[s] it as the paradigm of human activity' (ibid., p. 366). Just so, abnormal talk is not to be taken as the negation, in support of an alternative truth, of normal talk. Indeed, it would be incoherent to criticize systematic philosophy's pretensions to 'objectivity' on the basis of an entirely different idea of what 'real' philosophy is. Rather, what, in normal science, seemed to follow from the nature of the object of study, is now to be read as one choice among the many possible choices.

We can now see how McCloskey's attitude to the various options among economic theories, and in particular his continued adherence to neoclassicism, is not merely the upshot of his personal attachment to the old credo. Rather, it is one, though not the only one, among the legitimate implications of his philosophy. Economists will recall Ferguson's posture in the face of neo-Ricardian criticism of the marginalist notion of capital. Called on to write a textbook, which he set out in accordance with the old orthodoxy, he justified his own choice by announcing his 'faith' in the empirical validity of that notion even though it had been discredited in theory. Ferguson's faith now finds in McCloskey's Rhetoric its philosophical bona fides.

The second matter should by now be clear enough, so that we may be fairly swift about it. The Rortyan philosophical 'foundations' point to its not being a chance matter that McCloskey should have described the methodology consensual among economists as 'modernist'. As we have already noted, McCloskey picks up the term, 'to emphasize its pervasiveness in modern thinking well beyond science' (McCloskey 1985, p. 19). And he adds tellingly that '[m]odernism coheres, one part with another. There are modernist philosophers, modernist architects, modernist musicians, modernist politicians, and modernist economists. This is the reason for using so many-sided a word: the thing itself is many-sided' (ibid.)

In other words, McCloskey takes his own proposals to be not merely post-positivist, but post-modern, in the sense that modernism is taken to be the sort of arrogant project which wants an orderly or orderable world, and that post-modernism is the modest admission of the ineliminable plurality of viewpoints and lifestyles. For this reason, he, like Rorty, takes it to be the underlying scheme of our (American) democratic culture.

Our third element amounts to the following: we have seen that, like Feyerabend, McCloskey seems to be trapped in the same generality and prescriptiveness as he criticizes epistemology for. The trap is there whether the aim is merely negative or whether one tries to produce an antiepistemology with more (McCloskey) or fewer (Feyerabend) positive features. The link to Rorty assures us that McCloskey's proposal should not be taken, so to speak, too seriously. It does not displace the old methodologies, but can be set alongside them in a single, albeit prismatic, wishy-washiness. It is not 'better', except by being preferred – by those who accept it. And this is to come within an ace of tautology.

IS THERE SOME WAY OUT OF HERE?

> To the subject which has no genuine relation to the thing, which recoils from its strangeness and coldness, everything which it says about it becomes, both for itself and in itself, mere opinion, something reproduced and registered, which could also be otherwise. The subjectivist reduction to the arbitrariness of individual consciousness fits in precisely with the submissive respect for an objectivity which such consciousness leaves standing uncontested, and which it reveres even in the assertion that whatever it thinks is non-binding in the face of its power; according to its measure, reason is nothing. (Theodor Adorno)[8]

Some of the contradictions which had cropped up thus vanish. In particular, the appearance that McCloskey provides insufficient argument in favour of the rhetorical nature of economics, evaporates. It does so because we have found that in the book there is an extremely strong and wide-ranging argument in favour of the notion, deriving from Rorty, that all rational discourse is a sort of conversation. McCloskey's examples are therefore to be understood merely as spellings out which follow from the adoption of that notion. From what we have seen so far, the adoption of that notion is not capable of being given a 'foundation'; it can only be found more or less congenial. Moreover, the neutral standpoint from which one can inspect the various theoretical options that economics has to offer is neutral only in respect of being that of the hermeneuticist who has no intention of proposing himself as a legislator or of giving the 'correct' interpretation. What is important is the process of having a conversation.

It is worth being clear about the price to be paid for adopting such a stance, with all its radical feel and peculiar cogency. The price is spelt out with his customary clarity by Rorty, rather than by McCloskey, as follows:

> For my purposes, what matters is a distinction between two kinds of revolutionary philosophers. On the one hand, there are revolutionary philosophers – those who found new schools within which normal, professionalized philosophy can be practised – who see the incommensurability of their new vocabulary with the old as a temporary inconvenience, to be blamed on the shortcomings of their predecessors and to be overcome by the institutionalization of their own vocabulary. On the other hand, there are great philosophers who dread the thought that their vocabulary should ever be institutionalized, or that their writing might be seen as commensurable with the tradition. (Rorty 1980, p. 369)

Clearly, his preference is for the latter sort. They do something more important: they undermine the idea that there could be a better representation. Replacing the references to philosophers with references to economists, we get a formally similar argument. The only, though far from negligible, difference is that unlike Rorty, McCloskey sides with 'normal' discourse against the 'abnormal'. But in both cases it is accepted that when they begin the attack on the old paradigm, the supporters of the new cannot be making use of anything like an argument; nor indeed, can they do so afterwards. There have been and there will be revolutions. But they are arbitrary occurrences and change only the way that normal research is carried on inside a particular academic profession. They cannot aspire to greater faithfulness to an external reality which is the object of knowledge and manipulation.

In short the scholar wishes to persuade, in the ways that the Rhetoric describes, as an undertaking mostly within his own institutional environment. We may recall that '[t]he subject is the conversation economists have *among themselves*' (McCloskey, 1985, p. xviii, emphasis added).

But is this how things really stand? McCloskey, following Rorty, rightly trumpets anti-foundationalism, which for them leads unavoidably to relativism. That is, to the claim that truth is, at bottom, just what we feel most comfortable with. Have we really entered a post-modern world? Is man's individuating characteristic merely that of being able, 'poetically', to create new interpretations and new points of view?

Must we abandon the typically modernist wish to 'prove the truth' and power of knowledge changing ourselves and the world? Is there really no alternative to persuasion and Rhetoric leading to a specialism without ambition and to a bland arbitrariness?

No, I think not. After all, in a recent book on the experience of modernity, we find the following compelling observation: 'Being modern means being located in an environment which promises adventure, power, joy, growth, the transformation of ourselves and of the world; and which, at the same time, threatens the destruction of all that we have, all that we know and all that we are' (Berman, 1986 p. 25).

This contradiction is a distinctive feature of modernity. Giving up the correspondence account of truth underwritten by traditional epistemology does not commit us to relativism, which is the giving up of any notion of objective truth. Habermas, the very author to whom we saw McCloskey (misleadingly) appealing, seems to hold on to the possibility of a non-relativist anti-foundationalism. In *Lectures on the Philosophical Discourse of Modernity*, he writes in a closely related context to ours:

> It is clear today that the meaning of universal questions – such as questions about the necessary conditions of the rationality of an assertion, about the universal pragmatic presuppositions of communicative action and argumentation – had better be reflected in the grammatical form of universal propositions, but not in the unconditionalness of validity or of the 'ultimate foundation' which had been pretended for it and for its theoretical background. The fallibilist consciousness of the sciences has long since reached philosophy. With such a fallibilism, we, philosophers and especially non-philosophers, do not give up our claims to truth. These claims can be raised in the first person performative attitude in no other way than that in which – as claims – they transcend time and space. But we know that there is no zero-context in which to make truth-claims. They are made here and now and are exposed to criticism. For that reason we do have to take into account the trite *possibility* that they will have to be reviewed tomorrow or in another place. Philosophy claims to be prior in virtue of being the guardian of rationality, as a claim to rationality external to our form of life. But in practice, it privileges a set of strong propositions with weak claims as to their status, which is so little totalitarian that there is no need to appeal to a totalising critique of reason. (Habermas 1987, pp. 213–4)

In short, I wish to maintain that anti-foundationalism, and hence the abandonment of neo-Positivism and Popperianism, opens up new ground. On that new ground, there are many routes which can be taken, not only that of relativism. It is possible to retain the objectivity of knowledge within an anti-foundationalist framework. In the present century, this route has been tried very rarely not only within economic theory, but also in epistemology. The language and method of John Maynard Keynes represents one of those few attempts. It is worth seeing how he fared, because we shall find another 'rhetoric' (lower case) which has little to do with McCloskey's.

KEYNES'S RHETORIC

> We have to invent a new wisdom for a new age. And in the meantime we must, if we are to do any good, appear unorthodox, troublesome, dangerous, disobedient to them that begat us. (J.M. Keynes, *CW*, IX, p. 306)

Keynes's name crops up more than once in McCloskey's book, but always incidentally. When he is cited, it is generally only indirectly or he is given little importance. On page 71 (McCloskey, 1985), he appears as one of the 'authorities' to whom Samuelson appeals; on page 172, McCloskey is reporting a view on the 'Keynesian model'; on pages 17–18, he rightly notes that the Keynesian revolution would not have come about if the methodological cannons which most economists nowadays espouse had been strictly adhered to ('where was the evidence of an objective, controlled, statistical kind?' (p. 18)).

The remaining citation is in the 'Exordium' and it is to this that we shall give some attention. It is singular in being the quotation of the well-known closing sentences of the *General Theory*:

> The ideas of economists and political philosophers, both when they are right and when they are wrong, are more powerful than is commonly understood. Indeed, the world is ruled by little else ... madmen in authority, who hear voices in the air, are distilling their frenzy from some academic scribbler a few years back (quoted in McCloskey, 1985, p. xviii).

The singularity of this is that, though it is quoted with approval, Keynes's sentiment is clearly at odds with what McCloskey has said just a few lines before. That is to say, it is at odds with the fact that McCloskey proposes an analysis of the conversation of economists directed exclusively at the rhetorical modes employed within the profession. The only connection to be found between McCloskey and this passage of Keynes is an 'unfortunately': 'unfortunately' the conversation among economists has extra-academic implications.

It is worth looking more closely at this difference, at least of stress, between Keynes and McCloskey. We may begin by asking what role persuasion has in Keynes's writings. From Keynes's large output, I shall make use of the *Essays in Persuasion, The General Theory* and some of the articles leading up to the latter. This choice is not casual; it is dictated by the difference in the intended recipients in each case.

The first chapter of *A Revision of the Treaty* reappears in the *Essays in Persuasion* with a slightly different title: 'The Change of Opinion'. The subject under discussion is the relation between the statesman and public opinion; in the light of that relation, Keynes considers what is to be said about his earlier pamphlet, *The Economic Consequences of the Peace*. Keynes wonders whether, in a mass democracy, the public good can be pursued only at the cost of the truth, by the use of deception, flattery and trickery, on account of the public's ignorance: 'A preference for truth or sincerity *as a method* may be a prejudice based on some aesthetic or personal standard, inconsistent in politics, with practical good' (*CW*, IX, p. 34). In that case, perhaps, while granting its impracticability, Lloyd George was right to think that the Treaty of Versailles ought to be signed, given the vengeful spirit of the masses. Keynes does not seem convinced. It is hard to miss the fierce irony of a passage like this:

> In any event, private individuals are not under the same obligation as cabinet ministers to sacrifice veracity to the public weal. It is a permitted self-indulgence for a private person to speak and write freely. Perhaps it may even contribute one ingredient to the congeries of things which the wands of statesmen cause to work together, so marvellously, for our ultimate good. (ibid.)

However, Keynes's dissent is the result of a particular analysis of public opinion. He distinguishes 'outside opinion', which is that of the masses and which newspapers and politicians set themselves up to interpret; and 'inside opinion', which is what these latter unburden themselves of when they are in exclusive circles, out of the public view ('upstairs and backstairs and behindstairs'). In turn, 'outside opinion' is subdivided: 'that which is expressed in the newspapers and that which the mass of ordinary men privately suspect to be true ... there is under the surface a real difference between the dogmatism of the press and the living, indefinite belief of the individual man' (*CW*, IX, p. 35). The aim of the 1919 book was to persuade not only inside opinion, but also that outside, by trying to make the second sort of this latter overcome the first. Thus, Keynes's persuasion was addressed both to politicians and to the wider public, in an effort to make it ready to accept the truth. The practical harms which his 1919 analysis had picked out are now overcoming psychological needs, '*and everyone wishes to conform himself with the facts*' (*CW*, IX, p. 36).

Keynes's rhetorical strategy sets up the target of convincing its recipient as a means for changing the way things stand. In this, the faithful perception of the way things stand is necessary but insufficient. Inside opinion probably shared Keynes's judgement of the post-war situation and of the Treaty. But its inability to distinguish the two levels of outside opinion, and its unwillingness to accept outside opinion as an interlocutor capable of learning from experience and of changing itself, meant that inside opinion ended up bowing to outside opinion. Worse, it ended up bowing to the dogmatic and definite version of outside opinion, as represented by the press, and not to the living and indefinite belief of the individual man.

'Reality' and 'truth' are to be found, therefore, at the beginning and the end of Keynes's thought. He refers to the facts, to the objective situation in considering the possible consequences of the Treaty. Within this situation, there is still the outside opinion's attitude and inside opinion's predisposition to follow outside opinion. The two opinions make up a part of the reality that we want to understand and to change. Keynes directs his energies to changing the psychological and political conditions that brought about the signing of the Treaty. Persuasion is the means by which to bring states of mind and the way things stand back into line with each other. Allowing the dogmatic version of public opinion to get the upper hand would lead to practical harms. The detailed outline of these harms which Keynes had published is the cause of the public's greater willingness to revise its own attitude. A policy that gives way before the masses' wishes discounts the complexity of outside opinion and discounts the fact that the masses, too, can learn from experience. 'Changing' opinions thus means not denying the facts, but bringing about a modification of what the facts are; not denying the disastrous consequences of the Treaty, but a revision of the Treaty, as a choice from above which, however, can and must find democratic backing.

Here we have persuasion as means not as end; and we seem a long way from McCloskey. Perhaps the distance is due to the fact that we have chosen a non-economic text. How, whom and why does Keynes 'persuade' in his role as an economist?

The *General Theory* is a text explicitly directed at convincing his fellow economists: 'its main purpose is to deal with difficult questions of theory, and only in the second place with the applications of this theory to practice' (*CW*, VII, p. xxi). The economists who are declared to be the intended recipients of the book are those whom Keynes himself picks out as 'classical'. This is a word which, here and elsewhere, seems to mean virtually every English-speaking economist of Keynes's day. In the other prefaces, such as those to the French and German editions, he concedes that not all his contemporaries fall under the definition of 'classical'. In caricature, we can say that it applies to all economists who accept Say's Law – to those who accept that, in capitalism, there is a tendency to the full use of productive resources and to full-employment equilibrium; and that, if external forces produce a disequilibrium, that is a temporary aberration. It might be a matter for discussion whether, in fact, in Keynes's day, English and American economists really did fit so neatly into his category of the classical economist. Keynes himself, in later writings, to be found in volumes XIV and XXIX of the *Collected Writings*, seems to rethink and revise the description he had given in 1936 of English-speaking economic thought. Nevertheless, he does construct a 'classical' macroeconomic model against which to set up his own position, and he does ascribe to it an unquestioned theoretical dominance. The reason for this lies in the fact that he is seeking to change a practical situation in which economic policy is supported by outmoded and misleading theories which are, for all that, still powerful. 'Inside' opinion, made up in this case of politicians and civil servants, supports views which Keynes holds to be deeply mistaken and which have to be attacked at their roots, at their abstract theoretical foundations:

> Thus I cannot achieve my object of persuading economists to re-examine critically certain of their basic assumptions except by highly abstract argument and also by much controversy ... I have thought it important, not only to explain my own point of view, but also to show in what respects it departs from the prevailing theory. (*CW*, VII, p. xxi)

The persuasion of other economists at which Keynes is aiming, calls for the building of a new theory, for the translation of the old theory into the terms of the new, and for the spelling out of the different assumptions and conclusions of the two theories.

In this case the general public 'though welcome at the debate' is assigned the role of spectators. What is Keynes's reason for thus marginalizing the public from the discussion? 'The matters at issue are of an importance which cannot be exaggerated' (ibid.); they concern interests wider than those of academic lecture halls. But the reason for foregrounding the economists as his audience lies in the fact that Keynes recognizes that ideas are powerful, in this case powerfully harmful. 'Classical' ideas cast a shadow over the blind and damaging actions of politicians. It is by these means that they prolong and deepen the recession which everyone has to pay for. In this case too, Keynes does not regard his persuasion as an end in itself. It is a means for representing the way things stand, which itself is a product of the power that economic theories have to direct economic policies. And it is aimed at changing the way things stand, by showing the mistakenness of those theories and of those policies. The change from the deplorable situation to a desirable one requires a change of views: a new and (more) general theory. In any case, this seems to me to be the clear sense of the words which McCloskey himself quotes from the end of *The General Theory*.

We do not need to look very far to see why Keynes framed his persuasive and argumentative strategy in this way. We shall look at two of his writings which paved the way to *The General Theory*.

In 'Poverty in Plenty: Is the Economic System Self-Adjusting', Keynes points to a way of dividing economists into two camps:

> On the one side are those who believe that the existing economic system is, in the long run, a self-adjusting system, though with creaks and groans and jerks, and interrupted by time lags, outside interferences and mistakes. ... On the other side of the gulf are those who reject the idea that the economic system is, in any significant sense, self-adjusting. ... On which side does the essential truth lie? That is the vital question for us to solve. (*CW*, XIII, pp. 486–8)

The reply which meets this question is important. It is that the doubting heretics are right. But, even if 'they believe that common observation is enough to show that facts do not conform to the orthodox reasoning' (*CW*, XIII, p. 489), that is insufficient for them to defeat the orthodox believers. Classical theory has on its side not only a numerical advantage among economists, but also the advantage of being the 'habitual mode of thought' (*CW*, XIII, p. 488) among businessmen, bankers and politicians. Most of all, it also has the advantage of being (or at least seeming) a consistent and tightly-structured intellectual construction. Logic is on the side of the orthodox both as regards the abstract modelling of economic mechanisms and as regard the cogent derivation of conclusions for economic policy. It is against the heretics, who often start out, incoherently, from classical presuppositions.

> Thus, if the heretics on the other side of the gulf are to demolish the forces of nineteenth-century orthodoxy ... they must attack them in their citadel. No successful attack has yet been made. ... Now *I* range myself with the heretics. I believe that their flair and their instinct move them towards the right conclusions. But I was brought up in the citadel and recognise its power and might. ... For me, therefore, it is impossible to rest satisfied until I can put my finger on the flaw in that part of orthodox reasoning which leads to the conclusions which seem to me to be inacceptable. (*CW*, XIII, pp. 488–9 emphasis original)

In another pre-*General Theory* essay, 'A Monetary Theory of Production', it is made even clearer why the classical theory needs to be criticized and why the heretics' appeal to the classical theory's inconsistency with reality is not enough. In this article, Keynes maintains that a genuine monetary theory of production has to take account of the role which money plays in influencing the motives and decisions of economic agents. This is so because both in the long run and in the short, it is not possible to describe the economic process without referring to money's behaviour. Keynes stresses that on the contrary, in classical theory money is merely a neutral means of exchange and that, therefore, the economy which that theory describes is a real exchange economy. He concludes:

> Everyone would, of course, agree that it is in a monetary economy in my sense of the term that we actually live ... it is my belief that the far-reaching and in some respects fundamental differences between the conclusions of a monetary economy and those of the more simplified real-exchange economy have been greatly underestimated by the exponents of traditional economics; with the result that the machinery of thought with which real-exchange economics has equipped the minds of practitioners in the world of affairs, and also of economists themselves, has led in practice to many erroneous conclusions and policies. The idea that it is comparatively easy to adapt the hypothetical conclusions of a real wage economics to the real world of monetary economics is a mistake. It is extraordinarily difficult to make the adaptation, and perhaps impossible without the aid of a developed theory of monetary economics. (*CW*, XIII, p. 410)

This passage is of the greatest interest. It reaffirms Keynes's claim that, in order to get rid of a mistaken framework of economic policies, it is necessary to get beyond the mere registration of 'facts' which do not square with the orthodox framework and to construct a theoretical critique and alternative to it.

Three ideas are put forward in our passage: first, that it is common knowledge that we live in an economy in which money has a special role; second, that the traditional theory tries, unsuccessfully, to explain how a model which treats money as neutral can apply to a monetary economy; and third, that to understand why such an 'adaptation' is extraordinarily difficult, we have to have available a monetary theory of production, which is thus shown to be essential to the rejection of the classical framework. Only when we have fully developed an alternative theory, shall we be able to show up the tacit assumptions of the classical theory and to pinpoint which hypotheses are to be entertained in order to apply the theory to the real world. It is only once we have got what is hidden into the open that we shall be able to see both how the tacit assumptions exclude the possibility of crisis, and that the added hypotheses will be true only in specific cases which we cannot expect to be general or recurrent.

> If this is true, the real-exchange economics, on which most of us have been brought up and with the conclusions of which our minds are deeply impregnated, *though a valuable abstraction in itself and perfectly valid as an intellectual conception*, is a singularly blunt weapon for dealing with the problems of booms and depressions. For it has assumed away the very matter under investigation. (*CW*, XIII, p. 411, emphasis added)

In fact, these statements raise some fairly serious interpretative and epistemological problems. We may set aside Keynes's peculiar assertion that, '[e]veryone would, of course, agree that it is in a monetary economy in my sense of the term that we actually live'. A claim of this sort seems, at first sight, less than natural. Keynes's presentation of it as such ought therefore, to be explained, as we shall try to do later.

What calls for closer attention is the judgement Keynes gives of the classical theory, and the way that an appeal to reality ends up permeating what Keynes himself writes, albeit in a more sophisticated form than that of the other heretics. Can we read Keynes's alternative to the classical theory as a replacement of a false theory by a true theory? How is the claim that the classical theory can be toppled from its position of power only by a new and better theory, to be squared with Keynes's repeated appeal to the idea that the old theory does not match the new reality? How are we to understand the relation of language to reality in Keynes's theory?

The next two sections are given over to answering these questions. But first, it is worth noting parenthetically that what Keynes is explicitly proposing is a revolution, a new way of conceiving of the subject. Even though he has the support of only a thinly scattered tradition, however long and glorious, of heretics, he allots himself the task of resolving the disputes of the inter-war years. He says that his is 'an attempt by an economist *to bring to an issue* the deep divergences of opinion between fellow economists which have for the time being almost destroyed the practical influence of economic theory, and will, until they are resolved, continue to do so' (*CW*, VII, p. xxi, emphasis added). As we know also from the celebrated letter to Shaw, as well as from what we have seen in the present section, Keynes's aim is to bring it about that the classical theory should be the orthodoxy only for the nineteenth century. Keynes tries to persuade economists that the old theory is false and that his is the new wisdom for a new age. This is no small claim. It fits with a strong image of the explanatory and practical power of the new theory, and not with the weak proposals for edification which McCloskey and Rorty put forward.

KEYNES AND CLASSICAL THEORY

> Words are too solid
> They don't move fast enough
> (Suzanne Vega)[9]

At first sight, both in *The General Theory* and in the writings leading up to it, Keynes's verdict on the classical theory is inconsistent or, at least, ambiguous. He seems to waver between two distinct claims. The first is that the classical theory was true when it was first formulated, but that it is no longer true, as a result of changes in the economic and political situation in the aftermath of the First World War. The other is that the plain and simple falsity of the classical theory has been shown up by the post-war situation.

It seems that these two claims do represent a real doubt in Keynes's mind. But I shall try to extract a single attitude from them by showing how they can be rendered consistent in the light of an equivocation over the word 'true' in the two cases. Moreover, I shall try to show that neither claim can be harmonized with McCloskey's method (or with Rorty's philosophy). In the first case, it is because the classical theory no longer faithfully represents the post-war world, and therefore there is some correspondence theory of truth in play. In the second case, it is because Keynes depends on a notion of the objectivity of knowledge; therefore, truth cannot be glossed in the relativist and pragmatist way that McCloskey offers.

Once more, I shall have to select only a few among the many available texts. As a test case we may take the critique which, from his earliest writings through *The General Theory* and beyond, Keynes sustained of *laisser-faire* and of the gold standard. Keynes's hesitation shows up clearly if we compare the following passages.

In an article from 1925 collected in *Essays in Persuasion*, Keynes takes a stand against *laisser-faire*,

> not because I think that these doctrines were wrong in the conditions which gave birth to them (I hope that I should have belonged to this party if I had been born a hundred years earlier), but because they have ceased to be applicable to modern conditions. ... Half the copybook wisdom of our statesmen is based on assumptions which *were at one time true* or partly true, *but are now less and less true day by day* ('Am I a Liberal?' *CW*, IX, pp. 300–301; 305–6, emphases added).

Some years earlier, discussing the gold standard, one of the pillars of the free-market position, Keynes expressed himself in more forthright terms: 'in the modern world of paper currency and bank credit *there is no escape* from a "managed" currency *whether we wish it or not. ... Already before the war* the system was becoming precarious by reason of its *artificiality*' (*CW*, IX, p. 178, emphases added). But in *The General Theory*, he is more forthright still: 'the weight of my criticism is directed against the *theoretical* foundations of the laissez faire doctrine' (*CW*, VII, p. 339, emphasis original). And a few pages further on, there is no room for doubt: 'The extraordinary achievement of the classical theory was to overcome the beliefs of the natural man and, at the same time, to be *wrong*' (*CW*, VII, p. 350, emphasis added).

The conflict among Keynes's various judgements becomes clear if we look at his line of thought in the pre-war years. For instance, as early as *Indian Currency and Finance* (1913), Keynes's reasoning is absolutely clear on the performance of the gold standard. As I have argued elsewhere (Bellofiore 1985 and 1992), Keynes explains the success of the gold standard in terms of the exceptional circumstances which then obtained. First, there was the chance fact that gold production and the accumulation of capital had been growing at about the same rate. Second, there was the effectiveness of the discount rate mechanism as a regulator of capital movements within Britain. This effectiveness was attributable to Britain's position as international lender in the short-term loans market; her hegemonic position in the international financial system allowed her to control the movement of gold with small changes to the discount rate. And finally, there was the fact that, in many other countries, the ratio of gold reserves to the liabilities of the issuing banks was arbitrary and variable. In other words, the other central banks operated a policy of bringing the money supply into line with credit demand, rather than vice versa. What follows is a picture of the gold standard which is opposed to the classical conception. Instead of the exogenous factors of traditional theory, what we see is a 'regulated' and non-automatic system in which the money supply is endogenous.

We can thus see a single outlook behind the twin claims that the classical theory of *laisser-faire* and the gold standard was at one time true but is always false. Keynes's account of the matter is able to show how the traditional framework, despite offering a mistaken reconstruction of the economic mechanism, was cogent and in line with the facts of the last quarter of the nineteenth century. The agreement between theory and reality was secured by a set of conditions which were partly a matter of chance, and in any case unrepeatable, and of which the classical theorists were unaware. In was only within a different analysis that these conditions could be brought out. Given those conditions, and in the absence of a general framework, it is not surprising that the classical theory should have been taken to be 'true'. Crucial among these conditions was a peculiar attitude of intervention and not *laisser-faire* towards economic policy. It was towards this attitude that with the passing of time, Keynes's judgement became sterner, in view of the implications it had for the level of employment in the economy:

> Under the influence of this *faulty* theory the City of London gradually devised the *most dangerous* technique for the maintenance of equilibrium which can possibly be imagined, namely, the technique of bank rate coupled with a rigid parity of the foreign exchanges. For this meant that the objective of maintaining a domestic rate of interest consistent with full employment was wholly ruled out. Since, in practice, it is impossible to neglect the balance of payments, a means of controlling it was evolved which, instead of protecting the domestic rate of interest, sacrificed it to the operation of blind forces. (*CW*, VII, p. 339, emphasis added)

Once the peculiar conditions which had supported the classical economic policies no longer obtained, fidelity to a 'pre-war policy' was not only a theoretical error but also a practical disaster. By 1925, as we have already suggested, Keynes saw that after the war the motivations and objectives, what was reasonable and acceptable, had altered. Therefore, techniques and policies had to be altered too. To bring this about, a new theory was needed which could cope with the new circumstances by being more faithful to the features of a genuine monetary economy.

Keynes's posture towards the classical theory shows us the strong notion of truth which he defended. Truth is not restricted to time or place, even though the ascertainment of a theory's truth at a given time depends on the prevailing theoretical and practical circumstances. On this count, we find a further clear disagreement with McCloskey and Rorty. In addition, in order to explain the success or failure of a theory, we must refer, however indirectly, to extra-linguistic reality which can be taken on board prior to the formulation of a new theory. The very lapsing, after the First World War, of the conditions which favoured the classical theory, is to be cited as one of the causes of a widespread dissatisfaction among economists and others. The starting-point for the construction of an alternative paradigm is to be a connection, for the time being unexplained, between that dissatisfaction and the monetary nature of the economy which everyone recognizes. Also in this respect, we find in Keynes powerful recourse to an external reality, to some 'facts' which language and theory must take into account. This is a further marker of how far he is from McCloskey and Rorty.

We may therefore say that for Keynes, facing the 'facts' is necessary but not, as it was for many of the heretics, sufficient. To get clearer about this side of the matter, we ought to look in more detail at some of the more strictly epistemological aspects of Keynes's thought.

KEYNES'S EPISTEMOLOGY: OUTLINE

401. I want to say: propositions of the form of empirical propositions, and not only propositions of logic, form the foundation of all operating with thoughts (with language). – This observation is not of the form 'I know ...'. 'I know ...' states what *I* know, and that is not of logical interest.

402.   In this remark the expression 'propositions of the form of empirical
       propositions' is itself thoroughly bad; the statements in question are
       statements about material objects. And they do not serve as founda-
       tions in the same way as hypotheses which, if they turn out to be
       false, are replaced by others.
       (... and I write in confidence
       'In the beginning was the deed'
       [cf. Goethe *Faust* I]). (Ludwig Wittgenstein)[10]

In this quandary, our owners of commodities think after the manner of
Faust: 'In the beginning was the deed' – the action comes first. (Karl
Marx)[11]

In considering the epistemological question of the relation between
language and reality in Keynes's theory, we revert to the issues raised
in the first sections of this chapter. We saw how McCloskey's book sets
out from a typical upshot of discussions of the 'growth of knowledge',
which is the conclusion that every appeal to the facts or to an observational base is theory-laden. The only conception of truth which is
sustainable is the coherence view, to the detriment of the correspondence conception of truth as the correct representation of an extralinguistic
reality. The world is 'well lost', as Rorty would put it (Rorty, 1982); no
objectivist conception of truth is tenable – where 'objectivity' means a
guarantee by procedures of verification or falsification for factual statements. The acceptance of a relativist account of the process of knowledge-gathering seems to be unavoidable. Likewise unavoidable is the
abandonment of any absolutist conception of knowledge which requires that knowledge-claims have a 'foundation' independent of the
theoretical background against which they are put forward.

The account we have given of some of Keynes's beliefs does not
immediately clarify his attitude to this disputed crux. On the one hand,
Keynes seems to be committed to some form of philosophical realism
in as much as there is implicit in some of his moves an appeal to a
reality independent of the knowing subject. Some commentators such
as Tony Lawson (1986) have cited evidence from Keynes's writings in
favour of attributing to him an extension of this realism into empiricism, understood as the thesis in the theory of knowledge that sensory
input has a logical priority over conceptual constructions. It may be
that many of Keynes's assertions in his role as an economist, including
some which we have ourselves quoted, can be taken in this way. Those
which refer to 'the world we live in' seem to presuppose that, prior to
and independent of the theories which people formulate or end up

holding, there is a single basic description of it which everyone uses, because it is founded on common, direct and unquestioned perception. If so, then there is no doubt that Keynes's opposition to the views of McCloskey and Rorty would be total. But Keynes's epistemology would seem to be dated, because connected to philosophical presuppositions which have been broadly discredited.

On the other hand, reading Keynes this way is undermined, as Lawson himself has shown, by the presence of other passages which point, equally unambiguously and unsatisfactorily, to a rationalistic framework, understood as the claim that concepts are logically prior to sensation because the latter can only be learnt against a background of *a priori* categories. In that case, the basic description of the world in which we live would be founded not on the raw data of experience, but on evidence which was from the outset filtered by concepts known to be true by intuition. Even though this view seems to be less exposed to the criticism that it is impossible to justify propositions within a theory by reference to an extra-linguistic reality, it is not itself without its own difficulties. However for our purposes, this interpretation does not seem to take account of at least three views which Keynes held. First, any criticism of the classical theory which restricts itself to showing the disagreement of the theory with 'factual' evidence is insufficient to refute the theory. Second, in principle, nothing prevents a (necessarily abstract) theory from being adapted to the real world. And third, if we are to show that such an adaptation is impossible, or requires highly improbable supplementary hypotheses, we can only do so from the point of view of another theory.

This argumentative strategy commits Keynes to two things. One, as Lawson correctly points out, is that any background knowledge is subject to theoretical interpretation and therefore cannot be taken to be *a priori*. The other, which Lawson misses, is that the 'direct knowledge' which the *Treatise on Probability* discusses is not merely the 'basis' on which theoretical constructions, from which we derive 'indirect knowledge', are built and by which they are justified. 'Direct knowledge' also supplies one (but not the only) criterion by which we can judge the success of a theory, in terms of the agreement between the theoretical construction and the basic knowledge. It is therefore to be found not only at the beginning but also at the end of the process of knowledge-gathering. It supplies a criterion which we have seen Keynes operating when he admits that the classical theory seems to be not only well-constructed, but also to be in *prima-facie* agreement with the way the capitalist system works in a specific period of its history. But he holds that the criterion is insufficient as a guarantee of the truth of a theory when, as we have seen, he asserts that the classical theory is, nevertheless false, and that its temporary correspondence to the facts ought to be explained by a new, more general, theory.

Two issues arise which deserve closer treatment. One is whether Keynes has room in his theory of knowledge for some notion of objectivity, while recognizing that the background knowledge from which direct knowledge is derived is itself theory-laden. The other is what the precise relation is between direct knowledge and theoretical construction.

Before trying to give an answer to these questions, it is worth summarizing the account Keynes gives in the *Treatise on Probability*, in which he discusses most directly the question of relativity versus absoluteness and of the objectivity of knowledge. I claim that Keynes's approach leaves room for a notion of objectivity and rationality even when he is analysing behaviour under conditions of incomplete knowledge and uncertainty. Only when I have vindicated this claim shall I return to the initial questions and try to set out what seems to be a possible interpretation of the general epistemological position implicit in Keynes's thought.

From the very first pages of the *Treatise on Probability*, Keynes faces the question of the relativity or absoluteness of knowledge. It is worth recalling some of his well-known remarks; on page 18, he writes that 'we cannot speak of knowledge absolutely – only of the knowledge of a particular person'. And he continues a few lines further on:

> What we know and what probability we can attribute to our rational beliefs is, therefore, subjective in the sense of being relative to the individual. But given the body of premises which our subjective powers and circumstances can supply to us, and given the kinds of logical relations, upon which arguments can be based and which we have the capacity to perceive, *the conclusions which it is rational for us to draw, stand to these premises in an objective and wholly logical relation.* (*CW*, VIII, p. 19 emphasis added)

And a few pages earlier he says just as clearly:

> A proposition is not probable because we think it so, when once the facts are given which determine our knowledge, *what is probable or improbable in these circumstances has been fixed objectively, and is independent of our opinion.* ... What particular proposition we select as the premises of *our*

argument naturally depends on subjective factors peculiar to ourselves; but the relations, in which other propositions stand to these, and which entitle us to probable beliefs are objective and logical. (*CW*, VIII, p. 4; first emphasis ours; second original)

Jan Kregel has recently derived from these passages the claim that Keynes held that his theory was objective and rational in the sense that, given any pair of individuals faced with the same experience, they would place the same degree of rational belief in a proposition as expressed in an identical probability (Kregel 1987, p. 521). I agree with this view, and I think it can be expanded to take account of the diversity of theoretical interpretations of the facts. Individuals differ not only in respect of the evidence and experience they have, but also in respect of the interpretation to which they take these to point. But a given reading of the 'facts' ought to lead to only one conclusion.

We can unpack the situation as follows. On the one hand, 'certainty' is the state in which a secondary proposition is derived by argumentation from a primary proposition that expresses direct and certain knowledge. If such a case were possible, then the conclusions arrived at would be 'true' in the sense of being a faithful representation of the external world. On the other hand, 'uncertainty' is that state in which one begins with propositions that express incomplete knowledge. In that case, we may arrive at a secondary proposition whose probability can be calculated relative to the probabilities of other propositions. This is what Knight calls a situation of 'risk'. Alternatively, we may arrive at a secondary proposition whose probability either cannot be calculated, or cannot be calculated so as to allow comparison with the probabilities of alternative propositions. This is what Knight calls 'true uncertainty'.

It makes sense to speak of rational and objective choice, in the sense given, not only in the first case (that of certainty) but also in the second (insurable uncertainty or risk). But what ought we to say about the third case (that of true uncertainty)? Does every idea of rational choice, and hence of objectivity vanish when there is no comparability among the alternative propositions, or when a single basis of calculation is unavailable?

Given that, in the world of economics, situations of true uncertainty are the norm, as Keynes argues in Chapter XII of *The General Theory*, the importance of this question is not to be underestimated. On the one hand, such situations can come about because it is not possible to give a frequentist account of the relative probabilities, even though a quantitative comparison of the alternative propositions can be carried out. The results of such a comparison will be accepted with greater or less confidence according to the 'weight' given to the alternative arguments. The weight of argument depends on the totalling of the knowledge about the occurrence or non-occurrence of the event referred to by the proposition. On the other hand, situations of true uncertainty can also arise because of the novelty and singularity of an event whose occurrence is to be predicted. In such cases, any appeal to an evidential or experimental base is impossible. According to some interpreters, in cases of true uncertainty, a radical subjectivism takes over. In the former case, where no frequencies can be given, the weight of arguments for acting or for fending is an arbitrary matter, dependent on the individual's state of mind. In the case of absolute novelty, the very 'objective' basis of a probabilistic calculation is lacking.

There are two reasons why it does not seem to me that this reading is inescapable. The first is that on Keynes's account, subjectivity takes over in an individual's choice as a consequence of the features of the objective situation in which a person finds himself, in so far as he is capable of perceiving it. The second is that Keynes does not give up on the search for ways of dealing rationally with situations even of true uncertainty, including the extreme case of the lack of any evidential base for a probabilistic calculation. In particular, he underlines that in such situations, individuals' mimetic behaviour is not an aberration, but a rational choice. From imitations follows the setting-up of conventional rules; first of all, the hypothesis that things will continue as they are unless we are given definite reasons to believe that a change is on its way. Thus, a system of shared valuation imposes itself on the market which normally prevents instability, panic and a generalized 'flight' to money (for the details of a similar interpretation see Orléan 1987).

The conclusion which we were aiming at seems, therefore, to be confirmed: even in the extreme case of true uncertainty, Keynes's theory gives a role to objectivity and thus to a context-dependent rationality. Even when an individual's behaviour cannot appeal to even partial knowledge of the events to be predicted, the theory can still pick out both the rational line which the individual generally takes, and the circumstances in which he normally acts (when the conventions are being respected) and in which he bides his time (when the conventions are broken and speculation is rampant).

Putting these last remarks together with Keynes's argument reported above (pp. 97–107), and with the whole drift of his writings, we can suggest something like the following outline of Keynes's theory of knowledge.

Direct knowledge is the premise from which inductive reasoning must begin. But it is a premise which must be 'justified' deductively at the end of the process of knowledge-gathering. Justification is contextual, internal to the theory and involves both a coherentist aspect and a correspondence to the relevant 'facts', as is shown by the ability to manipulate experimentally the objects with which the theory deals. In economics, experiments are policies. Thus, we might say that the interpretation implicit in direct knowledge is guaranteed by the whole system of thought which includes it and which forms the indirect knowledge. It follows therefore, that the arising of a conflict between the theory and a new experience does not drive us to deny the earlier experiences, but to bring the whole conceptual structure into doubt. On the other hand, the argumentative process does not appear in Keynes's thought so much under the guise of formal deduction as under that of abduction. Instead of syllogistic argument, we find the invention of hypotheses to relate what is observed (direct knowledge) with what is not observable, and is thus able to explain the possibility, not the necessity, of the facts (indirect knowledge).

Economic reasoning has to do with motivations, expectations and uncertainty, and therefore with matters that are neither stable nor homogeneous. The relation between premises and conclusion must, then, be recognized as probabilistic. That relation is determined by the body of evidence available and by the state of confidence – which is why, for Keynes, economic policy has as one of its main tasks that of acting on the latter. The relation changes, therefore, not only in accordance with individuals' 'psychology', but also in accordance with the knowledge which we have available. Although such knowledge allows us to put forward epistemically, rather than ontologically, justified propositions, it is enlarged as a result of experience and experiment: as a result of humans' practical involvement with the world. That involvement is extralinguistic; it cannot be interpreted as any sort of 'mirroring', but only as active intervention. In this way, we have here a kind of causal primacy accorded to external entities, and therefore an objectivity of economic, and other, forms of knowledge, though the justification of knowledge never ceases to be a purely intradiscursive and epistemic matter.

Even from these few traces of Keynes's epistemology, it seems that we can draw answers to the questions with which we began. The nature of his epistemology seems to be rather distinctive. In the terms of a distinction made by Hacking (1983, pp. 27–8), it can be said to be a sort of realism about entities and not about theories. That is, Keynes denies that theories are true or false irrespective of what we know, but asserts that a whole set of theoretical entities really exist. Action and experimentation are what interest him, and what he will stake his own theories on. This sort of realism, which cannot pretend to derive from any absolute foundation, goes beyond the confines of epistemology and amounts to a metaphysics, or what might better be called a philosophical *prise de position*. One might say, quoting Wittgenstein, that it is the metaphysics of 'a community which is bound together by science and education' (Wittgenstein 1974, 298).

Thus, for Keynes, the truth of a theory has a non-propositional aspect, in the following sense: that the propositions among which the implicative relations hold from which knowledge is produced, are at least in part themselves produced in a practical involvement with the external world. In the case of economics, it is clear that the external world includes social relations as well as individuals' actions and motives. This is why Keynes does not dispense altogether with the notion of 'objective knowledge'.

Unlike the anti-methodology of McCloskey, Keynes seems to have carved out a position which is coherently critical of epistemology. Keynes's critique gives up the sort of methodologism which calls for 'external' guarantees of the truth of our knowledge on condition that that knowledge is acquired in accordance with the correct method. This is the sort of methodologism which McCloskey cannot get away from and whose possibility he simply denies, meanwhile remaining firmly entrenched in the problematic specified by the question of whether knowledge is absolute or relative. Keynes abandons the dream of an ultimate foundation of knowledge, adhering to a constructivist view on which truth has an objective meaning and justification is not external to the context of discovery. The objectivity in question is to be understood both in the sense that knowledge (partly) derives from and (partly) produces lines of action; and also in the connected sense that some items of putative knowledge must prove their 'goodness of fit' to the object which the theory discusses. The probable 'truths' which the enquiry comes up with are justified *within* the enquiry itself; they are neither absolute nor relative. Rather, the claims they make are rationally founded in the here and now, because they depend on universally applicable standards of judgement and action, even though the acceptability of a given judgement or a given action continues to depend on the incompleteness of our knowledge.

Such a non-relativist anti-foundationalism cashes objectivity out in terms not of the metaphor of representation, but of the practical relation which surrounds the process of knowledge-gathering and which does not create but changes reality by intervening on it. It seems to me to represent a challenge which is up to date though it raises more than a few problems of its own. But it should be borne in mind that what is in question is an underground current of thought, one which has been little developed or elaborated: it offers neither the consolations of dogmatic certainty, nor those of radical scepticism.

It might be useful, and even interesting, to bring out some voices which do not seem so very far from the account which we have seen Keynes giving. One in particular deserves to be mentioned here, because it was to be heard around Cambridge from the end of the 1920s: that of Ludwig Wittgenstein. The unsystematic, even anti-systematic, spirit of Wittgenstein's work should not be underestimated; and to that extent, it contrasts with Keynes's effort to build a new system. But that difference does not affect the significant similarities between Keynes and the later Wittgenstein. These similarities are most visible if we read Wittgenstein very differently from the popular exposition of him as one of the foremost modern supporters of relativism.

It is probably best if the reader decides for himself or herself, on the basis of a selection of passages taken from the work which seems to us to be closest to our present theme: *On Certainty*. This is one of Wittgenstein's last writings, being composed in 1950–51. It therefore cannot be used to make out a direct influence on Keynes, although the ideas which it contains are connected with those in the works which Wittgenstein was writing in the 1930s. The following passages are chosen only to show up a certain 'family resemblance' with Keynes's arguments and to render more explicit the philosophical moves involved.

87. Can't an assertoric sentence, which was capable of functioning as an hypothesis, also be used as a foundation (*Grundsatz*) for research and action? I.e. can't it simply be isolated from doubt, though not according to any explicit rule? It simply gets assumed, never gets called into question, perhaps not even ever formulated.

94.   But I did not get my picture of the world by satisfying myself of its correctness; nor do I have it because I am satisfied of its correctness. No: it is the inherited background against which I distinguish true and false.

105. All testing, all confirmation and disconfirmation of a hypothesis takes place already within a system. And this system is not a more or less arbitrary and doubtful point of departure for all our arguments: no, it belongs to the essence of what we call an argument. The system is not so much the point of departure, as the element in which arguments have their life.

130. But isn't it experience that teaches us to judge like *this*, that is to say, that it is correct to judge like this? But how does experience *teach* us, then? *We* may derive it from experience, but experience does not direct us to derive anything from experience. If it is the *ground* of our judging like this, and not just the cause, still we do not have a ground for seeing this in turn as a ground.

204. Giving grounds, however, justifying evidence, comes to an end; – but the end is not certain propositions' striking us immediately as true, i.e. it is not a kind of *seeing* on our part; it is our acting which lies at the bottom of the language-game.

248. I have arrived at the rock bottom of my convictions. And one might almost say that these foundation-walls are carried by the whole house.

292. Further experiments (*Versuche*) cannot *give the lie* to our earlier ones, at most they can change our whole way of looking at things. (Wittgenstein 1974, in all cases emphases original)

And at this point we might also quote the passage which serves as an epigraph for this section (see pp. 107–8).[12]

IN PLACE OF A CONCLUSION

Gravitation cannot be held responsible for people falling in love. (Albert Einstein)

Rather than bring to a close the present enquiry, which began with a critique of McCloskey's Rhetoric and led to a reconstruction of Keynes's different argumentative and persuasive strategy, it seems better to point to a possible area in which the account we have given could be further developed and enriched: the language and narrative structure of the *General Theory*.

The notion of objectivity which we have seen to be central to his reasoning is corroborated and spelt out by Keynes himself in the way he recounts, in the Preface to *The General Theory*, his own intellectual trajectory from the *Treatise on Money* to the later book, and in the considerations which he takes to have been operative in the growth of his own theoretical beliefs while writing his two major works. He writes:

> what in my own mind is a *natural evolution* in a line of thought which I have been pursuing for several years, may sometimes strike the reader as a confusing change of view. ... When I began to write my *Treatise on Money* I was still moving along the traditional lines of regarding the influence of money as something so to speak separate from the general theory of supply and demand. When I finished it, I had made some progress towards pushing monetary theory back to becoming a theory of output as a whole. (*CW*, VII, p. xxii, emphasis added)

The process of the writing of the earlier book thus appears as the site of the creation of an object of analysis which enjoys a life of its own, separate from that of the real object to which it is hitched. The development of the new object appears as 'natural evolution' – as if it were dictated by an internal logic. Keynes's theoretical enquiry sets out employing partly inherited notions which serve as the materials for the new conceptual construction. But they then come into conflict with it in such a way that they have to be replaced by new building-blocks in order to shore the whole construction up: 'my lack of emancipation from preconceived ideas showed itself in what now seems to me to be the outstanding fault of the theoretical parts of that work' (*CW*, VII, p. xxii). Keynes wrote, 'showed *itself*': the conceptual construction seems to be independent of the writer. It returns to him objectivized in what is written. Its independence is so marked as to bring about not merely a separation of the writer and the written, but to make the written return actively to the writer. This process is also seen in operation a few lines later in the same Preface:

> This book, on the other hand has evolved into what is primarily a study of the forces which determine changes in the scale of output and employment as a whole; and whilst it is found that money enters into the economic scheme in an essential and peculiar manner, technical monetary detail falls into the background. (ibid.)

This is the book-as-subject which interacts with the author. Alessandra Marzola rightly notes:

> In the act of writing the book, he therefore has undergone an evolution which has changed him. The autonomy of this development is witnessed by the presence of the neuter pronoun, 'it', which refers to the exercise of writing as the source of revelations for the writer. (Marzola, 1988 p. 9; also in her contribution to the present volume, pp. 192–223)

Keynes's epistemological thought is also mirrored in his decision to write in ordinary language, the relevance of which we now turn to clarify.

It is well known that Keynes gives precedence to ordinary language over formalized language. This is motivated by the fact that the former, unlike the latter, is capable of reflecting the complexities and interdependences of the real world and of keeping the account open for further qualifications. The precedence is not the product of any sense of ordinary language as providing a norm; rather it derives from the fact that we have reason for thinking that the matters with which economics deals are not in themselves smoothly or uniformly constituted. On the one hand, Keynes's position does not rule out formalized treatments, so long as they do not claim to provide irrefragable and definitive demonstrations, but aim only to provide the wherewithal for arriving at provisional conclusions on assumptions whose hypothetical character is kept to the fore. On the other hand, his position derives from what we know about the world and about the way we know about it. Here too, the rule is bound to the use, and does not precede it: not even by a simple overturning of the ordering which privileges formalized language relative to ordinary language.

The foregoing helps to explain the narrative structure of *The General Theory*. The order of the argument is set by the matter which is under discussion and which determines the important links among the interdependent variables in the organic whole that is the economic system itself. First, there is the specification of those quantities which are taken in this context to be given, and there are those that are independent and those that are dependent. Then there is the identification of the relations that are most likely to hold among those variables. And then there is the review, which Keynes provides in Chapter XIX, of the feedback effects resulting from variations in the variables which, to begin with, were taken as given or as independent.

Keynes's critical and persuasive goals further complicate the exposition because they involve a comparison with the classical theory. This leads to his translating the old theory into the terms of the new, and at times, to his simultaneously proposing and rendering acceptable the unorthodox elements of the new paradigm. There is no shortage of examples here. It is most of all in the first eighteen chapters of *The General Theory* that the 'internal' critique of the classical assumptions occupies the foreground: the old theory improperly extended to the whole system considerations which are valid only on the level of individual interactions. From this there follow many plain propositions, both positive and negative. Later in the book (but also to some extent earlier) Keynes carries out his comparison between the old theory and the new. This comparison takes the form of an analysis of the effects which the old theory's assumptions, such as price and wage flexibility, would have in the new framework, if they were adopted as economic policy. From this there issues forth a mass of conditional and interrogative propositions.

One innovative element which has to be rendered acceptable if the comparison with the classical theory is to go ahead, is the extreme precariousness of the building-blocks of knowledge which goes to make up the long-term expectations discussed in Chapter XII of *The General Theory*. As has often been noted, this is a peculiar chapter. It hammers home the radical uncertainty and potential instability of predictions about the prospective yield on capital goods. But at the same time, it argues that unless there are particular reasons to expect a change, in normal circumstances, long-term expectations are taken to be constant, as a result of the convention of supposing that the present state of affairs will continue indefinitely.

Undoubtedly, a radical break with the classical framework would have been implied by any stronger emphasis on the uncertainty of long-term expectations, in the direction of the claim that their future behaviour is unpredictable. But such a move would have carried the price of downgrading all entrepreneurial activity as mere irrationality, and of preventing the elaboration of the laws by which the capitalist system works under normal conditions. Keynes's theoretical choice is consistent with his own earlier analysis of probability. It is aimed at underlining the rational ways of facing, 'as best as we are able', the dark forces of ignorance and time, and therefore of functioning in conditions of limited knowledge on the basis of social conventions. This posture allows him to offer an alternative analysis of the normal working of the economic system, while also providing the groundwork for understanding the unstable situations which come about when the conventions cave in.

Thus, in Chapter XII of *The General Theory*, Keynes finds himself having to take account not only of the way that the classical theory treats uncertainty only in so far as it is reducible to calculable risk, but also of a possible 'extreme' version of his own 'true uncertainty'. The linguistic structure is hence complicated by the fact that Keynes is arguing on two fronts: with the 'classical' reader who is not yet convinced, and with the reader who so fully believes in true uncertainty as to overlook the possibility of rational action under such conditions. The proposal of the anti-classical material is full of qualifications and asides, and cannot go straight to the positive exposition of an alternative theory of long-term decision-making.

It seems therefore that we ought not to accept in full a recent account (Faverau, 1986) according to which the final version of *The General Theory* contains a 'pragmatic' research programme, which had been growing during the process of the book's composition. The claim is that this programme is less ambitious than the original scheme which centred on the notion of radical uncertainty. The move from the radical to the pragmatic programme would have been dictated by the desire to persuade the classical economists to abandon the orthodoxy of the nineteenth century which could not account for the fact of involuntary unemployment.

Faverau links this account to what he calls the 'Wittgenstein hypothesis'. This suggests that we can see the Keynesian revolution as having the aim of getting out of the blind alley of the 'language game' of classical theory. The aim would be fulfilled if the rules of that game could be changed as little as possible. Such a reading does not seem acceptable, because there is no obvious weakening of the notion of true uncertainty in *The General Theory*. The exogenousness of long-term expectations does not prevent their being further analysed. At the same time, that very feature allows us to pick out an equilibrium of unemployment for those given expectations, because of the normal fixing of too high an interest rate in the financial and monetary markets.

We can however suggest a view which is not too dissimilar from Faverau's, and which supports the 'Wittgenstein hypothesis' in another way: by replacing the exogeneity of long-term expectations with the exogeneity of the money supply. The exogeneity of the money supply makes the *General Theory* more straightforwardly comparable with the classical framework, but at the cost of losing sight of the banks' role in financing current production and therefore, of underrating the monetary

aspects of effective demand, thus allowing the impoverishing translation in terms of IS–LM curves.

When put in these terms, which we cannot develop here, Faverau's
reading of the limits of Keynes's attack on the limitations of the classical
'language game' shows itself to be fertile in questions. The one which at
the end of this already too long discussion, seems to me to be the most
worth asking is, borrowing and inverting one of McCloskey's chapter
titles: 'Why does Keynes *not* persuade?' For undoubtedly, it was only a
mangled and docked version of Keynes that was accepted by the profession. Anyone who studies the books which, in the immediate wake of
The General Theory, popularized his thought, cannot ignore the way he
undergoes a double dose of cosmetic surgery. Setting aside his warnings,
professional economists generally busied themselves with expounding
his views in resolutely formalized sets of simultaneous equations. And
publications for the non-specialist began with ritual complaints about
Keynes's confused and inaccessible style of writing (see also Gotti's
contribution to the present volume, pp. 152–92).

The Keynes who 'persuaded' the academic world was a Keynes who
never existed. This raises large doubts about what good it would have
done him to promote a 'compromise' in *The General Theory*, and about
his rhetorical strategy of aiming to persuade his 'fellow economists' at
the expense of completing the construction of the monetary theory of
production, whose foundations had been laid in the *Treatise on Money*.

AN ASIDE

Language is a virus from outer space. (Laurie Anderson)[13]

I do not hope that the foregoing should have convinced the firm be-
liever in McCloskey's anti-methodology that it is refuted by the case of
Keynes. How could I? It is possible that the way in which Keynes
actually persuades, if indeed he does, is different from the one we have
picked out, and even from the one Keynes could have supposed in
accordance with his own method. Yet, I am satisfied that I have made
out a plausible case that McCloskey's Rhetoric cannot claim to derive
from the author of *The Economic Consequences of the Peace* and *The
General Theory*. In short, *that* Rhetoric is not Keynesian.

What, then, is left of McCloskey's battery of arguments? Not a lot, I
think. All the same, I would like to suggest the possibility of revisiting

two of the cultural sites which bulk large in his thought, but which he has not really put to work and whose significance he has underestimated: pre-Socratic rhetoric and pragmatism.

To see, if only in outline, what these sites are, I begin with a reference to a slightly unusual source in the present context: a novel. This is Robert M. Pirsig's *Zen and the Art of Motorcycle Maintenance*, which carries the subtitle: 'An Enquiry into Values'. The book presents the story of the author's journey with his eleven-year-old son from Minnesota to San Francisco. He leaves at home a wife and another son who do not figure in the book. Until they reach Montana, the pair are accompanied by two friends of whom little is said. And though the difficulty of dialogue between father and son is one of the book's sometimes explicit and sometimes implicit themes, the son himself appears only in the background of the story and its narration.

The novel is mostly taken up with its main character's monologues. These quickly focus on two connected questions. On the one hand there is the dualism between classical, scientific, technological intellect and romantic, artistic, creative, intuitive intellect. On the other, there is 'that strange separation between what a man does and what a man is'. These monologues bring him to recover out of the past a personality, who is an earlier self, to whom he gives the far from fortuitous name of Phaedrus. Years before, Phaedrus had engaged himself against the same divisions, in a quest that brought him to isolation and madness.

This is not the place to set out how, throughout the story, within genuine high-level philosophical discussions, the reader comes to feel a tension created out of materials which seem to be linguistically meagre and, in terms of narrative, fragile. Nor is it the place to show how the resolution of the plot centres on the narrator's recovery of the reasons of the mad Phaedrus, against the mere words of Science and Philosophy, showing that Phaedrus was not wholly wrong. But he was not wholly right in seeking only words to defeat other words, as we see at the end of the book, when Phaedrus' flight from madness is found in and on the reactivation of his emotional relations with his son on the other side of silence.

What is of interest to us here is that Phaedrus was a teacher of rhetoric, and that there is an unmistakeable air of pragmatism in the narrator's stories. These are the same materials as McCloskey uses. But what greater difference could there be? With his stylish writing, McCloskey seeks to inveigle us with a calming message: we are only conversing; at bottom, this is just another specialization; we are not disputing with each other about the Truth. With his simple language, Pirsig creates unease: the unease of the search for Quality before Truth; a search which goes to the heart of what is essential and becomes a real mental, but perhaps not only mental, life-or-death struggle.

I wonder why I like Pirsig's novel and not McCloskey's essay. I do not believe the difference lies in the different genres of the two books. Perhaps some part of the explanation lies in the difference of the underlying philosophical attitude between the two writers, for all that they seem to share the same starting points. What is Pirsig's response to the dichotomies of modern consciousness? What is the stuff that his rhetoric is made of? What is his brand of pragmatism?

To answer the first question, the following passage may be useful:

> Yes and no ... this or that ... one or zero. On the basis of this elementary two-term discrimination, all human knowledge is built up. The demonstration of this is the computer machinery which stores all its knowledge in the form of binary information. It contains ones and zeros, and that's all.
>
> Because we're unaccustomed to it, we don't usually see that there's a third possible logical term equal to yes and no which is capable of expanding our understanding in an unrecognized direction. We don't even have a term for it, so I'll have to use the Japanese *mu*.
>
> *Mu* means 'no thing'. Like 'Quality' it points outside the process of dualistic discrimination. *Mu* simply says, 'No class; not one, not zero, not yes, not no'. It states that the context of the question is in error and should not be given. 'Unask the question' is what it says.
>
> *Mu* becomes appropriate when the context of the question is too small for the truth of the answer. (Pirsig 1974, p. 288)

It seems to me that the answer to be given to the classic epistemological question of whether there is an objective truth or not, is *mu*. At least this is the answer to be given so long as the answer 'yes' commits us to a vision of objectivity as representation, and the answer 'no' means that the world is 'well lost' as a part of the process of knowledge-gathering. What Pirsig has to say about Quality is not so far from what we have found in embryo in Keynes:

> eventually he saw that Quality couldn't be independently related with either the subject or the object but could be found *only in the relationship of the two with each other*. It is the point at which subject and object meet.
>
> Quality is not a *thing*. It is an *event*.
>
> It is the event at which the subject becomes aware of the object.

And because without objects there can be no subject – because the objects create the subject's awareness of himself – Quality is the event at which awareness of both subjects and objects is made possible.

This means that Quality is not just the *result* of a collision between subject and object. The very existence of subject and object themselves is *deduced* from the Quality event. The Quality event is the *cause* of the subjects and objects, which are then mistakenly presumed to be the cause of Quality! (Pirsig, 1974, p. 215, emphases original)

The availability of different ways within a pragmatist resuscitation of classical rhetoric can be made out if we distinguish different lines in each of the traditions of pragmatism and of rhetoric. This approach has its supporters. For some time, students of the ancient sophists have been making a distinction between Gorgias' dialectical rhetoric and Protagoras' empirical pragmatism (see for example, Guthrie 1962, Vol III, pp. 176–99).

For Gorgias, even if something existed, we could know nothing about it; in that sense there is a wholesale fracture between words and things, between language and the world. For Protagoras, man is the measure of all things in accordance with the way he experiences them; in this way, the truth appears in the relation between language and the world in the reciprocity of knowing and acting.

As for American pragmatism, it is well known that C.S. Peirce described as suicidal the irrationalist twist which William James gave to it and which John Dewey further warped. While, for James and Dewey, truth dissolves into the notion of the useful, Peirce hung onto a strong sense of universal, though hypothetical and fallibilist, truth, towards which all enquiry is tending, and whose objectivity is sustained by continual testing against the imaginable practical effects which, for us, exhaust the meaning of reality.

From the foregoing, we might hazard the conjecture that McCloskey is captive to a vision of rhetoric inherited from Gorgias and to a version of James-Dewey pragmatism. This would account for the fact that he ends up embracing a relativist response to the current crisis about foundations. By contrast, the very different and more stimulating upshot of Pirsig's novel finds its roots in a different rhetoric and a different pragmatism. These point towards a redefinition of the role of objective truth in the enterprise of knowledge-gathering.

Thus dangling from a slender thread, how strong or how weak I do not know, of philosophical genealogy, I must stop.

NOTES

1. This article is a reworking of a paper presented to a study day held at the University of Pavia on 6 February 1988. For their many contributions, comments and disagreements to which I am indebted, I must mention at least Paolo Albani, Anna Carabelli, Francesco Ciafaloni, Valeria Egidi, Augusto Graziani, Alessandra Marzola, Marcello Messori, Andrea Salanti, Francesco Silva, Sandro Vercelli and Stefano Zamagni.
2. Wittgenstein (1974), adjunct to 387, 17th March 1951.
3. McCloskey's book is the tip of an iceberg. In the five years to the time of writing of the present article, the proposal of a Rhetoric of economics made considerable strides from its first appearance in the *Journal of Economic Literature* in 1983. It was followed up in such equally well-regarded mainstream journals as the *American Economic Review*, *Daedalus*, *Economic Inquiry*, the *Eastern Economic Journal* and the *New Palgrave*. The quality and variety of the contributions on the topic are no less than the sheer quantity, in journals ranging as widely as *Economics and Philosophy*, the *Review of Austrian Economics* and the *Review of Radical Political Economics*.
4. *The Leopard* tr. Colquhoun, London: Reprint Society, 1960, p. 29.
5. 'Protokollsätze' originally in *Erkenntnis* III 1932, reprinted in Schick's translation in Ayer (ed.) (1959), *Logical Positivism*, Chicago: Free Press.
6. We may note, incidentally, that we have already left behind the identification between falsificationism and crucial experiment which McCloskey maintains. Falsificationism now presents itself as methodological falsificationism; once scientists' decisions about the core of unproblematic knowledge – as with any other sort of knowledge – are regarded as fallible, any falsification is subject to revision when the unproblematic knowledge is subject to question.
7. G. Frege (1965), *Logica e aritmetica*, Turin: Boriugliseri.
8. *Meinung, Wahn, Gesellschaft* in *Eingriffe: Mein Kritische Modelle*, Frankfurt 1963, p. 163, quoted in Peter Dews (1987), *Logic of Disintegration. Post-Structuralist Thought and the Claims of Critical Theory*, London: Verso, pp. 230–1.
9. *Language*, A & M, 1987.
10. Wittgenstein (1974), 402, 19th March 1951.
11. Marx, K. (1930), *Capital* Vol I, Part I, ch. ii, tr. Eden and Cedar Paul, London: J.M. Dent, p. 61.
12. Valeria Egidi has pointed out to me that it is also possible to reconstruct a discussion about the notion of truth relative to psychoanalysis. The positions may be divided into three in the same way as in the economic–philosophical argument. According to the first, the 'truth' of the analysand's story would correspond to a reconstruction of past psychic facts. This picks up the idea of truth as representation. Second, there is the view that the analysand's story ought to be seen as a narration, and there is no way of discriminating a 'true' narration. This position is a version of the hermeneutical–pragmatist dissolution of truth *à la* Rorty and McCloskey, as we are presenting it here. And third, there is the view, which can be traced to one of Freud's 1937 writings, *Konstruktionen in der analyse*, according to which the truth of the analytic narration is demonstrated in practice in the relation between analyst and analysand, as efficacy in therapy and transformation within that relation. This is similar to the view of truth as objectivity which I have been trying to set out in terms which are anti-foundationalist but non-relativist.
13. *Home of the Brave*, Warner Brothers, 1986.

126   *John Maynard Keynes: Language and Method*

REFERENCES

Bellofiore, R. (1985) 'John Maynard Keynes: dall' instabilità del capitalismo all' economia monetaria della produzione', *Note Economiche*, **XVIII** (3–4).

Bellofiore, R. (1992) 'Monetary Macroeconomics before the *General Theory*: the Circuit Theory of Money in Wicksell, Schumpeter and Keynes', *Social Concept*, **VI** (2), June.

Berman, M. (1986) *All that is Solid is Melting into the Air*, London: Verso.

Bicchieri, C. (1988) *Ragioni per credere, ragioni per fare*, Milan: Feltrinelli.

Blaug, M. (1980) *The Methodology of Economics*, Cambridge: Cambridge University Press.

Boland, L. (1982) *The Foundations of Economic Method*, London: Allen and Unwin.

Bonadei, R. (1988) 'J.M. Keynes. Il contesto del metodo', *Il Piccolo Hans*, **59**, Milan: Media Presse.

Caldwell, B. (1982) *Beyond Positivism: Economic Methodology in the Twentieth Century*, London: Allen and Unwin.

Carabelli, A. (1988) *On Keynes's Method*, Oxford: Blackwell.

Faverau, O. (1986) 'L'incertain dans la révolution keynesiénne: l'hypothèse Wittgenstein', *Oeconomia*, **XIX** (5).

Feyerabend, P. (1975) *Against Method*, London: New Left Books.

Freud, S. (1937) 'Construction in Analysis' in Strachey, L. (ed.), Standard Edition, vol 22, London: Hogarth Press.

Guthrie W.K.C. (1962 ff.) *A History of Greek Philosophy* (6 vols), Cambridge: Cambridge University Press.

Hacking, I. (1983) *Representing and Intervening*, Cambridge: Cambridge University Press.

Habermas, J. (1987) *Lectures on the Philosophical Discourse of Modernity*, Cambridge, Mass.: M.I.T. Press.

Kregel, J. (1987) 'Rational Spirits and the Post Keynesian Macrotheory of Microeconomics' *De Economist*, **CXXXV** (4).

Kuhn, T. (1970) *The Structure of Scientific Revolutions* (2nd ed), Chicago: Chicago University Press.

Lakatos, I. and Musgrave, A. (1970) *Criticism and the Growth of Knowledge*, Cambridge: Cambridge University Press.

Latouche, S. (1984) *Le procès de la science sociale*, Paris: Anthropos.

Lawson, T. (1986) 'The Absolute/Relative Nature of Knowledge and Economic Analysis' *Economic Journal*, **XCVII** (4).

Lawson, T. and Pesaran, H. (eds) (1985) *Keynes' Economics. Methodological Issues*, London: Croom Helm.

Marconi, D. (1987) *L'eredità di Wittgenstein*, Bari-Roma: Laterza.

Marzola, A. (1988) 'Letterarietà e immaginario nel discorso economico di J.M. Keynes' typescript presented to seminar at Pavia 6 February 1988.

McCloskey, D. (1985) *The Rhetoric of Economics*, Madison: University of Wisconsin Press.

Mingat, A., Salmon, P. and Wolfelsperger, A. (1985) *Méthodologie économique*, Paris: PUF.

Mirowski, P. (1987), 'Shall I Compare Thee to a Minkowski–Ricardo–Leontief–Metzler Matrix of the Mosak–Hicks Type? Or Rhetoric, Mathematics and the Nature of Neo-Classical Theory', *Economics and Philosophy*, **III** (1).

O'Donnell, R.M. (1989) *Keynes: Philosophy, Economics and Politics*, London: Macmillan.

Orléan, A. (1987) 'Anticipations et conventions en situations d'incertitude', *Cahiers d'economie politique*, (13).

Pesante, M.L. (1986) *Economia e politica*, Milan: Franco Angeli.

Pirsig, R.M. (1974) *Zen and the Art of Motorcycle Maintenance*, New York: Bantam.

Popper, K.R. (1980–10th rev. of 1934 trans.) *The Logic of Scientific Discovery*, London: Hutchinson.

Rorty, R. (1980) *Philosophy and the Mirror of Nature*, Oxford: Basil Blackwell.

Rorty, R. (1982) *Consequences of Pragmatism*, Brighton: Harvester.

Schmidt, C. (1985) *La sémantique économique en question*, Paris: Calmann-Lévy.

Vercelli, S. (1987) *Keynes dopo Lucas: I fondamenti della macroeconomia*, Rome: La Nuova Italia Scientifica.

Vicarelli, F. (1983) 'Dall' equilibrio alla probabilità: una rilettura del metodo della Teoria Generale' in Vicarelli, F. (ed.), *Attualità di Keynes*, Bari: Laterza.

Wittgenstein, L. (1974) *On Certainty*, Oxford: Basil Blackwell.

Zamagni, S. (ed) (1982) *Saggi di filosofia della scienza economica*, Rome: La Nuova Italia Scientifica.

4. The Methodology of the Critique of Classical Theory: Keynes on Organic Interdependence

Anna Carabelli

KEYNES'S METHODOLOGICAL CRITIQUE OF THE CLASSICAL THEORY

This chapter considers the critique which, most prominently in *The General Theory* (1936), Keynes directed at what he calls the 'classical school', a term which he uses to cover the convergence of views maintained by David Ricardo and his followers as well as, for example, John Stuart Mill, Alfred Marshall and A.C. Pigou (*CW*, VII, p. 3n).

The traditional way in which this critique has been considered is in terms of its *content*. Here, it is approached from a different angle. We shall try to show that Keynes's critique is, in line with his overall approach to economic theory, of an essentially *methodological* charac-ter.[1] By taking this line, we shall be able to show the interrelations between his critical argumentation and the expository form of *The General Theory*. Indeed, we shall see that for Keynes, the method he operates and the argumentative language he uses are one and the same, and least in so far as his critique and his exposition bear closely on methodological problems.[2] Seen in this light, *The General Theory* is a text of considerable importance both from the linguistic and literary point of view, and as a contribution to scientific understanding. It is of linguistic and literary interest because Keynes uses ordinary language to convey and argue for his theory.[3] And, as a scientific text, its interest lies in the fact that ordinary language is the only means by which to bring out the single underlying logic of the epistemological problems of economic theory faced both by the students of the subject and by the objects of study, namely economic agents.[4] In Keynes's view, both economists and economic agents employ non-demonstrative argument forms which are based on ordinary language.[5]

Thus, so far as is possible, we shall reconstruct Keynes's critical methodology independently of all questions of the content of his doctrines. Even though their content was essential to Keynes's attack on the classical theory, we shall proceed on the assumption that this is not where the critique's strength principally comes from (cf. also Marzola in this volume).

Keynes himself frequently stresses the importance of methodological issues for a proper understanding of his opposition to the classical theory. We may cite remarks which he makes in the various Prefaces to *The General Theory*. In the English version, of 13 December 1935, he writes: 'I have thought it important, not only to explain my own point of view, but also to show in what way it departs from the prevailing theory' (*CW*, VII, p. xxi). Likewise, in the Preface to the German edition of 7 September 1936, he emphasizes the importance of his critique: 'My emphasis ... upon the points of my divergence from received doctrine' (*CW*, VII, p. xxv). And, again, in the Preface to the French Edition, of 20 February 1939, he makes the same point: 'It may, therefore, be helpful to my French readers if I attempt to indicate very briefly what I take to be the main *differentiae* of my approach' (*CW*, VII, p. xxxii).[6]

The first two chapters of *The General Theory* are taken up with the methodological issues. And the main claim of the first chapter, which is only half a page long, is that there is a pressing need for a methodological overhaul of the classical theory. There, we are also given an explanation of (among other things) the book's title, when Keynes says that his aim is, 'to contrast the character of my arguments and conclusions with those of the *classical* theory' (*CW*, VII, p. 3; cf. also p. 257).[7] Likewise, Chapter 2 and the appendix to Chapter 19 of *The General Theory* can be singled out as passages which are wholly concerned with question of methodology; but they are by no means isolated in the corpus of Keynes's writings.

Two Errors in Earlier Critiques of the Classical Theory

First, Keynes saw that the classical theory was not easy to refute. Indeed, although it had often been attacked, it had survived and held up well over a considerable period. It was a cogently structured theory which did not show obvious weaknesses to a cursory inspection. Its strength derived from its being a well-organized system of thoughts and doctrines which had been widely accepted as a result of its persuasive power. As a result, it had come to pervade the habits of thought both of economists and of businessmen. In *Poverty in Plenty: is the economic system self-adjusting?* (1934), Keynes writes:

> The strength of the self-adjusting school depends on its having behind it almost the whole body of organised economic thinking and doctrine of the last hundred years. This is a formidable power. It is the product of acute minds and has persuaded and convinced the great majority of the intelligent and disinterested persons who have studied it. ... For it lies behind the education and the habitual modes of thought, not only of economists, but of bankers, business men and civil servants and politicians of all parties. (*CW*, XIII, pp. 488–9)

Nevertheless, despite being endowed with this impressive intellectual backing, Keynes thought that it led to conclusions which were repugnant to common sense, and he expresses this in terms of 'a cleavage between the conclusions of economic theory and those of common sense' (*CW*, VII, p. 350; cf. p. 33).

Keynes was fully aware that many thinkers before him had attempted to refute the classical theory. So, it will be helpful to examine the methodological errors which Keynes held responsible for the failure of these attempts and which he wished to avoid repeating. We shall thus learn how, in Keynes's view, one should *not* proceed in mounting a critique of a theory.

Among the classical theory's opponents of whom he takes notice, Keynes includes those authors whom he calls 'the brave army of heretics' (*CW*, VII, p. 371). And he distinguishes between the old heretics and 'the heretics of today', taking the latter to be 'the descendants of a long line of heretics' (*CW*, XIII, p. 488), including Mandeville, Malthus, Marx, Hobson and Mummery, Gesell, Major-Douglas, Dalton, Orage and Wootton.[8]

Keynes took it that the criticisms which they levelled at the classical theory were in the main of an empirical nature and that the critics believed that straightforward observation would suffice to show that the theory did not fit the facts and that, therefore, observation would undermine the theory: 'The heretics of today ... are deeply dissatisfied. They believe that common observation is enough to show that facts do not conform to the orthodox reasoning' (*CW*, XIII, p. 488). But for Keynes, a critique of this sort could not do the work. His lack of faith in the idea of a simple appeal to the facts of experience grows out of his whole epistemology of the relation between theory and observation, as set out in *A Treatise on Probability* (published in 1921, but begun in 1905–6). On this account, observation is theory-laden (cf. *CW*, VIII, p. 231).[9] That being so, how could the observation of facts bring the theory on which it was based into doubt? Thus, a purely empirical critique, based on the observation of facts in conflict with the conclusions of the theory, was of no use.[10] Therefore, the mere exhibition of empirical facts which did not fit the orthodox theory was doomed to failure (cf. Bonadei in this volume).

Keynes included in this group of heretics the German economic school headed by W.G.F. Roscher and G. Schmoller. Unlike the bent for theoretical thought which they showed in other fields and to which, for example, in *The Treatise on Probability* Keynes is ready to defer, the German economists are accused of being 'sceptical, realistic', of being satisfied with historical facts and results, of employing 'empirical methods' and of setting aside 'formal analysis' (*CW*, VII, p. xxv).

In contrast with the approach of earlier critics, Keynes took it that only reasoning, rather than observation of matters of fact, could raise doubts about a theory's status. And by reasoning, as we have already noted, Keynes meant the non-demonstrative logic which was of a piece with ordinary language.

The second mistake which Keynes picked out in the heretics' critiques was that of having accepted the premises of the classical theory, though they rejected its conclusions. In *Poverty in Plenty*, he writes, 'Indeed, many of them [the heretics] accept the orthodox premises' (*CW*, XIII, p. 489).[11] In his view, this meant that their position was inconsistent, because they maintained the right conclusions and the wrong premises. For this reason, they were doomed to failure and to 'have made no impression on the citadel' of the classical theory (*CW*, XIII, p. 489); this inconsistency meant that their criticisms were null and void. Here, Keynes's attitude indirectly, but clearly, shows that he held the classical theory to be a coherent system of premises from which conclusions had been validly drawn.

The Views of Keynes's Contemporaries

Keynes subjected his own contemporaries, in particular Henderson, Brand and Robbins (*CW*, XIII, pp. 487 and 491) as well as Pigou and

Robertson, to similar criticisms. In his view, their approach was, if anything, more ambiguous than that of the earlier 'heretics', and it involved them in the same incoherence: 'Post-war economists seldom ... succeed in maintaining this point *consistently*: for their thought today is too much permeated with the contrary tendency and with facts of experience too obviously inconsistent with their former view' (*CW*, VII, p. 20).[12] And others, even though they did not accept the premises of the classical theory, seemed to Keynes to accept its results: 'Contemporary economists, who might hesitate to agree with Mill, do not hesitate to accept conclusions which require Mill's doctrines as their premiss' (*CW*, VII, p. 19; cf. also *CW*, XIV, p. 79). With the almost sole exception of Robbins, who does not count as a critic of the classical theory (cf. *CW*, VII, p. 20 n.1), Keynes held that economists were prone to inconsistency as between premises and conclusions because they failed to derive the proper consequences from their methodological position. Indeed, none of them saw that to reject the conclusions of the classical theory it was necessary to instigate a revolution in economic theory: 'But they have not drawn sufficiently far-reaching consequences and have not revised their fundamental theory' (*CW*, VII, p. 20). This situation had the result that they were disabled from proposing any alternative theory. And even when such proposals were made, they fell into a third type of error, which Keynes called 'incompleteness of theory' (*CW*, VII, p. 370; cf. also pp. 340, 350, 355–6, 368–9).

KEYNES'S ACCOUNT OF THE EARLIER CRITICS' FAILURE

We have seen that the fundamental mistake which Keynes diagnosed in earlier, and some contemporary, critiques of the orthodox theory as the cause of their failure was that they involved the acceptance of that theory's premises and the rejection of its conclusions. Thus, they departed from mistaken premises and arrived at correct conclusions. What were the causes of this inconsistency? How could these critics simultaneously maintain these two positions without seeing that they were in conflict?

In Keynes's view, the rejection of the classical theory's conclusions was caused by the critics' 'instinct, by flair, by practical good sense, by experience of the world' (*CW*, XIII, pp. 489). Although, in *A Treatise on Probability* Keynes did not make a sharp distinction between logic and flair, he held that flair without logic (and vice versa) was sterile. Nevertheless, he recognized that it was logic rather than flair that was needed to destroy the classical theory and to attack it in its 'citadel' (*CW*, XIII, p. 488). Thus, Keynes adopted the position of the heretics, that is, 'those standing on [his] side of the gulf, whom [he] ventured to describe as half-right and half-wrong' (*CW*, XIII, p. 490). In *Poverty in Plenty*, he writes, 'Now *I* range myself with the heretics. I believe their flair and their instinct move them towards the right conclusions. But I was brought up in the citadel and recognise its power and might' (*CW*, XIII, p. 489 emphasis original). Dissatisfied with the methodological standing of the criticisms which had been raised, he set about finding and identifying 'the flaw in that part of orthodox reasoning which leads to the conclusions which for various reasons seem to me to be inacceptable' (loc. cit.). And it was logic, rather than flair, empirical methods, experience of the world or practical good sense, which was to be the intellectual tool for the criticism of the classical theory.

The 'Proper' Mode of Criticism: Attacking the Premises

Earlier critics had adopted a methodologically inconsistent approach which was 'essentially superficial and ultimately dangerous' (*CW*, XIII, p. 492). It was all the more untenable because in Keynes's view, as against that of the heretics, the relation between premises and conclusions in the classical theory was thoroughly cogent. He frequently underlines the fact that the classical theory was well constructed: 'the superstructure [of orthodox economics] has been erected with great care for logical consistency' (*CW*, VII, p. xxi; cf. also pp. 33 and 192) Keynes went so far as to claim that, if the fundamental tenets of the classical theory were in good order, as seemed to be built into the heretics' procedure, then, if the heretics were to be consistent, they ought to accept the theory's conclusions (cf. *CW*, XIII, p. 491). Thus, if what was wrong with classical economics was neither a lack of empirical fit nor any defect in the logical link as between the premises and the conclusions, where do we look?

But, there was something amiss with the classical theory and it should have been attacked at its core. Therefore the flaw had to be in some part of the theory at which the heretics had not looked. But where was its 'citadel', which had given the theory its 'power and might' and on which alone a successful attack would bring about a revolution in economic theory? It was clear to Keynes that the premises of the theory constituted this 'citadel'. Thus, the attack had to be launched against the acceptability of the premises; only in this way could the essential change in theory be brought about (*CW*, VII, pp. 489 and 492).

Explicit and Tacit Premises

Keynes observed that the premises of the classical theory were flawed because they lacked 'clearness' (*CW*, VII, p. xxi). This was where the 'proper' critique of the classical theory should be aimed; and in this way, Keynes could put his finger on the flaw in the orthodox reasoning which had led to unacceptable conclusions (*CW*, XIII, p. 489).

As we shall see, (pp. 135–7), Keynes held that the classical theory failed to make as explicit as it should have some crucial assumptions on which the generality and scope of its conclusions depended. For Keynes, it was necessary to distinguish among the classical theory's various premises and to sort them into the explicit and the tacit. Since the tacit assumptions made up the foundation of the classical theory, spelling them out was of the greatest importance. We can thus say that it was in his making this distinction and setting this task that the real *differentia* between Keynes's approach and that of the classical theory lies (cf. *CW*, VII, p. xxxii). And we find him saying in *The General Theory* that the tacit assumptions smoothed the way for the conclusions of the classical theory: 'granted this, all the rest follows' (*CW*, VII, p. 21).

Unlike earlier critics of the classical theory, Keynes held that the relation between premises and conclusions was in perfectly good logical order (cf. *CW*, VII, p. 371); thus there was nothing to be gained from searching for inconsistency in it. The relation in question was guaranteed by the tacit assumptions which underlay the theory:

> Thus writers in the classical tradition, overlooking the special assumption underlying their theory, have been driven inevitably to the conclusion, perfectly logical on their assumption that apparent unemployment ... must be due ... to a refusal by the unemployed factors to accept a reward which corresponds to their marginal productivity. (*CW*, VII, p. 16)

TACIT PREMISES

Thus we see that the first job of a methodologically well-conducted critique of the classical theory is to show that the theory contains tacit premises. The second job is that of providing a taxonomy of them; the third that of picking out their common characteristics and, in general, of discerning the epistemological role they play in the theory-building.

All Keynes's writings on economics are pervaded by his search for the tacit premises lurking in the classical theory. We may provide a few examples from the period in which he was preparing *The General Theory*. In 1933, in 'A Monetary Theory of Production', he writes,

> One of the chief causes of confusion lies in the fact that the assumptions of the real-exchange economy have been tacit, and that you will search treatises on real-exchange economics in vain for any express statement of the simplifications introduced or for the relationship of its hypothetical conclusions to the facts of the real world. (*CW*, XIII, p. 410)

In *The General Theory* itself, we find the following two observations, the first from Chapter 2, and the second from the beginning of Keynes's critique of the tacit premises in Pigou's theory in the Appendix to Chapter 19:

> This strange supposition ... is what all members of the orthodox school are tacitly assuming ... the classical school have slipt in an illicit assumption. For there may be *no* method available to labour as a whole. (*CW*, VII, p. 13; cf. also the French Preface p. xxxv)[13]

> Since the tacit assumptions, which govern the application of analysis, slip in near the outset of the argument, I will summarise his treatment up to this crucial point. (*CW*, VII, p. 272; cf. also pp. 274–5 and 277)

The Varieties of Tacit Premises

As we have noted, once the tacit premises within the classical theory have been identified, the second job is that of describing the varieties of them. Keynes differentiates at least three main varieties, although he does not himself give a clear taxonomy.

The first sort of tacit premise on which Keynes lights is the assumption of independence from changes in the value of money. The fact that the classical theory made this assumption carried with it the idea that money is a neutral means of exchange and allowed the theorists to move, without appropriate adjustments in the form of reasoning, from discussion of real-exchange economies to monetary economies. On the assumption in question, the two types of economy are counted as equivalent. This sets up a false analogy between them. In Keynes's view, the classical theory can rest on either of two versions of the

assumption. On the one hand, there is the assumption of the uniform
purchasing power of money, as if money were like 'a mean sun'. In
respect of this version, Keynes cites Marshall's reference to Cournot's
idea that it is convenient to assume the existence of a standard of
uniform purchasing power, as astronomers assume that there is a 'mean
sun' 'which crosses the meridian at uniform intervals, so that the clock
can keep pace with it; whereas the actual sun crosses the meridian
sometimes before and sometimes after noon as shown by the clock'
(*CW*, XIII, p. 409). On the other hand, there is the version which
neglects possible changes in the general purchasing power of money. In
respect of this version, Keynes refers to Pigou's assumption that the
supply of labour is independent (or 'virtually independent') of changes
in the value of money (*CW*, XIII, pp. 409–10).[14]

The second sort of tacit assumption which Keynes picks out concerns the alleged independence from changes in the level of output and
unemployment. Within the classical theory, this assumption implies
that the economic system is operating at full capacity, which in turn
implies an independence from the level of output and of employment.
According to Keynes, it was this assumption which allowed classical
theorists to assimilate, without appropriate riders or changes of argumentative style, full-capacity economies to economies in which there is
unemployment. What we find is a single form of reasoning applied to
the two different cases.[15]

The French Preface to *The General Theory* suggests that Say's basic
assumptions, such as that demand is created by supply, entailed an
independence from the level of output:

> J.B. Say ... [has been] abandoned by most economists; but they have not
> extricated themselves from his basic assumption and particularly from his
> fallacy that demand is created by supply. ... Say was implicitly assuming
> that the economic system was always operating up to its full capacity, so
> that a new activity was always in substitution for, and never in addition to,
> some other activity. Nearly all subsequent economic theory has depended
> on, in the sense that it has required, this same assumption. (*CW*, VII, p.
> xxxv)

Likewise, the tacit premises which Keynes picks out in the classical
theory of employment in Chapter 2 of *The General Theory* all lead
back to a single form of independence (*CW*, VII, pp. 21–2). And it is an
easy step to infer that this is the independence from changes in the level
of output and unemployment.

Finally, Keynes considers the assumption of independence from changes in the level of income. This premise does its work in the move from the analysis of single cases, whether of an individual person, a particular industry or part of the economic system, to the analysis of the collective predicament considered as a whole or system. The work it does is to imply the independence from changes in the collective or aggregate income. It is therefore crucial in allowing the classical theorist to apply unmodified thoughts which are only valid at the singular level to the collective level.

However, in Keynes's view, the fact that aggregate income is not independent of individuals' propensities to spend, means that we cannot pass straightforwardly from an analysis of (or an argument about) the individual level to one at the collective level. If we try, we shall run into logical paradoxes and fallacies. What is independent at the level of individuals may not be so at the level of the collective. It was built into the classical theory that the overall or aggregate income of an economic system as a whole was given and unchanging.[16] Keynes spells this out in the French Preface to *The General Theory*:

> Quite legitimately we regard an individual's income as independent of what he himself consumes and invests. But this ... should not have led us to overlook the fact that the demand arising out of the consumption and investment of one individual is the source of the income of other individuals, so that incomes in general are not independent, quite the contrary, of the disposition of individuals to spend and invest. (*CW*, VII, pp. xxxii–xxxiii; cf. also *CW*, VII, pp. 21 and 378; *CW*, XIII, p. 278)

Features of the Tacit Premises of the Classical Theory

The three types of tacit premises have in common a general assumption of 'logical independence of changes in the value or level of ...' Such a formula means that the classical theory holds good *always* and for *all* and *any* value of the variables considered. That is, it holds good for all values of money, for all levels of output, for all levels of capacity, for all levels of employment and for all levels of aggregate income. And all of this adds up to the tacit claim that the classical theory holds good universally, throughout space and time.

Keynes's targeting of this universalizing feature of the classical theory – the fact that it claimed to hold good *always* and for *all* and *any* values of the variables – comes out in the following passages. As to 'all', we find in the 1934 draft of Chapter 6 of *The General Theory*: 'The reader will remember that according to the classical theory, $\Delta Dw = \Delta N$ for *all* values of N [employment]' (*CW*, XIII, p. 427 emphasis original). We find the word 'always' in the French Preface to the book: 'Say was implicitly assuming that the economic system was *always* operating up to its full capacity, so that a new activity was *always* in substitution for, and never in addition to, some other activity' (*CW*, VII, p. xxxv emphasis added). And the words 'any' and 'always' appear in a single passage of Chapter 21: 'The view that *any* increase in the quantity of money is inflationary ... is bound up with the underlying assumption of the classical theory that we are *always* in a condition where a reduction in the real rewards of the factors of production will lead to a curtailment in their supply' (*CW*, VII, p. 304 emphases original).

Thus far, we can arrive at the following two assertions:

1. that, for Keynes, the classical theory's universality implied independence *always* and for *all* values and levels of the variables considered;

and

2. that the alleged universality of the classical theory presupposed also the generality of the tacit premises.

The Limits Set to the Tacit Premises of the Classical Theory

If, as we have seen, the tacit premises of the classical theory really were universal across all space and time, then that theory would be unassailable. If however, they were not, then a line of attack on the theory would be available.

As a matter of fact, Keynes held that the tacit premises about independence did not hold good *always* and for *all* values of the variables in question. As a result of this line of criticism, he came to think that the tacit premises of the classical theory held good only in an extremely limited range of circumstances (*CW*, VII, p. 378).[17] He went so far as to think that they held good only for *some* values or levels of the variables and only at *some* times and in *some* situations and contexts. This clearly represents a serious limitation on the theory.

We may take as an example Keynes's discussion of the limiting conditions on the premise of independence from changes in the value of money – that is, the classical assumption of the neutrality of money – where he says in *A Monetary Theory of Production* (1933):

We are not told what conditions have to be fulfilled if money is to be neutral. Nor is it easy to supply the gap. Now the conditions required for the 'neutrality' of money ... are ... precisely the same as those which will insure that crises *do not occur*. If this is true, the real exchange economics ... is a singularly blunt weapon for dealing with the problem of booms and depressions. For it has assumed away the very matter under investigation. (*CW*, XIII, pp. 410–11 emphasis original)

Likewise, in considering the level of output, Keynes showed that the tacit premises of the classical theory did not hold good for *all* levels but only for *one* level of the given variable. In the 1934 draft of Chapter 6 of *The General Theory*, he writes:

The innovation of the present theory is, at this stage, purely negative. Its significance will depend on our establishing our contention that there is, in general, only *one* level of output at which equality holds between marginal prime cost and the anticipated price, so that under competition the aim of maximising profit will cause entrepreneurs to choose that level of employment for which this equality holds. Only if the equality held good, as the classical theory assumes, for *all* levels of output, would it be true that there is nothing to check the increase of employment. (*CW*, XIII, p. 427 emphases added)

Thus, for Keynes, the 'lack of clearness in the premises' (cf. *CW*, VII, p. xxi) carried with it a similar lack of generality in the range of situations of which they held good. As a result, the results which were drawn from them were also limited. And this meant that the limited generality of the premises of the classical theory set limits to the general applicability of the theory itself. As we shall see in the next section, the narrow range of cases of which the premises held good implied that the classical theory was only a particular case of a more general theory.[18]

What Keynes Means by a 'General' Theory

We are now in a position to get a grip on what is meant by the word 'general' which may baffle the reader who reads as little as the title of *The General Theory*. In Chapter 1, Keynes writes: 'I have called this book the *General Theory of Employment, Interest and Money* placing the emphasis on the prefix *general*. The object of such a title is to contrast the character of my arguments and conclusions with those of the *classical* theory' (*CW*, VII, p. 3). Thus, for Keynes, a general theory is one which does not rest upon tacit premises positing any 'independence from'.[19] In this way, his use of the word 'general' is in reality connected with the methodology of his critique of the classical theory. And it is here that we find the difference between the 'character' of Keynes's arguments and those of the classical theory (*CW*, VII, p. 3 and 276).

Only a theory which does not introduce premises of independence, which are of limited applicability, at the outset of its analysis can be counted a general theory.[20] All other theories – including the classical – which did introduce such premises were simply special cases of general theories: 'Thus we are led to a more *general* theory, which includes the classical theory with which we are familiar, as a special case' (*CW*, VII, pp. xxii–xxiii; cf. XII, p. 420).[21]

The Fallacy in the Classical Theory: *Ignoratio Elenchi*

To get a better grip on the difference between a general theory and one of its cases, we may lay stress on the fact that Keynes held that the introduction of the tacit premises was a fallacy generally recognized in classical logic. And in *The General Theory* Keynes refers to it as the fallacy of *ignoratio elenchi* (*CW*, VII, p. 259).[22]

This was the fallacy that induced the classical theory into committing 'false inference', a 'fallacy of composition', into offering an 'optical illusion, which makes two essentially different activities appear the same', a 'false analogy', a 'paradox', in short, into applying the analytic tools appropriate to one part of a system to the system as a whole (*CW*, VII, pp. xxxii; 20–1; VIII, p. 191; XIII, p. 278); or, alternatively, which induced the classical theory into the mistaken 'idea that it is comparatively easy to adapt the hypothetical conclusions of a real wage economics to the real world of monetary economics (*CW*, XIII, p. 410; cf. also p. 278).

More specifically, Keynes attributed to the classical theorists the mistake of ignoring the dependence of the system as a whole on changes in the variables considered, and, what amounts to the same, of ignoring the relevance of the *changes* in those variables for the system considered as a whole.[23]

The Epistemological Role of the Tacit Premises

By now it should be clear that Keynes's criticism of the classical theory's premises was not concerned with their empirical relevance. Rather, it was directed at their 'logical standing'.[24] We shall now turn to the epistemological implications of this.

As we have seen, the three tacit premises each posited a 'logical independence from'. To this we may add the fact that according to *A Treatise on Probability*, the notions of 'logical irrelevance' and 'logical independence' played a central role in Keynes's theory of knowledge. In particular, with regard to causality and the 'atomic hypothesis', they were identical with each other. Indeed, in the *Treatise*, a judgement of logical independence ('independence for knowledge') was the very same thing as a judgement of logical irrelevance to the organic nature of the variables in question. Such a judgement of logical irrelevance justified the introduction of the 'atomic hypothesis' in the mathematical theory of probability (cf. *CW*, VIII, pp. 182–3; and 466).[25]

In the classical theory, the premises about 'logical independence from' played several roles. First, they represented a straightforward denial of the logical relevance of changes in the value of money, level of output and level of aggregate income. And as we have seen, one corollary of this judgement of irrelevance was the implicit generality of the theory: it is supposed to hold good for all levels and values of the variables. Second, they constituted the crux at which the 'atomic hypothesis' about the factors under consideration was inserted into the theory. That is, they made up the claim about the numerical measurability of those factors, their divisibility, time-reversibility, homogeneity, exhaustiveness, completeness, the permanence of forces and the primariness of primary qualities. In this respect, there is a close parallel with the mathematical theory of probability which Keynes criticizes in *A Treatise on Probability* (*CW*, VIII, pp. 276–8; cf. also Carabelli 1988, Ch. 6). And, third, these premises did not function merely like the 'atomic hypothesis' in probability theory, but had a position like that of the axiom of parallels in Euclidean geometry: 'it is, then, the assumption ... which is to be regarded as the classical theory's "axiom of parallels"' (*CW*, VII, p. 21; cf. p. 16). Once the premise is admitted 'all the rest follows' (*CW*, VII, p. 21).

Complex Systems: Organic Interdependence

By incorporating the premises of logical independence, the classical theory was able to treat economic systems *as if* they were *always* isolable at *all* levels and values of the variables in question. In this way, it aimed to isolate the economic system from the effects of *changes* in some variables. But Keynes held that such an attempt at isolation was not feasible relative to the economic systems with which economic theory deals, or ought to deal (cf. *CW*, VII, p. xxxii; V, p. 77).

The classical theory's premises of independence, considered as groundless hypotheses of the isolability of phenomena, were comparable with similar moves made in Newtonian physical theory (cf. Lakatos 1970, p. 124). By employing this sort of hypothesis, the classical theory was in a position to speak of economic individuals, of industries and of systems *in isolation* from each other. Indeed, when considered in isolation, individuals, industries and systems do behave in much the same ways. They are, after all, systems which can be isolated from changes in variables which have been judged to be irrelevant by the adoption of the premises of logical independence. Under those conditions, they behave as *simple* or *closed* systems, in which the functional relationships among the variables are atomic in character.

Set against these simple systems, there are the systems in which Keynes was most interested. These are the systems to which a *general* theory applies. They are the non-isolable systems, which are genuinely *complex* or *open*, and in which the non-independent variables are connected to each other in an organic interdependence (cf. *CW*, XIII, pp. 312–3; XXIX, p. 100).[26] It thus emerges that one of the leading methodological elements in Keynes's assault on the classical theory was provided by the concept of organic interdependence which grew directly from his approach to probability theory (cf. *CW*, VIII, pp. 276–8).[27] Moreover, this concept underlay his positive contribution to the study of the economy; it is the basic notion in the discipline of macroeconomics.

CONCLUSION

Even for a theoretical thinker of Keynes's calibre, the business of building up a theory of complex and open economies was no easy matter. It is enough to think of the difficulties faced by him in presenting such a theory and the economy which it reflects in *The General Theory* (cf. Carabelli 1984, pp. 190–92; and 1988, pp. 155–7).

Keynes found that he had to introduce provisional assumptions of logical independence to cope, in *The General Theory*, with the organic interdependence of the variables (or 'non-homogeneous complexes') or of 'incommensurable collections of miscellaneous objects' (*CW*, VII, p. 39), such as net output, the purchasing power of money, probability and so on. The introduction of such assumptions was performed by mobilizing the idea that such independences could be supposed for the purposes of the analysis in question. Keynes utilized his concept of *causa cognoscendi* (independence for knowledge) put forward in *A Treatise on Probability*. The operation of this process is clearly in view in Chapters 4 and 18 of the finished version of the book and in the following passage of the 1933 draft: 'these partly insoluble difficulties of quantitative description do not arise in our causal analysis, which is *strictly logical* in itself and is subject, in practice not to essentially insoluble difficulties, but only to the actual imperfections of our knowledge' (*CW*, XXIX, p. 73, emphasis original). Its role was provisionally to isolate the factors which were 'relevant-for-knowledge', in such a way as to provide 'practical intuition' with 'a less intractable material on which to work' (*CW*, VII, p. 249). These simplifying assumptions were due to be discharged at a later stage in the analysis. We may, for example, recall the discharging, in Chapter 19, of the assumption of the independence from changes in money wages, or the isolation of the five factors which complicate the analysis and whose probable mutual interrelation is taken up in Chapter 21 (pp. 295–303). What is more, these assumptions of independence are introduced as relative to 'this place and context' and to the *quaesitum* under discussion. More specifically, as noted above, the independence which is being assumed is closely connected to the notion of its being logically 'relevant ... [to] our *quaesitum*' (*CW*, VII, pp. 245, 247; cf. Gotti in this volume and Varese 1989, p. 47). In Keynes's view, such a process of assumption and discharge could only be carried out in ordinary language, which is an open language, rather than in closed artificial languages such as that of mathematics (*CW*, VII, p. 297).[28]

We might note in conclusion how similar this process is to that which Keynes adopts in *A Treatise on Money*. Again, simplifying assumptions are temporarily taken on board in order to cope with complexity: 'the method and the ideas of the preceding chapters will ... be better illustrated. ... The chapter is, therefore, an essay in the internal mechanics of the price–wage–employment structure' (*CW*, V, p. 274). As the analysis progresses, these assumptions are discharged. And, at the end, the reader who has grasped Keynes's 'general system of thought' is left to go ahead alone with the generalization of the results as an exercise which, in an open and organic theory like this, has no definite end (cf. *CW*, V, pp. 274–5; 280; 284; 292; XIII, pp. 469–70). In addition, in order to exhibit the malleability of his own methodology, Keynes points out that, even before breaking down the initial simplifying assumptions, there are eight other ways of getting to his results. These other options are picked out from among the many possible argumentative byways and digressions which the exposition of the theory offers.[29]

From our brief notes on Keynes's expository structure, we can see how what Gotti calls the 'vision of the theory as open-ended' is closely dependent on the methodological vision which underlies the theory. We conclude therefore, with the claim that Keynes's language and method are organically interdependent on each other.

NOTES

1. Keynes's methodological approach to economic theory is discussed in Carabelli, 1988.
2. In speaking of 'method' we mean the underlying epistemology of the theory. In other words, it is what Keynes meant by saying that something counts as a theory. We may recall Keynes's explicit methodological insistence on the use of ordinary (as opposed to artificial mathematical) language for conceiving and setting out economic theory.
3. These matters are discussed by Roncaglia and Rossini-Favretti 1979, 1989, Rossini-Favretti 1988, 1989b, and Varese 1989 as well as in the contributions of Gotti and Marzola in the present volume. Whereas Marzola emphasizes the rhetorical aspect of Keynes's literary performance, in which the rhetoric and the method are indivisible, and the act of writing is part of the heuristic process, Rossini Favretti attributes a cognitive value to Keynes's writing, one which reflects the problems discussed in *A Treatise on Probability*.
4. See Bellofiore (1988) on recent discussions of the role of rhetoric in economics and their relation to Keynes. On the shared logic of the scientist and of the economic agent, see Carabelli 1988, pp. 162–3.
5. Keynes viewed logic as the logic of ordinary language, rather than that of formal systems. Such a vision is coloured by the notion of reason as what is contingently reasonable, or as variable in relation to differing circumstances and much closer to a logic of opinion (the classical *doxa*), which is the hallmark of the logic of rhetoric, as against a logic of knowledge (*episteme*). See Carabelli 1982 a and b, 1984, 1988 ch. 8.
   Our account of *A Treatise on Probability* is at variance with that put forward by O'Donnell (1982, 1989, pp. 34, 38, 47, 90, 93, 97–8) by Lawson (1987, pp. 961–3; 1989 pp. 244–8) and by Fitzgibbons (1988, pp. 26–8, 85), all of whom read

Keynes as the champion of universal truth and absolute knowledge. They have tended to overestimate Keynes's debts to Moore (e.g. the realist-Platonic vision of the existence of abstract objects) and to Russell (e.g. the formalist vision of the project in logic); and they have tended to overshadow his differences from them. For my part, to understand *A Treatise on Probability*, it seems more important to bear in mind the differences than the similarities. I have tried elsewhere to show that Keynes sought to escape from Moore's Platonism and from Russell's formalism. It may be useful to sketch the basic points.

In line with the Platonic tradition, Keynes held that logical relations are real objects. But he did not think of them as supported by an immanent non-spatial and atemporal metaphysical reality with its static and universal categories of infallible *a priori* intuition. He sought to overcome the limits of universalistic abstractions which tended to marginalize from theoretical concern all the things of greatest importance. And these included the uniqueness, contingency, mutability, and space- and time-dependence of things. He bridled at two of the conditions of metaphysical realism: the unidimensionality of existence and the permanent fixity of concepts. For him, both reality and thought are multidimensional. The categories of theoretical thought are, therefore, not determined in advance by an independent reality, but nor are they imposed on reality once and for all by the free action of the *a priori*. Thus, Keynes sought to overcome this dichotomy as he did many of the dichotomies dear to positivism. He did not envisage a universal and absolute point of view: neither Platonic metaphysical realism nor Kantian transcendental idealism.

In this way, theoretical categories are to be selective. On the basis of what is already known about reality and giving reasons for the choice, the theorist has to choose a particular and relative point of view for further knowledge-gathering within the contingent situation. Modelling reality, which is the same thing as introducing theoretical abstractions, is a procedure which cannot be universal. Likewise treating reality as relative to changing circumstances does not mean that it is not objective, relative to those circumstances, unless, of course, objectivity and universality are to be automatically associated. And Keynes did not associate them in any such way (cf. also Note 24, and Putnam 1981, pp. 201–3).

Following an Aristotelian rather than Platonic line, *A Treatise on Probability* seeks to build up a form of non-demonstrative and contingent reasoning which is relative to changing contexts, which Keynes calls 'the variable flux' or 'the shifting picture' of experience (cf. Carabelli 1988, pp. 126, 149–50, 279). In the face of such changing and merely contingent contexts, rationality lacks both an ontological underpinning and the necessity of the *a priori*. While he was writing *A Treatise on Probability*, Keynes was dissatisfied with the theories of knowledge proposed by his contemporaries which he thought were unable to take account of these features of the situation. One of the main characteristics of his thought about probability was the (not always successful) attempt to overcome the positivist dichotomies: rationalism–empiricism, rationality–irrationality, science–art, science–ethics, theory–experience, mind–reality, primary versus secondary qualities and so on. He would surely have appreciated the styles of epistemological thought which have paid due attention to complexity, such as those put forward by Morin 1977–86, 1984, 1985, by Prigogine, 1980 and by Prigogine and Stengers 1984. See also the view of logic put forward by Dow 1988, p. 104.

For Keynes's views on the relation between theory and experience, see Bonadei in this volume. Reiss notes (1988, pp. 5–8) that Virginia Woolf is critical of the rationalist–analytic view – attributed to Mr Ramsey and criticized by Lily Briscoe in *To the Lighthouse* – which separates subject from object and mind from matter. For Woolf, as for Keynes, the actual target of the criticism was Moore's Platonic realism.

6. This passage follows Keynes's observation that the method and presuppositions of classical economic thought had remained unchanged for a century. Thus, 'I was wanting to convince my own environment and did not address myself ... to outside opinion' and consequently to state 'my own position in a more clear-cut manner' (*CV*, VII, p. xxxi).

7. Likewise,we find at the beginning of Chapter 19 the following passage: 'My difference from this theory is primarily a difference of analysis; so that it could not be set forth clearly until the reader was acquainted with my own method' (*CW*, VII, p. 257).

8. For Keynes's views on Mandeville, Malthus, Gesell and Hobson, see *CW*, VII, p. 371; on Major-Douglas *CW*, VII, p. 370; and on Dalton, Hobson, Orage and Wootton *CW*, XIII, pp. 487–8. In *The General Theory*, Keynes gives over fully five pages to the 'unjustly forgotten' Gesell (*CW*, VII, pp. 353–8).

9. See also Carabelli 1988 pp. 69–71. On observation see Shapere 1982, and Hacking 1983, ch. 10.

10. It may be useful to consider the criticisms Keynes levelled at the approach of Malthus, perhaps the greatest opponent of the classical theory and certainly top of the list of 'heretics'. Keynes regarded him as one of his own great predecessors.

    It is generally thought that the methodological approaches of Keynes and Malthus are fairly similar to each other. But the similarity is at best broad-brush. In *The General Theory*, Keynes takes Malthus to task for having criticized Ricardo on empirical grounds and for having offered only a partial theory as an alternative (*CW*, VII, p. 32).

    However, in the *Essay on Malthus* and the *Allocution*, he is less reductive. In these writings, Keynes nuances his account to take in the differences of nuance among the three main phases of Malthus's intellectual development. First, there is the first version of the *Essay on Population* (1798), which Keynes thought of as '*a priori*' and 'philosophical'. In Malthus's subsequent revisions of the book (1803, 1817 &c.), Keynes detects a shift towards the proposal of inductive arguments and in the direction of mere empiricism (*CW*, X, p. 86). And, third, there is the phase of Malthus's mature writings, in particular *An Investigation into the Cause of the Present High Price of Provisions* (1800), the *Principles of Political Economy* (1820) and the correspondence with Ricardo. Keynes's discussions of these writings, in the latter part of the *Essay on Malthus* (*CW*, X, pp. 71–103) and in the whole of the *Allocution* (*CW*, X, pp. 104–8), throw light not only on Malthus's methodology, but also on Keynes's. In those places, he puts the accent on Malthus's combination of formal thought with the intuition necessary 'to keep a hold on what may be expected to happen in the real world' (*CW*, X, p. 88; cf. pp. 107–8). In this respect, Keynes also draws comparisons with Newton's method (cf. *CW*, X, p. 364); see also Parsons 1985 and Carabelli 1988, p. 109.

    The present account of Keynes's position is supported by Winch's book *Malthus* (1987). Although Malthus's method is not Winch's primary focus, he tries to clarify his 'method of approach and choice of questions that need to be answered' (p. 78), such as those concerning irregular fluctuations and the 'immediate and temporary effects of particular changes' (letter to Ricardo in *Works and Correspondence of David Ricardo*, VII, p. 120). In particular, Winch subscribes to Keynes's account of the *Essay on Population*, as beginning with 'an exposition of the principles of population treated as a set of deductive propositions' and as proceeding to 'how the historical and empirical evidence lend support to the abstract principle' (Winch 1987, p. 18). Furthermore, Winch notes that the *Essay* 'amounts to a short treatise on scientific method according to the Newtonian model' (loc. cit.). And, in discussing the later writings, such as the *Principles*, Winch observes that Malthus, unlike Ricardo, assimilates political economy to the moral sciences and to 'the art of legislation' rather than to mathematics and the natural sciences. The crucial passage from p. 2 of the *Principles* is appropriately cited (Winch 1987, p. 76) and associated with Malthus's 'conviction that one of the chief faults of economists lay in their "precipitate attempt to simplify and generalize"' (Winch loc. cit., quoting *Principles* p. 6).

Unlike the view Keynes puts forward in his writings devoted to Malthus, but like that found in *The General Theory*, Winch also suggests that, in later life, Malthus tended towards an empiricist methodology, despite recognizing the indispensability of theory and the impossibility of getting by with mere appeals to common sense. 'But', Winch adds, 'he lacked Ricardo's confidence in thinking that economics was a 'strict science like mathematics' (Ricardo, VIII, p. 331), and his commitment to experience as the ultimate arbiter was consequently stronger, whatever the result might be in terms of tidiness' (pp. 92–3).

11. We may recall that Keynes criticized Gesell not for inconsistency as between premises and conclusions, but for the incompleteness of the alternative theory which he proposed. Gesell's view is contrasted with Marx's methodological incoherence: 'The purpose of [Gesell's book was] a reaction built on theoretical foundations totally unlike those of Marx in being based on a repudiation instead of an acceptance of the classical hypotheses (*CW*, VII, p. 355). As to Marx, Keynes wrote to Shaw that a time would come when the 'Ricardian foundations of Marxism will be knocked away' (*CW*, XIII, p. 493). On Keynes's criticism of the methodology of contemporary Labour writers, see Carabelli 1987.

12. The most striking example among them was Pigou. He shared Keynes's attitude to economic policy and practice. Evidence for this agreement is to be found in *The Times* in 1932 and 1933, which published jointly-signed letters from them advocating countercyclical fiscal policy (*CW*, XXI, pp. 126, 137–40). On this see Moggridge 1988, pp. 54–5. But note also Keynes's remark from as late as October 1937, à propos Pigou's *Socialism versus Capitalism* (1937): 'As in the case of Dennis [Robertson], when it comes to practice, there is really extremely little between us. Why do they insist on maintaining theories from which their own practical conclusions cannot possibly follow? It is a sort of Society for the preservation of Ancient Monuments' (*CW*, XIV, p. 259).

13. There was nothing new in Keynes's search for and attempt to make explicit the tacit premises in the theories he criticizes. It is operative in *A Treatise on Probability* in relation to the mathematical theory of probability, Bernoulli's principle of indifference, induction and statistical inference (cf. for example, *CW*, VIII, p. 66). On Keynes's procedure here see Carabelli 1988, pp. 75, 267–8. Favereau (1985 p. 39) has dubbed this attitude 'the Wittgenstein hypothesis' and stressed the modernity of Keynes's approach to epistemology in trying to show the limits of formal language. It must, nevertheless, be remembered that this attitude is present in Keynes's thought long before *The General Theory*, prior to and independent of Wittgenstein.

14. It is worth remembering that, unlike the classical theory, Keynes's theory of value had to be expressed in monetary terms. See Chapters 4 and 21 of *The General Theory*, esp. pp. 41, 293–4. On Keynes's attitude, prior to *The General Theory*, to a monetary theory of money, see his 'The Economic Consequences of W. Churchill', *CW*, IX, pp. 208–9 and *A Treatise on Money*, *CW*, V, pp. 120–24, 137, 149–53. See also Wells 1986, pp. 12–14, Rotheim 1981, Chick 1985, Weeks 1988 and Note 16 below.

15. In the view of Varese (1989, pp. 36, 44) Keynes gives fresh epistemological value to non-formal languages and is concerned with various and heterogeneous universes of discourse. On Keynes's criticisms of Russell's account of implication and on the multiplicity of universes of discourse, see Carabelli 1988, pp. 136–8.

16. It was on this point that Keynes grounded his criticism that the classical savings and investment schedules could not 'shift independently of one another' (*CW*, VII, p. 179); they were interdependent. Likewise, supply and demand curves for loanable funds were not independent. One 'could not obtain a determinate conclusion without introducing some additional equation or datum' (*CW*, XXIX, p. 228). Keynes linked the interdependence of supply and demand with his theory of value (*CW*, VII, pp. xxii–xxiii). Surrey (1988) pp. 110–3) suggests that at the heart of Keynes's criticism of the non-independence of classical supply and demand schedules lay a problem for the classical theory of systematic under-identification at the macro level.

17. We ought continually to bear in mind that, as Keynes says in the English Preface, *The General Theory* was addressed to 'his fellow economists' and had as a principal object the study of 'difficult questions of theory' with the aim of 'persuading economists to re-examine certain of their basic assumptions' (*CW*, VII, p. xxi).

18. In his *Tract on Monetary Reform* (1923) Keynes had already raised a similar objection, based on the illicit premise of independence against the quantitative theory of money (cf. *CW*, IV, p. 65). And he voices similar criticisms at the theory of purchasing power parity and against the alleged intrinsic stability of the value of gold (*CW*, IV, pp. 75, 133–4). In *A Treatise on Money* (1930), the point is re-asserted (*CW*, V, pp. 73, 75, 77).

19. A theory which is in this sense *general*, is not meant to hold universally in time and space. In this respect it differs from what was alleged on behalf of the tacit premises of the classical theory. For Keynes, economic theory was a 'logic, a way of thinking', a 'method' (*CW*, XIV, p. 296, XII, p. 856). And, as we have seen in note 5 above, it is a non-demonstrative form of reasoning adapted to circumstances. In this way, a theory is general if it is capable of dealing with a variety of hypothetical cases in which the variables are differently dependent on each other, and if it gives a central place to *change* and *variability*. There is nothing universal about the choice of the level of abstraction at which the theory is employed, nor about which model, out of the many available, is applied in practice. These are matters which are relative to the circumstances of time and place. Obviously, the conclusions drawn from different models vary according to circumstance. Keynes describes the skill of choosing the particular model as an 'art' (*CW*, XIV, p. 296). In the light of this, we can see how unfounded it was of Hayek to call Keynes's general theory 'scientistic' (Hayek 1978, p. 287).

20. Independence also plays a prominent role in decision theory and, in particular, in the theory of subjective expected utility. We have in mind the recent debate, aimed at clearing up the paradox of rational behaviour in conflict with utility-theory, about whether to give up the so-called principle of independence or to weaken the axiom of ordering, which requires that preferences form a complete set (see Seidenfeld 1988; Sen 1977).

21. In her contribution to this volume, Marzola shows how Keynes makes frequent use of the 'dissociation' of ideas as an argumentative strategy. She also brings out the way that the antithesis of change and permanence is a central metaphor in *The Economic Consequences of the Peace*. Rossini-Favretti draws attention to the antithesis of the general and the special (1989b, p. 24).

22. *Ignoratio elenchi* is one of the thirteen fallacies listed by Aristotle in *Sophistical Refutations* (*De Sophisticis Elenchis* 167 a.20), which is concerned with contentious reasoning. In English, the term covers not only ignorance, but the ignoring, of what is in dispute. On this type of fallacy see Hamblin (1970, pp. 31–2, 87–8).

23. In logic *ignoratio elenchi* is counted as an informal fallacy of relevance. It is informal because the error is due not to the form of the argument, but to a defect in

the content. It is a fallacy of relevance because there should be some relation between the meanings of the premises and the conclusion. See Greenstein, 1978, pp. 112, 132, 141). Keynes stresses the connection between relevance and meaning in *A Treatise on Probability* (*CW*, VIII, p. 62).

24.   Despite his recognition that the classical premises are 'inappropriate to the facts' (*CW*, VII, p. 371), Keynes's criticism of them is not reducible to the claim that they are unrealistic or empirically unfounded. Rather, it is that they lack generality (*CW*, VII, p. xxi). That is, they are logically inadequate to meet the questions and problems which arise. They therefore led their supporters to 'ignore' or 'dismiss' real problems instead of solving them (e.g. *CW*, VII, pp. 350, 364).

Keynes gives an account of direct judgements of *logical relevance* in *A Treatise on Probability* in his discussion of Bernoulli's principle of indifference (*CW*, XVIII, pp. 58–60, 62, 113). There, he distinguishes between judgements of preference or indifference and judgements of relevance or irrelevance. The former concern situations in which the evidence is the same but the conclusions different; the latter concern situations in which the evidence is different but the conclusion the same. In particular, direct judgements of logical relevance concern the effect which specific factors included in the argument have on the probability of the outcome. He further discusses the effects which different amounts of relevant evidence (or relevant knowledge) have in dealing whith the notion of the 'weight of argument' (*CW*, VII, pp. 77–85). On the role of judgements of relevance, see Sperber and Wilson 1986, pp. 70, 77–84, 120–42.

In Keynes's view, judgements of logical relevance are not absolute, but relativized to the *quaesitum* and to the specific circumstances in which it arises (cf. *CW*, VII, pp. 245, 247, VIII, p. 113; and, on relevance as adequacy and perspicuity, Putnam 1981, pp. 201–3).

It is worth noting that Keynes's critique of the classical theory in terms of its logical relevance has no bearing on the longstanding debate over realism and instrumentalism about the hypotheses of a theory or of one of its models; see Boland 1989 Ch. 4 and bibliography; also Morgenbesser 1969, Nagel 1963, Mongin 1988 and the associated debate in *Philosophy of the Social Sciences* (1988). For Keynes, verification, confirmation, falsification or predictive power have no role to play in the attack on the classical theory's premises. For this reason, there is something misplaced about the emphasis which O'Donnell (1989 pp. 228–9) and Lawson (1987 and 1989) put on the empirical realism – as opposed to instrumentalism – of Keynes's assumptions. After all, these sorts of disputes are internal to positivism which might be thought to have been exemplified in the arguments between Friedman and Samuelson in the 1950s and 1960s. Keynes had already got beyond that dichotomy. Furthermore, in reference to the specific authors cited, it might seem that Lawson confuses two distinct notions of realism (Platonic metaphysical realism and empirical realism) which do not bear any very close relation to one another.

25.   In *A Treatise on Probability*, Keynes decided to define independence by reference to the concept of logical relevance rather than to that of causality. The problem of the relation between logical relevance and empirical relevance – or material cause as he called it – he left unsolved (*CW*, VIII, pp. 182–3).

So Keynes was not interested in material ontology – that is, how things are in reality – but in how things are actually *known* (or rather, probably known) by us. The distinction he made was between the '*causa essendi*' ('cause of why a thing is what it is') and the '*causa cognoscendi*' ('cause of our knowledge of the event') (*CW*, VIII, Note on the Use of the Term 'Cause' pp. 305–8). In this I disagree with Lawson's reading of Keynes as a 'realist', attempting 'to understand causal things and the ways in which they act' and 'to analyse causal structures at their own level of being' (Lawson 1989, p. 239). Keynes considered cause a relative cognitive concept – that is, a logical ground or a reason for believing which is relative to particular circumstances (see the reference to 'causal analysis' as '*strictly logical*' in the 1933 draft of *The General Theory* (*CW*, XXIX, p. 73).

He therefore connected the concept of relevance with probable knowledge of or about things rather than with things themselves. To clarify this point, there is the following quotation from *A Treatise on Probability*: 'this conclusion cannot be reached unless *a priori* ... we have some reason for thinking [i.e. a *causa cognoscendi*] that there may be such a causal connection between the quantities [i.e. a *causa essendi*]' (*CW*, VIII, p. 466).

Relevance was connected with the first type of cause (*causa cognoscendi*) and not with the second (*causa essendi*). On the connection between irrelevance and independence and on their role in Keynes's concept of *causa cognoscendi* see Carabelli (1985, pp. 154, 157; 1988 sections 3.5, 3.6 and 6.1).

26.   We can now also fully grasp Keynes's methodological criticism of Pigou. According to Keynes, Pigou was taking 'out of a complex system' two variables (employment and real wages) which were not logically 'independent' (*CW*, XIII, pp. 312–13).

That *both* employment and real wage rates were functions of the level of effective demand – in particular an inverse relation not to be confused (according to Asimakopoulos 1988, p. 79) with a demand curve for labour – was equally stressed by Keynes in the 1933 draft chapter of *The General Theory*: 'we may well discover empirically a correlation between employment and real wages. But this willl occur, not because the one causes the other, but because both are consequences of the same cause' (*CW*, XXIX, p. 100). On this see also Brothwell (1988, p. 54).

27.   In recent years a number of authors have been paying attention to the importance of this concept in Keynes's approach to economics, even if no consensus about it has yet emerged. See Brown-Collier 1985, Brown-Collier and Bausor 1988, Davis 1988 and 1989, Fitzgibbons 1988, Lawson 1989, O'Donnell 1982 and 1989, Winslow 1986 and 1989, Carabelli 1984 and 1988. We may also mention two early contributions which discuss the notion of open and complex systems, though without reference to Keynes: Grunberg 1966 and 1978.

28.   On this aspect, see Carabelli 1984, 1988 pp. 141–4, 152–7; also Walker 1985 p. 176, which criticizes Keynes's claim that mathematics is associated with the 'atomic hypothesis' and that it is unable to deal with problems of organic unity. Simon (1962) and Gottinger (1983) take pains to cope with complexity in mathematical terms.

29.   We may therefore notice the relation between argumentation 'by digression' and the open-ended, organic structure of Keynes's theory. The theory seems to be structured like the altogether singular novel, Lawrence Sterne's *Tristram Shandy* (1760). It has often been observed that this novel is structured as a series of digressions: 'Digressions, incontestably, are the sunshine, – they are the life, the soul of reading!' (Bk I ch. xxii). On digression in Keynes, see also Bonadei and Gotti in the present volume.

REFERENCES

Asimakopoulos, A. (1988) 'The Aggregate Supply Function and the Share Economy' in Hamouda, O.F. and Smithin, J.N. (eds), *Keynes and Public Policy after Fifty Years*, vol. II, Aldershot: Edward Elgar.

Bellofiore, R. (1988) 'Retorica ed economia. Su alcuni sviluppi recenti della filosofia della scienza economica e il loro rapporto con il metodo di Keynes', *Economia Politica*, **V**, December.

Boland, L.A. (1989) *The Methodology of Economic Model Building*, London: RKP.

Bonadei, R. (1988) 'J.M. Keynes: La costruzione di un metodo' *Il Piccolo Hans*, **59**.

Brothwell, J. (1988) 'The *General Theory* after Fifty Years – why are we not all Keynesians now?', in Hillard, J. (ed.), *J.M. Keynes in Retrospect: The Legacy of the Keynesian Revolution*, Aldershot: Edward Elgar.

Brown-Collier, E. (1985) 'Keynes' View of an Organic Universe', *Review of Social Economy*, **13**.

Brown-Collier, E and Bausor, R. (1988) 'The Epistemological Foundations of *The General Theory*', *Scottish Journal of Political Economy*, **35**, (3).

Carabelli, A.M. (1982a) 'J.M. Keynes e *A Treatise on Probability* in *Modelli di rationalità nelle scienze economico-sociali*, Venice: Arsenale.

Carabelli, A.M. (1982b) 'On Keynes's Method: Practical Rationality', Cambridge: mimeo.

Carabelli, A.M. (1984) 'Causa, caso e possibilità', *La scienza impropria: Metodi e usi della teoria economica*, Milan: Franco Angeli (a 1985 abridged version of this paper appears in Lawson, T. and Pesaran, H. (eds)).

Carabelli, A.M. (1987) '"Il solo socialista presente": Keynes e i laburisti', *Il Ponte* **42**, (6).

Carabelli, A.M. (1988) *On Keynes's Method*, London: Macmillan.

Chick, V. (1985) 'Time and the Wage-unit in the Method of *The General Theory*: History and Equilibrium' in Lawson,T. and Pesaran, H. (eds), *Keynes's Economics. Methodological Issues*, London: Croom Helm.

Davis, J.B. (1989) 'Keynes on Atomism and Organicism', *Economic Journal*, **99**.

Davis, J.B. (1991) 'Keynes' Critique of Moore: Philosophical Foundations of Keynes's Economics', *Cambridge Journal of Economics*, **15**.

Dow, S.C. (1988) 'What Happened to Keynes's Economics?' in Hamouda and Smithin (eds), *Keynes and Public Policy After Fifty Years*, vol. I, Aldershot: Edward Elgar.

Faverau, O. (1985) 'L'incertain dans la "révolution kéynesienne". L'hypothèse Wittgenstein', *Economies et Sociétés*, 3.

Fitzgibbons, A. (1988) *Keynes' Vision: A New Political Economy*, Oxford: Clarendon Press.

Gotti, M. (1988) 'Il modello argomentativo di J.M. Keynes nella *General Theory*' *Quaderni del Dipartimento di Linguistica e Letterature Comparate*, Vol. 4, Bergamo: Istituto Università degli Studi.

Gottinger, H.H. (1983) *Coping with Complexity; Perspectives for Economics, Management and Social Sciences*, Dordrecht: Reidel.

Greenstein, C.H. (1978) *Dictionary of Logical Terms and Symbols*, New York: Van Nostrand Reinhold.

Grunberg, E. (1966) 'The Meaning and Scope of External Boundaries in Economics' in Krupp, S.R. (ed.), *The Structure of Economic Science*, Englewood Cliffs, N.J.: Prentice-Hall.

152   *John Maynard Keynes: Language and Method*

ographyGrunberg, E. (1978) '"Complexity" and "Open Systems" in Economic Discourse', *Journal of Economic Issues*, **12** (3).
Hacking, I. (1983) *Representing and Intervening*, Cambridge: Cambridge University Press.
Hamblin, C.L. (1970) *Fallacies*, London: Methuen.
Hamounda, O.F. and Smithin, J.N. (eds) (1988) *Keynes and Public Policy After Fifty Years*, (2 vols), Aldershot: Edward Elgar.
Hayek, A. (1978) *New Studies in Philosophy, Politics and Economics*, London: RKP.
Hillard, J. (ed.) (1988) *J.M. Keynes in Retrospect: The Legacy of the Keynesian Revolution*, Aldershot: Edward Elgar.
Lakatos, I. (1970) 'Falsification and the Methodology of Scientific Research Programmes' in Lakatos, I. and Musgrave, A. (eds), *Criticism and the Growth of Knowledge*, Cambridge: Cambridge University Press.
Lawson, T. (1987) 'The Relative/Absolute Nature of Knowledge and Economic Analysis', *Economic Journal*, December.
Lawson, T. (1989) 'Realism and Instrumentalism in the Developments of Econometrics', *Oxford Economic Papers*, **41** (1).
Lawson, T. and Pesaran, H. (eds) (1985) *Keynes' Economics. Methodological Issues*, London: Croom Helm.
Malthus, T.R. (1986) *The Works*, Wrigley, E.A. and Souden, D. (eds), London: Pickering and Chatto.
Marzola, A. (1988) 'Letterarietà e immaginario nel discorso economico di J.M. Keynes', paper presented to the seminar held at Pavia, 6 February 1988.
McQueen, D. (1988) 'The Hidden Microeconomics of J.M. Keynes', in Hamouda, O.F. & Smithin, J.N. (eds), *Keynes and Public Policy After Fifty Years*, vol. I, Aldershot: Edward Elgar.
Moggridge, D.E. (1988) 'The Keynesian Revolution in Historical Perspective', in Hamouda, O.F. & Smithin, J.N. (eds), *Keynes and Public Policy After Fifty Years*, vol. I, Aldershot: Edward Elgar.
Mongin, Ph. (1988) 'Le réalisme des hypothèses et la "Partial Interpretation View"', *Philosophy of the Social Sciences,* **18**.
Morgenbesser, S. (1969) 'The Realist–Instrumentalist Controversy' in Morgenbesser, Suppe and White (eds), *Philosophy, Science and Method*, New York: St. Martin Press.
Morin, E. (1977–86) *La Méthode* (3 vols), Paris: Le Seuil.
Morin, E. (1984) 'Epistemologie de la complexité', in Atias, C. and Le Moigne, J.L. (eds), *Edgar Morin: Science et conscience de la complexité*, Aix-en-Provence: Librarie de l'Université.
Morin, E. (1985) 'Le vie della complessità', in Bocchi, G. and Ceruti, M., *La sfida della complessita*, Milan: Feltrinelli.
Nagel, E. (1963) 'Assumptions in Economic Theory', *American Economic Review: Papers and Proceedings*, May.
O'Donnell, R. (1982) *Keynes: Philosophy and Economics. An Approach to Rationality and Uncertainty*, Cambridge PhD dissertation.
O'Donnell, R. (1989) *Keynes: Philosophy, Politics and Economics. The Philo-

sophical Foundations of Keynes's Thought and their Influence on his Economics and Politics, London: Macmillan.

Parsons, D.W. (1985) 'Was Keynes Kuhnian? Keynes and the Idea of Theoretical Revolutions', *British Journal of Political Science*, **15**, October.

Pigou (1937) *Socialism versus Capitalism*, London: Macmillan.

Prigogine, I. (1980) *From Being to Becoming*, San Francisco: Freeman.

Prigogine, I. and Stengers, I. (1984) *Order Out of Chaos*, London: Collins.

Putnam, H. (1981) *Reason, Truth and History*, Cambridge: Cambridge University Press.

Reiss, T.J. (1988) *The Uncertainty of Analysis. Problems in Truth, Meaning and Culture*, Ithaca N.Y.: Cornell University Press.

Ricardo, D. (1951) *The Works and Correspondence*, Sraffa, P. (ed.), Cambridge: Cambridge University Press.

Roncaglia, R. and Rossini-Favretti, R. (1979) *Reading Keynes's* General Theory *within a Linguistic Framework*, Bologna: Pitagora.

Roncaglia, R. and Rossini-Favretti, R. (1989) 'Reading *The General Theory*: a Linguistic Perspective' in Rossini-Favretti (ed.), *Il linguaggio della* Teoria Generale. *Proposte di analisi*, Bologna: Patron Editore.

Rossini-Favretti, R. (1988) 'L'argomentazione nella comunicazione e nell'epistemologia Keynesiana', *Studi italiani di linguistica teorica ed applicata*, **XVII**, (1).

Rossini-Favretti, R. (ed.) (1989a) *Il linguaggio della* Teoria Generale. *Proposte di analisi*, Bologna: Patron Editore.

Rossini-Favretti, R. (1989b) 'Communicazione e metodo scientifico nell' opera di J.M. Keynes. Da *The General Theory* a *A Treatise*', in Rossini-Favretti (ed.), *Il linguaggio della* Teoria Generale. *Proposte di analisi*, Bologna: Patron Editore.

Rotheim, R.J. (1981) 'Keynes's Monetary Theory of Value (1933)', *Journal of Post Keynesian Economics* **3** (4), Summer.

Seidenfeld, T. (1988) 'Decision Theory without "Independence" or without "Ordering"', *Economics and Philosophy*, **4**.

Sen, A. (1977) 'Social Choice Theory: a Re-examination', *Econometrica*, **45**.

Shapere, D. (1982) 'The Concept of Observation in Science and Philosophy', *Philosophy of Science*, **49**.

Simon, H. (1962) 'The Architecture of Complexity', *American Philosophical Society, Proceedings*, vol. 106 April.

Sperber, D. and Wilson, D. (1986) *Relevance. Communication and Cognition*, Oxford: Basil Blackwell.

Sterne, L. (1760) *Tristram Shandy*.

Surrey, M. (1988) 'The Great Recession 1974–84: Is a "Keynesist" Approach Plausible?' in Hillard, J. (ed.), *J.M. Keynes in Retrospect: The Legacy of the Keynesian Revolution*, Aldershot: Edward Elgar.

Varese, F. (1989) 'J.M. Keynes 'apostolo' della probabilità' in Rossini-Favretti (ed.), *Il linguaggio della* Teoria Generale. *Proposte di analisi*, Bologna: Patron Editore.

Walker, D.A. (1985) 'Keynes as a Historian of Economic Thought: the Biographical Essays on Neoclassical Economists', *History of Political Economy*, **17** (2).

Watt, I. (1957) *The Rise of the Novel*, London: Hogarth Press.

Weeks, J. (1988) 'Value and Production in "The General Theory"' in Hillard, J. (ed), *J.M. Keynes in Retrospect: The Legacy of the Keynesian Revolution*, Aldershot: Edward Elgar.

Wells, P. (1986) '"Mr. Churchill" and "The General Theory"' in Cohen, J.S. and Harcourt, G.C. (eds), *International Monetary Problems and Supply-Side Economics*, London: Macmillan.

Winch, D. (1987) *Malthus*, Oxford: Oxford University Press.

Winslow, E.G. (1986) '"Human Logic" and Keynes's Economics', *Eastern Economic Journal*, **12**, Oct–Dec.

Winslow, E.G. (1989) 'Organic Interdependence, Uncertainty and Economic Analysis' paper presented to History of Economics Society Meeting 10–13 June 1989, Richmond, Virginia.

5. 'The General Theory' as an Open-ended Work

Maurizio Gotti

In an earlier discussion, we examined the argumentative format in which Keynes set out *The General Theory* (Gotti 1988).[1] There, we tried to bring to light his formidable powers of expression and the broad range of rhetorical tropes which he employed. These highlighted our author's impressive stylistic richness and his mastery of the linguistic and metalinguistic principles which determine the efficacy of his persuasiveness in economic argument.

The aim of this chapter is to provide an analysis of the criticisms that have been levelled at Keynes in respect of the stylistic errors and fallacious arguments of which he has been accused in the composition of his *magnum opus,* and which have been held to blame for the arising of misunderstandings and ambiguities. In some cases, these features of Keynes's writing have undermined the persuasiveness of the theory itself. Our enquiry is aimed at evaluating the weight which is due to these criticisms, with a view to determining the real effectiveness of Keynes's book, given the purposes which it was meant to serve.

THE PURPOSES OF KEYNES'S ARGUMENTATION

In order to get a better grasp on the importance to be given to the alleged imperfections of Keynes's book, it is worthwhile to begin with an account of the purposes which *The General Theory* was set to fulfil. In its turn, the goal of Keynes's argumentative activity depends on his conception of the theoretical study of economics and of the methodological context in which that study is embedded.

Keynes's methodological thought is subservient to a vision of economics as one of the 'moral sciences'. It therefore falls outside the positivistic assumptions typical of the empirical sciences. For Keynes, it is the strong subjective element in the very object of study which blocks off the assimilation of economics to the experimental sciences and which brings it into line with philosophical enquiries.[2] He deploys a powerful image to illustrate the difference between the methods of economics and those in Newtonian science:

> Economics ... deals with motives, expectations, psychological uncertainties. One has to be constantly on guard against treating the material as constant and homogeneous. It is as though the fall of an apple to the ground depended on the apple's motives, on whether the ground wanted the apple to fall, and on mistaken calculations on the part of the apple as to how far it was from the centre of the earth. (*CW*, XIV, p. 300)

The behaviour of the economy cannot but be influenced by this strongly subjective element which is itself a product of the arbitrary behaviour of Economic Man. The latter often ignores or is ignorant of classical economics, and so behaves in ways which are quite unpredictable and sometimes irrational. For example, among the features which Keynes attributes to investors are that they

> know almost nothing whatever about what they are doing. They do not possess even the rudiments of what is required for a valid judgment, and they are the prey of hopes and fears easily aroused and as easily dispelled. This is one of the odd characteristics of the capitalist system under which we live, and is not to be overlooked. (*CW*, VI, p. 323)

By giving status to this irrational side of economic agents Keynes distances his own view from that of the classical theory. For the classical theorists were emphatic that the choices which are made are normally made in accordance with the rational and logical principles of the maximization of profit and economic utility. By contrast, Keynes's vision is more realistic in that he takes account of the operation of the 'insane and irrational springs of wickedness in most men' and of their 'deeper and blind passions' (*CW*, X, pp. 447 and 450).[3] It is the irrational and instinctual behaviour of Economic Man[4] which introduces instability into the working of the economy and which makes it unreliable and unpredictable.

According to this vision of the economy, the purpose of Keynes's argumentative activity must be found not so much in absolute and certain demonstrations of the validity of a theory by means of declarative procedures based on objective facts and irrefutable arguments; rather, he aims at the persuasion of his particular audience by means of the high perlocutionary force of the format of his argumentation.[5] While hanging on to all the features of rationality, a polemic of this sort, and with these aims, sets aside the procedures typical of positivistic argumentation. To fulfil its purpose, it sets itself to guiding the reader to the acceptance of its conclusions by presenting them as the most plausible and credible in the terms of its own logical framework. In his introduction to the *Cambridge Economic Handbooks*, Keynes spells out these features of economic argumentation: 'The theory of economics does not furnish a body of settled conclusions immediately applicable to policy. It is a method rather than a doctrine, an apparatus of the mind, a technique of thinking, which helps its possessor to draw correct conclusions' (*CW*, XII, p. 856).

On this conception, economic theory loses its dogmatic character and takes persuasion as its only goal. Keynes himself explicitly accepts this consequence: 'In economics you cannot *convict* your opponent of error; you can only *convince* him of it' (*CW*, XII, p. 470). The fact that economic argument is aimed at persuasion has as an obvious result the call for greater logical rigour and for greater precision in the expression of thoughts. As Keynes says: 'Even if you are right, you cannot convince him, if there is a defect in your own powers of persuasion and exposition' (loc. cit.).

The matter of the clarity of exposition comes to have the greatest importance in evaluating the persuasive power of a contribution to economics. The unbreakable bond which already links thought to language is thus further strengthened. As a result, greater importance is given to the role of the linear form relative to the content in achieving perlocutionary success for the whole line of thought. We find confirmation of the importance which Keynes gives to exposition in ensuring the persuasive effectiveness of polemical writing when he criticizes Marshall's style in the *Principles of Economics*:

> [His] method has, on the other hand, serious disadvantages. The lack of emphasis and of strong light and shade, the sedulous rubbing away of rough edges and salients and projections, until what is most novel can appear as trite, allows the reader to pass too easily through. Like a duck leaving water, he can escape from this douche of ideas with scarce a wetting. The difficulties are concealed; the most ticklish problems are solved in footnotes; a pregnant and original judgment is dressed up as a platitude. The author furnishes his ideas with no labels of salesmanship and few hooks for them to hang on in the wardrobe of the mind. (*CW*, X, p. 212)

In order that a piece of writing should achieve its goal of being persuasive, the move from 'signification' to 'communication' should be made in such a way that the reader not only understands, but agrees with the author's thought (cf. Merlini Barbaresi 1988, p. 147). Keynes's enriched understanding of the importance of expository technique leads him to a detailed scrutiny of the linguistic and rhetorical regulations of polemical writing and to make his own stylistic and lexical choices with care and precision.[6]

THE RECEPTION OF 'THE GENERAL THEORY'

If Keynes's aim in argument is not so much the demonstration of his theory's validity by reference to irrefutable facts as it is to convince the reader of the acceptability of the views put forward, then one way of gauging the effectiveness of *The General Theory* as a persuasive performance would be by reviewing the extent to which it was actually accepted among economists. As is well known, *The General Theory* was immediately and widely successful and it further confirmed Keynes's popularity and intellectual dominance. From the very start, the book caught the attention of economists and was generally accepted as a landmark in economic thought.[7] As Keynes had hoped, the revolutionary significance of his work was picked up straight away; and nowadays many commentators see in the publication of *The General Theory* something of a Kuhnian revolution.[8]

Nevertheless, in parallel to the widespread acceptance of Keynes's theory, various economists took a decided stance violently critical of *The General Theory* and attacked both the theoretical underpinnings and the methodological outlook on which the book is based. Such readers have not died away with the passage of time; indeed, they have been reinforced and renewed by some influential figures who have not been sparing in their criticisms of the book's conceptual and formal shortcomings. Here, for example is what Samuelson has to say, recognizing Keynes's genius at the same time as having to express deep reservations about his book:

> It is a badly written book, poorly organized. ... It is arrogant, bad-tempered, polemical, and not overly generous in its acknowledgments. It abounds in mares' nests or confusions. ... Flashes of insight and intuition intersperse tedious algebra. An awkward definition suddenly gives way to an unforgettable cadenza. When finally mastered, its analysis is found to be

obvious and at the same time new. In short, it is a work of genius. (Samuelson 1964, pp. 318–19).

And more recently, very critical judgments have been expressed of *The General Theory* which highlight the limitations of its persuasiveness. For example, Yeager puts his worries about the book's overall defects in these terms:

> Keynes, likewise, hardly deserves credit for what he supposedly may have meant but did not know how to say. If, more than 50 years later, scholars are still disputing the central message of the *General Theory*, that very fact should count against rather than in favour of Keynes's claim to scientific stature. Whatever the *General Theory* was, it was not great science. It was largely a dressing-up of old fallacies. Worse, for many years it crowded better science off the intellectual scene. (Yeager 1986, p. 40)[9]

The book's shortcomings are mostly put down to Keynes's excessive haste and to his writing habits. As Murad puts it:

> Keynes was a man of many ideas and he was impatient to put his ideas before his fellow economists and before the public as soon as he conceived them and often without giving them time to ripen. In this he was at opposite poles from his teacher Alfred Marshall, who was reluctant to publish anything until he had satisfied himself that he had thought through his problems thoroughly and left no contradictions or loose ends to confuse the reader. Marshall spent twenty years preparing his *Principles of Economics*, Keynes probably spent no more than three years in writing the *General Theory* and revising it in response to criticisms from friends and colleagues, and all this time he was busy with a thousand and one other things besides. No wonder that the *General Theory* is not as smooth a finished piece of work as is Marshall's *Principles*. (Murad 1966, p. 196)[10]

For all that excessive haste was a feature of Keynes's way of writing, it seems not to have been operative in the case of *The General Theory*, which was put together over a relatively long period during which Keynes was less than usually distracted by commitments in public affairs. As Patinkin reports,

> after the completion of the Macmillan Report in June 1931, Keynes seems to have been much less occupied than before with activities on behalf of the government. Similarly, after 1933 there was a falling-off in the intensity of his journalistic activities. Correspondingly, I would conjecture that in the last two years before their respective publication, Keynes was able to concentrate far more on the writing of the *General Theory* than he had been able to on the writing of the *Treatise*. (Patinkin 1977, pp. 8–9)

Moreover, the final composition of *The General Theory* was preceded by long discussions and exchanges of correspondence between the author and his Cambridge colleagues which made the production of the book longer and more painstaking.

Even though the book's failure to persuade is generally put down to both its and its author's shortcomings, the suspicion immediately arises that that lack of success may in some cases be attributable to readers' ways of approaching the text. As a result of insufficient willingness or inadequate interpretative strategies, they may have lacked the knowledge or the desire to understand and accept Keynes's proposals. Hence, to understand the causes of the failure to persuade of Keynes's book, it is useful to look both at the argumentative features of *The General Theory* and at the accounts which have been given of it.

In order to provide an account of the lack of conviction on the part of many readers, we might take either of the following two postulates as premises:

1. In general, persuasion requires an understanding of the locutionary and illocutionary force of the utterance.
2. Necessarily, understanding of the locutionary and illocutionary force of an utterance carries with it acceptance of its perlocutionary force.

The first premise presupposes that there are responsibilities devolving either on the utterer (who might have failed in respect of clarity, organization, etc.) or on the recipient (who might have decided not to co-operate with the utterer, not to take account of his methodological premises, etc.). In some cases, we might find that both parties in the process of creation–reception of the utterance are responsible for failure. On the other hand, the second premise presupposes that once he has interpreted it correctly, the recipient is always free to accept or reject what the utterer is proposing. Nevertheless, if we base our account on this second premise, we must be prepared to bring to light a given recipient's interpretive motives and to set out his reasons for not accepting the views which he is considering. However, the assessment of these reasons would involve an appraisal of the contents of the text which, in the present case, would require economic expertise to which we lay no claim.

The analysis which we shall seek to provide will depend only on the first premise and will highlight the ways in which *The General Theory* was poorly understood due either to the expressive and argumentative shortcomings in the text which cramp its persuasive power; or to the reader's insufficiencies in approaching the text which obstruct a full understanding of its locutionary and illocutionary force.

The Matter of Method

A survey of the various critical comments which *The General Theory* attracted shows that one very common reason for Keynes's theories not being accepted was the failure to grasp his methodological innovations. Even though he set out clearly the ways in which his particular methodological principles differed from what had traditionally been accepted, many economists undertook their reading of *The General Theory* on the basis of very different premises from those set out in the book. On the whole, these economists were attached to the idea of economics as a positivistic science which employs objective demonstrations from concrete facts; they therefore did not fully understand Keynes's novel methodological proposals. In some cases however, the novelties were recognized but not accepted, so that the very procedure of the argument and its results were objects of harsh criticism. This was for example, Beveridge's view:

> Keynes neither starts from facts nor returns to them. ... Mr. Keynes starts, not from any fact, but from the definition of a concept. ... He proceeds to a fresh set of concepts and of their definitions. ... Mr. Keynes does not return to facts for verification. There is no page throughout his work on which a generalisation is set against marshalled facts for testing. (Beveridge 1937, p. 464)

Beveridge's methodological starting-point is the exact opposite of Keynes's. Indeed, he is explicit that any theoretical line of thought, in economics as in any other science, must be based on the facts (loc. cit.). This presupposition, common among economists at that time, creates clear expectations which, if not met, will lead to the book's failing to persuade. This being so, the accusation which is most often levelled at Keynes is that he was trying to change the very nature of the study of economics and to apply to it epistemological canons which were characteristic of other branches of knowledge. As Beveridge concludes,

> If many who are not professional economists have read it and have read the discussion of it by other economists, I do not see how they can avoid the

conclusion that economics is not a science concerned with phenomena, but a survival of medieval logic, and that economists are persons who earn their livings by taking in one another's definitions for mangling. (Beveridge 1937, pp. 465–6)

We might diagnose in this misunderstanding of Keynes's methodological innovations the presence of the attitude of a certain type of reader who approaches the book not so much with the aim of interpreting it correctly in accordance with the author's premises, but with that of finding in it a confirmation of his own opinions and expectations. In the framework of such an exegetical pattern, the reader interprets the various things said in terms of the categories which he has ready prepared.

One clear example of this attitude can be found in the heated debate about the assimilation of Keynes's theories to the pre-existing trends of epistemological thought, that is to say, Rationalism and Empiricism. Keynes's theory was interpreted by many commentators in terms of one or other of these trends in the philosophy of science; as a result, his own epistemological presuppositions were misrepresented and their theoretical and practical consequences were falsified. Such critics thus failed properly to notice that Keynes's position cannot be assessed in terms of the two traditional theories; although it is coloured by features of both methods, it is quite independent of each. Even when other critics did not overhastily assimilate Keynes's position to either of the standing epistemologies, it was misinterpreted and 'narcotized' (Eco, 1979) and robbed of its own scientific autonomy.

Another example of the way that Keynes was misread is provided by the debate about whether his analysis is dynamic or static. Here again, readers were unable to give a correct interpretation because their view was obscured by the official options offered by economic analysis; they thus did not see the novelty of Keynes's method. In an effort to harmonize the varying needs that arose from his desire to describe the different equilibrium situations which come about as a result of various economic factors, Keynes employs a mixed method which is sometimes static and sometimes dynamic. Indeed, given the need to treat the various factors both separately and in terms of their mutual interplay, Keynes had to evolve a new analytic method to perform this function. An inability to see the novelty of Keynes's choice here has led some writers to think of this analytic procedure as a sort of uneasy compromise between the method of comparative statics and the concerns of process dynamics (cf. Chick 1983, p. 16).

The lack of a clear understanding of the novelty of Keynes's analytic tools led necessarily to a fragmentary reading of the book. As a result, the differences between the various levels of his analysis were smoothed over and the high degree of interconnectedness among the book's different parts was obscured. This aberrant sort of reading[11] caused Keynes to be accused of having misused the term 'general' in describing his own theory, which some have thought 'cannot do more than individuate very special cases' (Schumpeter 1952, p. 286).

Another matter which may have caused a discrepancy between readers' expectations and what is to be found in the text arises from the method of setting out causal connections. As has been shown (e.g. by Vercelli, 1987), Keynes's mode of exposition is constructivist. It dictates that the central problem be analysed first by enquiry into the direct and determining causes, and then into the primary indirect causes; we thus arrive at the variables which can be planned for and controlled by central authority. This order of investigating the various causal factors, which is the opposite of the natural order of such connections, may have proved a serious obstacle to the reader's work of intepretation.

THE BOOK'S SHAPE

The need to discuss the various factors, first separately and then in their complex interplay, imposed on Keynes an unusual way of structuring his work, one which runs against readers' expectations. Keynes's analytic method is based on the notion that there is an organic interdependence among economic variables, and in this way it aims to overcome the limits of the atomistic approach which had been characteristic of the classical theory. Keynes himself explains the systematic nature of the new analytic method at the point in *The General Theory* at which he clarifies what the new methodology amounts to:

> The object of our analysis is, not to provide a machine, or method of blind manipulation, which will furnish an infallible answer, but to provide ourselves with an organised and orderly method of thinking out particular problems; and, after we have reached a provisional conclusion, by isolating the complicating factors one by one, we then have to go back on ourselves and allow, as well as we can, for the probable interactions of the factors amongst themselves. This is the nature of economic thinking. (*CW*, VII, p. 297)[12]

Keynes's heuristic method thus sets itself to get over the narrowness of the classical approach by dealing with two opposed needs. On the one hand, there is the need to examine the various economic variables in isolation. And, on the other, there is the need to bring these independent studies together and to show up the close interrelations among the various variables which have been examined. This alternation between linear atomistic analyses and complex systemic integrations is reflected at the level of the expository form of the book. At that level, we find recurrent references back and forth to other parts of the book. Chick has vividly compared this technique to the expository language of cinema: 'Keynes's method is more like a film, a moving picture, made from snapshots (as films are), each snapshot systematically related to what has gone before. It is a story full of flashbacks – and flashes forward' (Chick 1983, p. 14). Keynes uses this continual referring of the reader to other parts of the book as a compromise between, on the one hand, the complexity and systemic interdependence of the parts of his analysis and, on the other, the linearity of the lay-out of the book as written. We can see how this compromise operates in *The General Theory* with a few quotations in which Keynes steps out of the text to help the reader to grasp the overall scheme of the book. What he provides are indications that different aspects of a given economic problem have to be discussed in different chapters:

> The theory of wages in relation to employment, to which we are here leading up, cannot be fully elucidated, however, until chapter 19 and its Appendix have been reached. (*CW*, VII, p. 18)

> We shall return to the aggregate supply function in chapter 20, where we discuss its inverse under the name of the *employment function*. But, in the main, it is the part played by the aggregate demand function which has been overlooked; and it is the aggregate demand function that we shall devote Books III and IV. (*CW*, VII, p. 89)

> It may be mentioned, in passing, that the effect of fiscal policy on the growth of wealth has been the subject of an important misunderstanding which, however, we cannot discuss adequately without the assistance of the theory of the rate of interest to be given in Book IV. (*CW*, VII, p. 95)

> Only at the conclusion of Book IV will it be possible to take a comprehensive view of the factors determining the rate of investment in their actual complexity. (*CW*, VII, p. 137)

In other places, before launching on the analysis of the parts of a given theory, Keynes gives a summary sketch of it, even though he is aware that the reader will have some difficulty in understanding the novel theory before it has been presented in full and its terminology explained:

> A brief summary of the theory of employment to be worked out in the course of the following chapters may, perhaps, help the reader at this stage, even though it may not be fully intelligible. The terms involved will be more carefully defined in due course. (*CW*, VII, p. 27)

On occasion, he has to break up the discussion of some economic variables, leaving the exposition suspended, to introduce further explanations which the reader might think of as mere digressions:

> In this and the next three chapters we shall be occupied with an attempt to clear up certain perplexities which have no peculiar or exclusive relevance to the problems which it is our special purpose to examine. Thus these chapters are in the nature of a digression, which will prevent us for a time from pursuing our main theme. (*CW*, VII, p. 37)

Sometimes the clarifications follow insistently one on another and produce the appearance of digressions on digressions. For instance, as we have seen in our last quoted passage, Chapters 4–6 are counted as a digression to which is added an appendix which itself serves as a digression:

> User cost has, I think, an importance for the classical theory of value which has been overlooked. There is more to be said about it than would be relevant in this place. But, as a digression, we will examine it somewhat further in this appendix. (*CW*, VII, p. 66)

Occasionally Keynes finds himself unable to hold up the discussion of some matter and has to introduce some aspects or terminology without being able adequately to clarify them:

> In some passages of this section we have tacitly anticipated ideas which will be introduced in Book IV. (*CW*, VII, p. 112)

> It would seem (following Mr. Kahn) that the following are likely in a modern community to be the factors which it is most important not to overlook (though the first two will not be fully intelligible until after Book IV has been reached). (*CW*, VII, p. 119)

The recurrent alternation between the presentation of new material and recourse to matters already discussed gives Keynes's work its peculiar quality, which is very different from that of the traditional polemical essay. Victoria Chick finds that the expository manner of *The General Theory* is in many ways like the typical structure of a play for the theatre:

> it might be helpful to compare the book to a play. When characters go off-stage, you do not presume them to be dead – they are likely to pop back at any time. The *General Theory* is rather like that. Early on (*G.T.* Chapter 3) you are given a sketch of the plot, but it is only much later (*G.T.* Chapters 19–21) that the full story is revealed. (Chick 1983, p. 28)

Unless he grasps Keynes's methodology, the reader is not likely to understand why matters which have once been treated keep on coming back. He is likely to read the alternating treatment of different matters as indicating, by its halts and swerves, a tentativeness in the line of thought being pursued. Hansen gives a reading of this sort:

> Book II of the *General Theory* is a detour. The argument which was commenced in Book I is interrupted and resumed in Book III. The intervening chapters, 4 to 7, are devoted to preliminary definitions and concepts which logically might better have been treated at the outset of the volume. But Keynes wanted the reader to get a taste of what was coming first. Accordingly, he postponed to Book II the dry and rather uninteresting consideration of the concepts and terms employed in the argument which followed. (Hansen 1953, p. 39)

Unless he sees how the various parts of the book work together, the reader is likely to think the worse of it. Hansen's comment that, if some of the chapters of *The General Theory* had not been written, not a great deal would have been lost (op. cit. pp. 155) is an emblematic instance of this sort of reading. And Hansen's is not the harshest of interventions.[13] Even when the reader is not tempted to eliminate parts of the text, when it is not understood or when it is in conflict with his own views, the value of the author's words tends to shrink in importance. For example, we find this at work in Friedman's attitude toward Chapter 19 of *The General Theory*. For him, the chapter adds nothing to Keynes's apparatus; but merely illustrates the application of that apparatus to a specific problem and provides grounds for thinking that downwards stickiness in salary levels is not only observable but politically desirable (Friedman 1972, p. 948).

However, even when the author's motivations for arranging his material in a given way escape the reader's immediate understanding, there is always some reason why the various parts of the text are disposed as they are. For instance, Chapter 23 is often thought of as 'superfluous'. In that chapter, Keynes reviews the views of various economists with whom he does not agree. Because it does nothing to support Keynes's own views and expounds theories which have already been subjected to criticism earlier in the book, the chapter has been thought of as redundant or merely repetitive. Nevertheless, in Keynes's scheme for the work, it is of the greatest importance because it does serve to shore up his own position. Indeed, Keynes presents the economists discussed in Chapter 23 as 'heretics' who, like Keynes himself, 'following their intuitions, have preferred to see the truth obscurely and imperfectly rather than maintain error, reached indeed with clearness and consistency and by easy logic but on hypotheses inappropriate to the facts' (*CW*, VII, p. 371).

The breadth of the analysis and the variety of factors taken into account require that the discussion should be of a high level of complexity. This leads to an occasional artificiality in Keynes's argumentative structure. Faced with this, the reader's response has sometimes been to look for a way of arriving at a reading of it which renders the text reasonable. As an example of this sort of repair work by the reader, we may cite Chick's analysis of Keynes on the supply curve:

> The structure of his argument, in effect, is the following:
> (i)   the labour supply curve of Classical theory is open to challenge.
> (ii) Even if we accept the supply curve and the partial-equilibrium framework of Classical theory, wages are sticky downward and employment is not always full because the adjustment mechanism presumed in Classical theory is not in fact present in modern industry.
> (iii) The partial equilibrium framework is, in any case, inappropriate.
> Perversely, however, he presented (ii) after (i), and (iii) does not appear until Chapter 19. (iii), if valid, would make discussion of (i) and (ii) unnecessary. (Chick 1983, p. 134)

The peculiar fragmentation of the book's structure has often been seen as an excuse for taking it apart and reassembling it. Indeed, in the decades after the publication of *The General Theory*, many ways of dealing with the text were proposed and as a result, many versions of Keynes's work were in circulation. Some examples can be seen from the following passage:

> Hicks and Hansen reduced him to a page and a diagram; Tobin, Modigliani and their heirs fitted him into the corsets of choice theory. By such rhetori-

cal moves the text was permanently transformed. Economists have known for some time how the book should be read (Leijonhufvud 1968) but do not want the old meanings back. They have made up their own text. (Klamer & McCloskey 1988, p. 14)

Understandably, readers' manoeuvrings had consequences. Widely differing accounts of the central strands of Keynes's theory were born out of the various proposals for organizing the material. For example, Blaug cites at least three distinct versions of Keynes's theory which can be arrived at by assembling the various lines of thought in the book in different ways:

(1) *hydraulic Keynesianism* – the 45 degree diagram type of income–expenditure theory and the IS–LM interpretation, which treats the Keynesian model as a special case rather than a general theory – also known as the 'neoclassical synthesis' or 'bastard Keynesianism', depending on your point of view; (2) *fundamentalist Keynesianism* – an emphasis on shifting expectations and pervasive uncertainty, as found in chap. 12 of *The General Theory* and Keynes's 1937 article 'The General Theory of Employment', implying that Keynes's approach cannot be reconciled with the neoclassical tradition; and (3) *disequilibrium Keynesianism* – a GE formulation of Keynes without a Walrasian auctioneer, incomplete and imperfect information, false price signals, and income-constrained quantity as well as price adjustments. (Blaug 1980, p. 222 n. 119)

THE TONE OF THE POLEMIC

The structure of Keynes's argumentation has often been criticized. He has been accused of not having always respected the logical sequence of the stages of his thought and of sometimes having left out parts which are necessary for an understanding of what he is putting forward. The result has sometimes been harshly described:

[*The General Theory*] is a work of profound obscurity, badly written and prematurely published. All economists claim to have read it. Only a few have. The rest feel a secret guilt that they never will. Some of its influence derived from its being extensively incomprehensible. Other scholars were needed to construe its meaning, restate its propositions in intelligible form. Those who initially performed this task – Joan Robinson in England, Alvin Hansen and Seymour Harris at Harvard – then became highly effective evangelists for the ideas. (Galbraith 1975, p. 218)

Keynes too felt that he had not always made his exposition as clear as it could be, as we see from this letter of August 1936 to R.G. Hawtrey: 'I am thinking of producing in the course of the next year or so what might be called *footnotes* to my previous book, dealing with various criticisms and particular points which want carrying further. Of course, in fact, the whole book needs re-writing and re-casting' (*CW*, XIV, p. 47).

Keynes's awareness of some lack of clarity at certain points in the book led him to choose a forthright tone in expounding his ideas. Indeed, he took it that a certain measure of conviction in putting forward new ideas was necessary to convince the reader of their goodness. Any hesitancy in the propounding of new theories would have been seen as a sign of uncertainty and so would have sacrificed the perlocutionary force of the argument. Keynes goes so far as to assert that, 'the author must, if he is to put his point of view clearly, pretend sometimes to a little more conviction than he feels. He must give his argument a chance, so to speak, not be too ready to depress its vitality with a wet cloud of doubt' (*CW*, VIII, p. 467). Even the advice of his friends was to no avail in getting him to tone down the combative style of his exposition.[14] Instead, it produced the opposite effect. Here for example, is how he responded in a letter to a colleague: 'The general effect of your reaction, apart from making me realise that I must re-write this drastically, is to make me feel that my assault on the classical school ought to be intensified rather than abated' (*CW*, XIII, p. 548).

Keynes's employment of this polemical tone shows his grip on the rhetorical techniques of argumentative practice. He exploits the prime trope of vehemently attacking the opposition's views so as to make his own argument all the more persuasive (cf. Govier 1987). However when *The General Theory* was published, its strongly disputatious tone was partly responsible for its not being properly understood. For it produced strong emotive reactions in the economists belonging to the Classical School which Keynes so violently attacked. These emotive reactions hindered a detached reading of the book and a rational interpretation of the new theory which it put forward. Many commentators at the time thought that a less aggressive tone would have got *The General Theory* more widely accepted among economists. In Pigou's view, it would have had a deeper influence on economic thought in the long run if it had been less concerned to raise the flag of revolution, emphasizing the points of agreement more and the points of disagreement less (quoted in Harris 1955, p. 10).

In any case, Keynes was not afraid of debate, but even sought it, because he was sure that it would bring about a wider public discussion which would smooth the way to a better understanding of his book. Keynes's clear-cut choice in this matter is clearly expressed in a letter to Roy Harrod: 'I *want*, so to speak, to raise a dust; because it is only out of the controversy that will arise that what I am saying will get understood' (*CW*, XIII, p. 548).

THE SHAPE OF KEYNES'S ARGUMENTS

Keynes himself was aware both that the organizational shortcomings of his book sometimes made his reader's job quite difficult, and that gaps in the structure of the argument created problems for the understanding of parts of the theory.

The accusation most frequently levelled at him has been that he omitted to shore up the argument for some of his assertions.[15] This sort of criticism bears out the impression that, in the process of construing the book, the reader brings to bear conventional patterns of interpretation which Keynes does not respect.

One of the commonest structures which arguments have been seen to take by the tradition of rhetoric is set out by Toulmin (1958). A claim, *C*, is generally taken to be based on some data, *D*, defended by a warrant, *W*. If there is some rebuttal, *R*, the claim may be weakened by a qualification, *Q*. In that case, some backing, *B*, may be added to underwrite the claim. Toulmin's example of this structure (cf. Toulmin 1958, p. 105) is as follows:

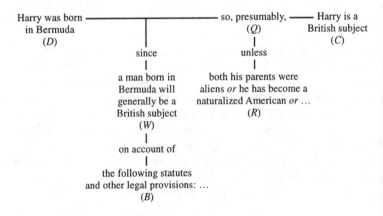

The reader frequently finds himself confronted with claims that are not given adequate backing in *The General Theory*. It is no wonder that Keynes was accused of being cryptic or ambiguous. Here, for example, is an instance that has been singled out:

> Thus in one place (p. 110), Mr Keynes declares, in paradoxical denial of what is 'commonly supposed', that 'we can be certain that a rise in the rate of interest will have the effect of reducing the amount actually saved'. But he neither gives facts to show that interest and saving have been related in this way in the past nor refers to some other work where this relation is established. (Beveridge 1937, p. 465, n. 3)

Again, Patinkin points out that in the theory of employment put forward in Chapter 3 of *The General Theory*, many of the assumptions of the theory are not spelt out in the discussion of that chapter. In order to understand the relations between the level of employment and the level of prices, we have to look at the contents of Chapter 21. Patinkin claims:

> But though all this is fairly clear from Chapter 21, in Chapter 3 itself we are in the most unhappy situation of having the logical consistency of the argument depend on a crucial assumption at whose existence in the chapter Keynes does not even hint! Furthermore, Keynes does not specify the details of the dynamic market mechanism which lies behind this assumption; nor does he always strictly adhere to it in the course of his subsequent exposition. (Patinkin 1976, p. 91)

We can see from the various interpretations which have been given of Keynes's theory that, when the reader finds himself in difficulties because of the lack of explicit authorial justification, he tries to reconstruct the text using the co-operative principles which underlie all communicative processes (cf. Grice 1975). In general, and if he is being rational, the reader takes the following steps:

(*a*)   The utterer asserts that p;

(*b*)   There is no reason to think that he is not observing the principles of cooperation;

(*c*)   He could not both assert that p and observe the principles of co-operation without also believing that q;

(*d*)   He knows (and knows that I know that he knows) that I am able to see that I must suppose that he believes that q;

(*e*)   He has done nothing to prevent me believing that q;

(*f*) It is his intention that I believe that *q*, or at least, he has no objection to my believing that *q*;

(*g*) Therefore, there is an implicature that *q*.

(Cf. van Eemeren and Grootendorst 1984, p. 120)

If this is the rational procedure for readers to take, the main causes of misunderstanding of a text's argument can be identified as the failure of one or other of the steps we have set out. The reader's failure to understand can, therefore, come about as a result under any of the following conditions:

(*A*) The reader has wrongly understood the meaning of the assertion that *p*;

(*B*) The writer has not respected the co-operative principles;

(*C*) In asserting that *p*, the writer has followed ideas of information which do not coincide with the reader's; for this reason, the reader unhesitatingly thinks of *q*, when the writer was thinking of *r*;

(*D*) The reader was unable to see that, from *p*, one must necessarily suppose that *q*; or

(*E*) The writer has prevented the reader from believing that *q*.

Thus far, we have already seen cases of (*A*), (*C*) and (*D*). Readers have not properly understood the meaning of the text or have followed interpretative schemes different from Keynes's and have thus made inferences which the author had not programmed for. These sorts of cases help explain only the failures of understanding which arise essentially from reader inability or uncooperativeness. Our overview of Keynes's writings has led us to the conclusion that we should not expect cases of (*E*), since Keynes repeatedly asserts that the mainspring of his polemical activity is to get readers to believe that *q*.

At the outset, we envisaged the need to take account also of failures of persuasiveness which could be attributed to the author's shortcomings. We are thus left with case (*B*). That is, we ought to turn our attention to Keynes's willingness to respect the principles of co-operation which underlie communication. Principles of this sort have been set out by Grice (1975, pp. 45ff.) in a set of maxims:

1. The author ought to say only what he thinks is true (Principle of Quality)

2. He ought not to give too much or too little information given the accepted purpose of the exchange (Principle of Quantity)
3. He ought to make his contribution appropriate to the context, including what has already been said (Principle of Relation)
4. He ought to express himself clearly and in an orderly way, avoiding ambiguity and other causes of misunderstanding (Principle of Manner).

Taking Keynes's respect for (1) and (3) for granted, we may proceed to consider how far he applies the other co-operative maxims. One of the commonest accusations levelled at Keynes is that of having broken (2) by providing less information than the reader needs. Specifically, the largest gaps which have been pointed out concern the lack of explanation of data, and the shortage of justification of some of his assertions. This latter is often put down to the immediacy of his writing and his strong desire to persuade: 'It was Keynes's object, in presenting his basic propositions, to avoid the qualifications and complications which were called for by a comprehensive treatment. In his burning anxiety to convince he did enormously oversimplify' (Kahn 1984, p. 159). In a letter to J.K. Hicks in June 1935, Keynes underlines the urge to convince the reader: 'I deliberately refrain in my forthcoming book from pursuing anything very far, my object being to press home as forcibly as possible certain fundamental opinions – and no more' (quoted in Moggridge 1976, p. 91). And within the book itself, Keynes sometimes warns the reader that he does not want to go so far into certain subjects whose complexity would call for a detailed analysis. He justifies himself in terms of making the argument leaner and easier:

> For the sake of simplicity of statement I have slurred the point that we are dealing with complex rates of interest and discount corresponding to the different lengths of time which will elapse before the various prospective returns from the asset are realised. But it is not difficult to re-state the argument so as to cover this point. (*CW*, VII, p. 137)

As Fouraker properly notes, Keynes often seems to be in a hurry to get to his conclusion. As a result, he takes what Fouraker calls 'short cuts'. In this respect, he thinks that Keynes resembles Marshall: 'Instead of leading the reader through the intricate analytical processes that their own minds had recently traversed, they would provide a short cut of an assumption whose purpose was to eliminate consideration of the difficult problem they had faced and solved' (Fouraker 1958, p. 66).

Drawing on what Coats (1988) has to say about Marshall's use of this sort of implicit argumentation, it might be thought that the fact that some of Keynes's assertions lack a fully worked-out justification can be explained in terms of the way that in Cambridge new ideas were discussed over a long period and circulated among the University teaching staff before being set down in writing. When written up, some of the logical scaffolding which had been expounded orally would be taken for granted and could be left out. Having in mind an audience like that, made up of his Cambridge colleagues, Keynes could think that not every single argumentative move was important for his exposition.

We can see here a conflict between, on the one hand, a principle of naturalness, according to which the author should provide all the information on a given subject in its *ordo naturalis* (cf. Merlini Barbaresi 1988), and, on the other, a principle of quantity, such as our (2) cited above from Grice. In accordance with the demands of relevance (cf. Sperber and Wilson 1986), it is the principle of quantity which prevails, allowing the author to avoid spelling out knowledge which he takes to be shared with his audience. The application of this principle is complicated by the fact that *The General Theory* is aimed at a variety of different audiences, only one of which – made up of those in Keynes's circle in Cambridge – was already acquainted with his novelties, while the others were encountering them for the first time.[16] From inspection of the argumentative procedures of *The General Theory*, we can see that Keynes gave pride of place to the former,[17] making the business of interpretation much more difficult for the latter groups by requiring them to go in for all sorts of interpretive jugglery. Fouraker takes this line, referring to both Marshall and Keynes:

> The major works are infested with oblique passages that the novice dismisses as manifestations of a poor writing style. It is only after he has seized upon some apparent flaw in the system and followed its implications that such passages lose their opaque quality. They are then recognized as admirably constructed defenses of the author's flank, indicating that he has already considered and resolved the objection. Many a criticism of the *Principles of Economics* and *The General Theory* has been transformed into an interpretation of some obscure paragraph by a rereading of the pertinent chapters. (Fouraker 1958, p. 67)

The 'oblique passages' to which Fouraker refers are those in which Keynes and Marshall leave out some essential stages of the line of thought they are pursuing. Making sense of these passages calls for a great effort of interpretation in as much as they become clear only once the reader has found a weak point on his own, worked out the tacit presuppositions it is based on, set out those presuppositions, seen how they figure in the system as a whole, and then generalized the discovery.

Likewise, Leontief (1937) pays attention to the 'implicit theorising' in Keynes. He picks on the definitions of 'labour-unit' and 'wage-unit' (*CW*, VII, pp. 41–4) and the accounts of aggregate supply and aggregate demand as examples from *The General Theory*. Nevertheless, he adds that it is so widespread a phenomenon that the embarrassment of riches makes the choice of appropriate examples particularly difficult (cf. Leontief 1937, p. 349; in 1966 reprint Vol I, p. 70). Within a few months of the publication of *The General Theory* Leontief underlined the risks which this sort of 'implicit theorising' carried. With great foresight, he anticipated the flurry of interpretations to which it would give rise:

> Ironically enough those who most often use the method of implicit solutions very seldom undertake themselves the onerous task of explicit interpretations. They formulate a number of implicit theorems, extend the argument one or two steps forward or backward, and then let the reader find the way home by himself. If an uncautious critic ventures to express some doubts as to the 'correctness' of the whole procedure, the short-cut theorist triumphantly points out that his implicit definition necessary has *some* explicit meaning. If the critic follows a path of his own, makes a serious attempt to find his way and gets lost, the theorist rightly but uncharitably accuses him of logical inconsistency and of inability to understand the correct meaning of the theorem. Scientific discussion degenerates into a comedy of errors and mistaken identities. (Leontief 1937, pp. 343–4; in 1966 reprint Vol I, pp. 64–5)

Our references to Fouraker and Leontief highlight the importance of the reader's task in decoding the text. It is his attentive rereading of various parts of the book which reconstructs the passages missing from the argumentative structure, and which provides a unified meaning to the assertions in the text.

There arises at this point an alternative hypothesis to account for the argumentative incompleteness of *The General Theory*. This depends on the thought that Keynes wished to stimulate the reader into a co-operative effort of interpretation of the book. Keynes's own words give support to this hypothesis:

> It is, I think, of the essential nature of economic exposition that it gives, not
> a complete statement, which, even if it were possible, would be prolix and
> complicated to the point of obscurity but a straight sample statement, so to
> speak, out of all the things which could be said, intended to suggest to the
> reader the whole bundle of associated ideas, so that, if he catches the
> bundle, he will not in the least be confused or impeded by the technical
> incompleteness of the mere words which the author has written down,
> taken by themselves. ... An economic writer requires from his reader much
> goodwill and intelligence and a large measure of cooperation. (*CW*, XIII, p.
> 470)

It is interesting to note how, in this passage, Keynes describes economists' mode of arguing as a succession of 'sample statements' which
work by suggesting to the reader a 'whole bundle of associated ideas'.
In this way, Keynes attributes to argumentative writing definitely literary properties: the reader takes cues from the weave of the text for
various personal associations, rather than for unambiguous conclusions
determined by an orderly and analytic set of premises and reasonings.

Another feature on which Keynes depends is the heuristic value of
insights. These allow both reader and writer to see matters which might
escape notice by the application of deductive and observational methods: 'Our practical intuition ... can take account of a more detailed
complex of facts than can be treated on general principles' (*CW*, VII, p.
49). Thus, Keynes was counting on the intuitive ability of his readers to
supply the background for the development of his argument. And he
was apt to lose patience when his thought was subjected to detailed
logic-chopping. One of his pupils attests to this attitude:

> He drew a distinction between the process of original thought in which one
> really relied on intuition and the process of scholastic thought in which one
> tidied up the mess and wrote out the results with some precision. I guess
> my interpretation of the transition from the *Treatise* to the *General Theory*
> was that he was trying to carry on these two procedures simultaneously and
> this was what made him, I think, quite impatient with a lot of people who
> were not prepared to follow him into it intuitively (as some of us were), but
> who wanted to see the thing written down precisely. (Bryce 1977, p. 41)

These intuitive capacities are important not only in the understanding of the text, but also in the process of its composition, for they
suggest the developments of the thought which is being set out and
clarify its details and application. The act of writing itself is part of
Keynes's heuristic activity which allows him to keep moving ahead, by
means of chains of intuitions and deductions, in the uncovering and

understanding of the facts of economic life. We can see the result of this process not only in what he has to say about the influence the act of writing has on him, but also in his claim that the object of his creative effort has its own separate existence independent of the person of the writer. As he says in the English Preface to *The General Theory*:

> This book, on the other hand, has evolved into what is primarily a study of the forces which determine changes in the scale of output and employment as a whole; and whilst it is found that money enters into the economic scheme in an essential and peculiar way, technical monetary detail falls into the background. (*CW*, VII, p. xxii)[18]

Claims about the creative and interpretative power of both the author's and the reader's intuitive abilities underwrite what we mooted earlier, that the polyvalency of *The General Theory* was not a chance matter, but the upshot of a deliberated choice.[19] Once again, we cannot help noticing how Keynes sets himself to upset the traditional canons of interpretation and to defeat the reader's expectations. The resources for finding Keynes's line of argument in the book depend entirely on the reader's capacity for giving an authentic interpretation to the 'mere words … taken by themselves'. As Keynes himself admits, the reader is asked to offer not just the usual sort of co-operation, but a much higher level of intuitive involvement and goodwill. Indeed, he refuses to extend to the reader too much concrete help in the business of interpreting the text. Rather, he is happy to discourage anyone who does not immediately grasp the meaning of what he says:

> How far is it worthwhile to anticipate objections or difficulties which will only be raised by someone who has not really followed the argument or taken the point? Where such further explanations may help to clarify the argument itself, yes. But beyond that, no. For there is no reasonable limit to the objections which can be raised by someone, who has misunderstood the argument, and an author is unlikely to be successful if he tries to anticipate beforehand what points will be taken by a critic whose mind is really running on another track. (*CW*, XXIX, p. 37)

Thus, Keynes operates an elitist conception of the writer's role which narrows the range of readers to those who are alert and highly motivated.

THE MATTER OF TERMINOLOGY

The ambiguities in Keynes's book and hence, the variety of interpretations that have been given of it, are also in part a result of the rather queer use *The General Theory* makes of technical terms. Indeed, Keynes has been accused of failing to limit his technical terms to one meaning each, and of having used a single word to refer to a variety of concepts. In so far as the reader has a reasonable expectation that, once a technical term has been introduced in one sense, it will continue to be used in that way until the author should decide otherwise, Keynes's attitude here can be regarded as an infringement of those expectations.

One term which crops up in *The General Theory* and which has been most frequently criticized for being used ambiguously is the word 'investment'. Keynes uses this word 'to mean both real investment and the purchase of Stock Exchange securities' (Kahn 1984, p. 150). Del Punta draws our attention to the fact that, after Keynes has given his definition of investment in Chapter 6, 'in subsequent chapters, up to the end of the book, the concept casts clouds over its surroundings, expands and contracts to expand and contract anew; so much so that the reader exhausts himself, often in vain, to understand what investment amounts to at any given point in the argument' (Del Punta 1977, p. 91). Indeed, three different meanings can be given to Keynes's uses of this term. The first is in Chapter 6, when saving is equated with investment. As Del Punta notes, this equation is 'arithmetic or, rather, definitional rather than conceptual' (Del Punta 1974, p. 764). Keynes's second account of the concept of investment comes in Book IV. There, he is discussing the relation between the rate of interest and the marginal efficiency of capital. Here, according to Del Punta, investment is understood in much the same way as is envisaged by the traditional marginalistic theory. A third account appears in Chapter 10, where Keynes considers the relation between investment and the multiplier:

> On this account, investment is further stripped – one might say wholly stripped – of the connotations attributed to it in the traditional meaning. The initial outlay which sets the multiplier going, which is referred to by the word 'investment', can be entirely different from investment understood in its true sense. (Del Punta 1974, p. 764)

Even though he is referring to three different concepts, Keynes does not feel the need to use three different words or to avoid ambiguity by tagging the one word with different adjectives.

Chick picks up a further passage in which the definition of 'investment' in Chapter 6 is tacitly modified in the following chapter:

> The result ... does *not* amount to the same thing as his definition of investment in Chapter 6, but differs in two respects: (i) the definition of Chapter 7 includes inventories ... which in Chapter 6 are excluded; and (ii) in the Chapter 7 definition, investment may be done by households as well as firms, while in Chapter 6, investment is strictly an entrepreneurial activity. (Chick 1983, p. 54)

Even the equation between the concepts of investment and saving which was set up in Chapter 6 has been a cause of disagreement among economists, which might have been avoided if Keynes had specified the equation more clearly:

> One source of confusion arose from the failure of his critics to realize that while investment and saving are always *equal*, they are not always in *equilibrium*. All this could have been avoided if Keynes had made it clear from the outset that the *equality* of saving and investment does not mean that they are necessarily in *equilibrium*. He was realistic enough to see this, as is revealed again and again in different sections of his book. But he never explicitly stated it, doubtless because the matter had not been clearly thought through. (Hansen 1953, p. 59)

On other occasions, Keynes uses two different words to apply to a single concept. However, since the two words refer to different aspects of the matter, it is no surprise that interpretation is made difficult. For instance, in Chapter 3 of *The General Theory*, the term 'aggregate demand price' is used in place of 'proceeds'. But, given that there are two sorts of 'proceeds' – those that are expected and those that come about at varying levels of employment – the reader is given no help in understanding which of the two sorts of 'proceeds' is in play. A reading of this passage is bound to be puzzling: 'The aggregate demand function which started out as expressing the proceeds expected by firms is suddenly converted into a function expressing the proceeds which firms actually realize at various levels of employment' (Murad 1966, pp. 59–60).

Marschak picks up a further case of Keynes's equivocal use of technical terms. Having recalled the two definitions of income given in *A Treatise on Money* and *The General Theory*, he points out that

> Mr. Keynes followed the 'second' definition of income (exclusion of windfall profits from income) in his *Treatise* of 1930, but emphatically aban-

doned it, in favour of the first definition in his *General Theory* of 1936. However, he occasionally relapses, in important places in the book, into speaking of 'savings = investment' as of an equilibrium condition, thus silently switching over to the other definition of income. (Marschak 1942, p. 65)

The accuracy of these criticisms is confirmed by what Keynes himself says. He is not overworried by attributing one *signatum* to each *signans*; on the contrary, elsewhere he explicitly says that he is happy to use technical terms in a less than rigorous way:

> A definition can often be *vague* within fairly wide limits and capable of several interpretations differing slightly from one another and still be perfectly serviceable and free from serious risks ..., provided that ... it is used consistently within a given context. If the author tries to avoid all vagueness and to be perfectly precise, he will become ... prolix and pedantic. (*CW*, XXIX, p. 36)

Once again, immediacy of expression is prized over precision of reference. Indeed, for Keynes, a vague definition will induce a certain polyvalency in a word so allowing the production of a larger number of associations of ideas. For this reason, Keynes prefers descriptive definitions to prescriptive ones,[20] so as to avoid setting up a univocal relation between the *definiens* and the *definiendum*, while leaving open the possibility, from time to time, of attaching a different *definiens* to the *definiendum*. While Keynes recognizes that definition is integral to any sort of specialist communication, he also sees it as a drag on the writer's creative expression and a brake on the range of the reader's intuitions. He writes in this vein to R.B. Bryce:

> In my book I have deemed it necessary to go into these matters at disproportionate length, whilst feeling that this was in a sense a great pity and might divert the readers' minds from the real issues. It is, I think, a further illustration of the appalling state of scholasticism into which the minds of so many economists have got which allow them to take leave of their intuitions altogether. Yet in writing economics one is not writing either a mathematical proof or a legal document. One is trying to arouse and appeal to the reader's intuitions; and if he has worked himself into a state when he has none, one is helpless. (Quoted in Patinkin and Clark-Leith 1977, p. 128)

Once more, Keynes stresses the literariness of economic writing and its clear difference from mathematics. Keynes's views on terminology are certainly in line with, and even follow from, the other theoretical and methodological novelties of *The General Theory*, and are themselves in some measure innovative.

In thinking about a taxonomy of definitions, Keynes refers to the trichotomy which Malthus had proposed (Malthus 1827). In this scheme, the three separate types of definition correspond to the three distinct types of discipline: mathematical sciences, natural sciences and moral sciences. Each type of science is distinguished by its own linguistic field and puts forward definitions in its own peculiar way. In mathematics, definition is an operation of naming which cannot stand on its own, since the definition of an entity is insufficient to guarantee that anything answers to the definition, which can only be established by supplying a proof. In the natural sciences, the coining of technical terms by nominal definitions refers to precise classifications which derive from the observation of natural phenomena or from empirical experimentation. In moral sciences, the definition of a term is the creation of the very concept which has been defined. Malthus gives 'freedom' as an example, which changes meaning according to who is using it, since each individual attaches the meaning of the term to the definition he has of it. Since Keynes conceives of economics as one of the moral sciences, he is committed to applying the type of definition which is specific to that sort of science.

There is also another motive which may have influenced Keynes to take up this attitude to the terminology he employs in his work. He may have thought that the adoption of a lexicon of words whose meaning and content is fixed in advance would be an obstacle to a discipline, such as economics, which he thought of as essentially dynamic.[21] His emphasis on the intrinsic dynamism of the various phenomena and on the interplay among the various economic factors dictated an overcoming of a static type of language.

Like any other evolving discipline, economics is continually involved in redefining its terms. As the contents of concepts are continually changing, so the form in which they are expressed must in turn bring itself up to date with those changes. As Kuhn has made clear (Kuhn 1970), every scientific revolution carries with it a restructuring of the semantic field in the discipline in which the revolution occurs. When that happens, the pre-existing terminology must be properly assigned new meanings, otherwise there will grow up misunderstandings and cross-purposes of the following sort: 'Two men whose discourse had previously proceeded with apparently full understanding may suddenly find themselves responding to the same stimulus with incompatible descriptions and generalizations' (Kuhn 1970, p. 210). Keynes frequently refers to the author's right to change the meanings of words introduced in earlier writings, and he pokes fun at those of his colleagues who criticized him for such changes of opinion: 'I seem to see the elder parrots sitting round and saying: "You can *rely* upon us. Every day for thirty years, regardless of the weather, we have said 'What a lovely morning!' But this is a bad bird. He says one thing one day, and something else the next"' (*CW*, XX, p. 502). Clearly, what Keynes had been taken to task for, was not so much exercising his right to alter the extension of a given concept or to redefine a given word; rather, it was the way he went about doing so. Some colleagues clearly felt that in order to prevent misunderstandings among the practitioners of a given discipline, it is necessary to declare openly every change of meaning and to ensure that every subsequent employment of a term reflects the new definition. This being so, the redefinitions of 'savings' and 'investment' which came about between *A Treatise on Money* and *The General Theory* are legitimate only if they are clearly spelt out in the latter book; otherwise ambiguity and puzzlement arise for the reader every time these words are used in *The General Theory* without appropriate discrimination among the various meanings given to them in the two books.

Keynes makes fairly clear the extent to which he is dissatisfied with the amount of completeness and accuracy which the process of definition can reach. He recognizes that, however complete a definition might be, it can accentuate only some of the aspects of a phenomenon or concept. Linguistic and semiotic research confirms this insight. C.S. Peirce arrives at similar conclusions about the process of definition. By reporting the following definition of lithium, he brings to light the way in which it points to the metal's other connotative as well as denotative properties:

> If you look into a textbook of chemistry for a definition of *lithium* you may be told that it is that element whose atomic weight is 7 very nearly. But if the author has a more logical mind he will tell you that if you search among minerals that are vitreous, translucent, grey or white, very hard, brittle, and insoluble, for one which imparts a crimson tinge to an unluminous flame, this mineral being triturated with lime or witherite rats-bane, and then fused, can be partly dissolved in muriatic acid, and duly purified, it can be converted by ordinary methods into a chloride, which being obtained in the solid state, fused, and electrolyzed with half a dozen powerful cells will yield a globule of a pinkish silvery metal that will float on gasolene; and the

material of *that* is a specimen of lithium. The peculiarity of this definition –
or rather this precept that is more serviceable than a definition – is that it
tells you what the word lithium denotes by prescribing what you are to *do*
in order to gain a perceptual acquaintance with the object of the word.
(Peirce 1931, 2.330)

All the properties listed by Peirce are specific to lithium. But they are
more or less important according to the use one wishes to make of the
element. According to the feature which is in question, we might refer
to its hardness, to its alkalinity, to its colour or to its lightness. Every
definition can include both the constitutive features – the monadic or
primary characteristics (Eco 1979) – of the concept, as well as ingredients which are indicative of the concept. Even though, as descriptions
of the way the substance behaves – in the case cited by Peirce, 'being
triturated with lime or witherite rats-bane, and then fused, can be partly
dissolved in muriatic acid' and so on – these indicative ingredients of a
definition can be properly attributed to the substance, they do not
represent its specific qualities and, therefore, are not definitional of it.
In this way, a definition which emphasizes indicative features over
constitutive features is likely to give rise to ambiguity.

There are other cases in which, as a result of the growth of knowledge in a given science, the constitutive features of a concept themselves undergo change and thus produce misunderstanding. We might
think, for example of the word 'atom', whose root is in the idea of
indivisibility, or 'hypnosis', which for the ancient Greeks was connected with sleep. As a result of scientific advances, the constitutive
features of these terms, which were written into the original definitions,
have changed. They no longer refer to the features which the etymol-
ogies of the words would suggest.

Keynes is alive to the multifariousness of the semantics of definition.
But he is not too concerned to ward off the danger of ambiguity in the
words he uses. Quite the contrary; he chooses to mobilize as fully as
possible the allusive and metaphorical potential of language. Indeed,
both in giving definitions and in proposing arguments, Keynes makes
considerable use of figurative techniques, such as metaphor, the better
to exploit his reader's emotive and cultural responses as well as their
intuitive and rational capacities.

Keynes is fully aware of the broad power of suggestion which metaphors offer and he uses them to stimulate not only his reader's emotions, but also their understanding and knowledge.[22] Metaphors are
particularly well adapted to embodying Keynes's polemical method in

so far as their highly evocative charge sets in train a series of references to different linguistic levels and to different ranges of experience. Mirowski points out this feature of metaphor very clearly: 'The use of metaphor sets up a field of secondary and tertiary resonances, contrasts and comparisons that do not merely describe, but also reconstruct and transform the original metaphorical material' (Mirowski 1988, p. 136).[23]

THE CHOICE OF ORDINARY LANGUAGE

In order to offer the reader a greater degree of discretion in the interpretation of the text, Keynes adopted a non-formal, ordinary language for the composition of *The General Theory*. He deliberately refused to employ a formalized language, with its narrow frame of reference and univocity. Such a choice would not only have hindered the development of the methodology which he wished to recommend, but would have been inimical to Keynes's aim of rousing up associations of ideas and interrelations among the various facets of the terms and concepts which underlie his systematic approach. As he himself says: 'Too large a proportion of recent "mathematical" economics are merely concoctions, as imprecise as the initial assumptions they rest on, which allow the author to lose sight of the complexities and interdependencies of the real world in a maze of pretentious and unhelpful symbols' (*CW*, VII, p. 298). What makes a formalized language inappropriate for the discussion of theoretical matters, not only in Keynes's thought but in economics in general, is that the univocal reference of each term in the vocabulary to a specified concept cannot take into account the need to give words different meanings in different contexts, and at different points in the procedure. Such a language can be useful only in those disciplines in which theoretical discussion does not call for multiple definitions of the concepts they employ. This does not apply to economics, where the complexity and interconnectedness of its parts do not admit of atomistic analysis.[24] As Keynes puts it:

> It is a great fault of symbolic pseudo-mathematical methods of formalising a system of economic analysis ... that they expressly assume strict independence between the factors involved and lose all their cogency and authority if this hypothesis is disallowed; whereas ordinary discourse, where we are not blindly manipulating but know all the time what we are doing and what the words mean, we can keep 'at the back of our heads' the necessary reserves and qualifications and the adjustments which we shall

have to make later on, in a way in which we cannot keep complicated partial differentials 'at the back' of several pages of algebra which assume that they all vanish. (*CW*, VII, pp. 297–9)

Translating thought into the precise and unequivocal terms of a symbolic–mathematical language is an obstacle to the further development of that thought itself. Keynes writes in a letter to Roy Harrod:

> In chemistry and in physics and other natural sciences the object of experiment is to fill the actual values of the various quantities and factors appearing in an equation or a formula; and the work when done is once for all. In economics that is not the case and to put a model into a quantitative formula is to destroy its usefulness as an instrument of thought. (*CW*, XIV, p. 299)

In view of these considerations, there is nothing haphazard about Keynes's choice of ordinary language. It is in line with and follows from the other methodological and theoretical innovations which we have been spelling out. By allowing his own words to have a number of meanings, Keynes changes the very concept of the language of economics and deprives it of the univocity and singleness of reference which are characteristic of the language used in mathematics and the natural sciences.

CONCLUSIONS

From our analysis of Keynes's text, we have seen that the ambiguity of *The General Theory* is not due so much to accidental or secondary factors such as haste, insufficient planning or negligent revision, but to a precise choice made by the author himself. Keynes meant his book to be an 'open-ended work', where we take that term to cover what Eco (1979) discusses in *The Role of the Reader*. *The General Theory* outlines the main themes of a new theory without stopping the reader from intervening actively in interpreting it and bringing the author's creation to fruition. Its final form was aimed at making it elastic, capable of being read in a variety of ways, and open to the critical and interpretative agency of the reader. A year after the book's publication, Keynes offered the following comment which supports the account we have been giving:

I am more attached to the comparatively simple fundamental ideas which underlie my theory than to the particular forms in which I have embodied them, and I have no desire that the latter should be crystallised at the present stage of the debate. If the simple basic ideas can become familiar and acceptable, time and experience and the collaboration of a number of minds will discover the best way of expressing them. (*CW*, XIV, p. 111)

We might wonder whether this way of structuring his material helped the fortunes of the book and author. It is certain that the innovativeness of Keynes's theory was powerfully emphasized by his various methodological and stylistic choices in composing *The General Theory*. The choices we have reviewed include his new methodological outlook, the use of a more literary style with less technical vocabulary, his highly polemical tone, and the strong persuasive aims of his argumentation. Its popularity was also certainly helped by the high level of ambiguity which Keynes introduced into the book; for, it has made the book a standard reference-point in specialist discussion for more than fifty years. As Samuelson rightly observes, 'It is not unlikely that future historians of economic thought will conclude that the very obscurity and polemical character of the *General Theory* ultimately served to maximize its long-run influence' (Samuelson 1983, p. 193). Moreover, by provoking this wide-ranging and longstanding debate, the ambiguousness of Keynes's book has allowed his economic theory to be more clearly defined and more fully formulated by the exegetical efforts of his many readers. *The General Theory* is one of the few non-literary texts in which the author, willingly and knowingly, gives the reader not merely the role of decoding the text and assenting to the views propounded, but an altogether more demanding and important role as the author's collaborator in the working out of the final form and the exact meaning of the new economic theory.

NOTES

1. In this chapter, we use '*The General Theory*' to refer to *The General Theory of Employment, Interest and Money*, first published by Macmillan, London, 1936. In accordance with practice in the rest of this volume, our references are to the text reprinted in Vol. VII of the *Collected Writings of John Maynard Keynes*. This edition is signalized with the initials *CW*.
2. In a 1938 letter to Roy Harrod, Keynes likens economics to a philosophical discipline, saying that it is a branch of logic, one way of thinking.
3. We can see how correct Keynes's view was from its high degree of balance. As Carabelli notes:

One of Keynes's merits was that of refusing the operation of removing and concealing the so-called irrational (or metaphysical) factors, which was tacitly performed by the positivist scheme. At the same time, he was also able to avoid the symmetrical reversal of the rationalist position, such as extolling irrational factors, as he did not fall either into mere historicism or subjectivism and pragmatism which were to characterise modern Bayesian developments in economics. (Carabelli 1988, p. 236)

4. Keynes frequently refers to the instinctual aspect of the behaviour of *homo oeconomicus*; for example, in the following passage from *Essays in Persuasion*:

The essential characteristic of capitalism [is] ... dependent upon an intense appeal to the money-making and money-loving instincts of individuals as the main motive force for the economic machine (*CW*, IX, p. 293).

5. The terms 'locutionary' and 'perlocutionary' are used in the sense suggested by Austin (1962) and Searle (1969). 'Locution' is the act of saying something; 'illocution' is the act performed in saying something; and 'perlocution' is the effect produced by saying something.

6. For examples of Keynes's argumentative strategies and stylistic choices in *The General Theory*, see Gotti (1988).

7. Fletcher emphasizes the great impact which *The General Theory* had on the world of economics:

Confounding its critics the book rapidly conquered professional opinion and established Keynesian economics as the orthodoxy for the following four decades. It also provided the main inspiration for policy-makers, who were able to preside over an era of such outstanding economic achievement, in employment, growth and relative stability of the price level, that it seems in retrospect a Golden Age. (Fletcher 1987, p. xvii)

8. A.W. Coats expresses a similar view, saying that the Keynesian revolution of the 1930s is one of the most impressive cases in economics of a change of paradigm in Kuhn's sense. Coats notes that Keynes's own achievement was preceded both by precursors who are not always credited and by a growing sense of the inadequacy of the existing theory. The acceptance of the new vision was accompanied in many cases by 'a conversion experience' and the revolution was carried out by a group of relatively young economists, if we allow Keynes to have been a Peter Pan figure. Cf. Coats 1969, p. 293; see also Leijonhufvud 1976, p. 83.

9. Patinkin expresses the same view:

And the best evidence of the existence of such ambiguities and obscurities is the fact that forty years later disagreements continue to go on in the literature about the role played in the *General Theory* by such crucial assumptions as wage rigidities, the 'liquidity trap', the interest elasticity of investment, unemployment equilibrium, and the like – not to speak of the protracted exegetical debate about the meaning of Keynes' aggregate supply function. (Patinkin 1976, p. 23)

10. This view is also expressed by, among others, Schumpeter:

The quality of [Keynes's] work suffered from its quantity and not only as to form: much of his secondary work shows the traces of haste, and some of his most important work traces of incessant interruptions that injured its growth. Who fails to realise this – to realise that he beholds work that has never been allowed to ripen, has never received the last finishing touch – will never do justice to Keynes's powers. (Schumpeter 1952, p. 271; cf. also Robinson 1964, p. 94)

11.   The word 'aberrant' is used without any negative connotation. It indicates merely a decodification which is far from faithful to the author's intentions and which undermines them. It is this sense that Eco has in mind in his *The Role of the Reader* (1979).

12.   Keynes makes frequent reference to the need for a systematic approach to economic variables; here is a passage from his memoir of Edgeworth:

We are faced at every turn with the problems of organic unity, of discreteness, of discontinuity – the whole is not equal to the sum of the parts, comparisons of quantity fail us, small changes produce large effects, the assumptions of a uniform and homogeneous continuum are not satisfied (*CW*, X, p. 262).

13.   Thus Patinkin:

Let us now return to Keynes' puzzling reference to the point of intersection of his aggregate demand and supply curves as the point where 'the entrepreneurs' expectations of profit will be maximised' (*G.T.* p. 25 quoted above) and suggest that these words should simply be deleted from the *General Theory.* (Patinkin 1976, pp. 92–3; contested by Musu 1977, pp. 44–5)

14.   For example Roy Harrod writes to Keynes:

What I think is important from the point of view of the effect and influence of the work is that you should minimise and not maximise the amount of accepted doctrine that your views entail the scrapping of. A general holocaust is more exciting. But everything you write now has such immense relevance that you no longer require these artificial stimulants to secure attention. Don't go out of your way to provoke dogged resistance on the part of professional economists! (*CW*, XIII, p. 537)

15.   See, for example Patinkin:

Keynes frequently failed to specify the exact nature of the assumptions that underlay his argument. (Patinkin 1976, p. 23)

16.   Bellofiore is one commentator who underlines the importance for Keynes of the different readers to whom his writing was addressed. Some of his considerations surface in section 6 of Bellofiore's first contribution to the present volume, and in Bellofiore 1988, p. 459.

17.   Keynes himself confirms the principal intended audience of his *magnum opus* in the Preface to the French edition of *The General Theory*, where he says:

I was wanting to convince my own environment and did not address myself with sufficient directness to outside opinion (*CW*, VII, p. xxxi).

18.   As Marzola notes in her contribution to this volume, the act of writing has its own evolution which itself changes. In the case of *The General Theory* it is the use of the pronoun 'it', which signifies the exercise of writing as the source of revelations for the writer himself. (Cf. also Marzola 1988, p. 9)

19.   This attitude has attracted sometimes fierce criticisms, such as Leijonhufvud's, in which Keynes is defined as a Delphic oracle who issues profound thoughts to shake the world while he is in a total trance (cf. Leijonhufvud 1968, p. 35).

20.   Naess (1981, p. 45) distinguishes a 'prescriptive' definition, in accordance with which a given term, *a*, ought, in a given context, always to mean *b*, from a 'descriptive' definition, in which *a* sometimes means *b*.

21.   Lindley Fraser expresses a similar view, noting the danger, if a uniform terminology were adopted by all economists, of being left behind by changing events – a

static terminology is not well adapted to dynamic phenomena (Fraser 1937, pp. vii–viii).
22. The importance of the experiential and cognitive aspect of metaphor is well highlighted by Lakoff and Johnson:

> The essence of metaphor is understanding and experiencing one kind of thing in terms of another (Lakoff and Johnson 1980, p. 5).

23. The close interrelation between linguistic and experiential aspects is stressed in Hübler's analysis (1990) of the metaphors used to refer to the Stock Market crash of October 1987.
24. Referring to Keynes's choice, Rossini-Favretti observes that the limitation of the 'atomic' hypothesis is the counterpart of the complexity of the natural world. This brings out the need for a logic which, unlike the logic of artificial languages, is 'organic' and made up of an indefinite number of parts: the logic of ordinary language (Rossini-Favretti 1988, p. 15).

REFERENCES

Austin, J.L. (1962) *How to Do Things with Words*, Oxford: Clarendon Press.
Bellofiore, R. (1988) 'Retorica ed economia. Su alcuni sviluppi recenti della filosofia della scienza e il loro rapporto con il metodo di Keynes', *Economia Politica*, **3**, December.
Beveridge, W. (1937) 'The Place of the Social Sciences in Human Knowledge', *Politica* **II** (9), September.
Blaug, M. (1980), *The Methodology of Economics*, Cambridge: Cambridge University Press.
Bryce, R.B. (1977) 'Keynes as Seen by his Students in the 1930s' in Pantinkin, D. and Clark-Leith, J. (eds), *Keynes, Cambridge and the General Theory*, London: Macmillan.
Burton, J. et al. (eds) (1986) *Keynes's 'General Theory': Fifty Years On*, London: The Institute of Economic Affairs.
Carabelli, A.M. (1988) *On Keynes's Method*, London: Macmillan.
Chick, V. (1983) *Macroeconomics after Keynes*, Oxford: Philip Allen.
Coats, A.W. (1969) 'Is there a Structure of Scientific Revolutions in Economics?', *Kyklos*, **XXII** (2).
Coats, A.W. (1988) 'Economic Rhetoric: The Social and Historical Context' in Klamer, A. (et al) (eds), *The Consequences of Economic Rhetoric*, Cambridge: Cambridge University Press.
Del Punta, V. (1974) 'L'investimento in Keynes: un concetto fuorviante per la politica economica' *Rivisita di politica Economica*, **LXIV** (6).
Del Punta, V. (1977) 'Keynes e la politica economica: aspetti controversi della politica economica keynesiana' in *La teoria keynesiana quarant' anni dopo*, Milan: Giuffrè, for the Italian Economic Society.
Eco, U. (1979) *The Role of the Reader*, Bloomington: Indiana University Press.
Fletcher, G.E. (1987) *The Keynesian Revolution and its Critics*, London: Macmillan.

190   *John Maynard Keynes: Language and Method*

Fouraker, L.E. (1958) 'The Cambridge Didactic Style', *The Journal of Political Economy*, **LXVI**.
Fraser, L. (1937) *Economic Thought and Language*, London: A & C Black.
Friedman, M. (1972) 'Comments on the Critics', *Journal of Political Economy*, **80**, Sept–Oct.
Galbraith, J.K. (1975) *Money: Whence it Came and Where it Went*, London: Andre Deutsch.
Gotti, M. (1988) 'Il modello argomentativo di J.M. Keynes nella *General Theory*', *Quaderni del Dipartimento di Linguistica e Letterature Comparate*, vol. 4, Bergamo: Università degli Studi.
Govier, T. (1987) *Problems in Argument: Analysis and Evaluation*, Dordrecht: Foris.
Grice, H.P. (1975) 'Logic and Conversation' in Cole, P. and Moregan, J.L. (eds), *Syntax and Semantics: Speech Acts*, New York: Academic Press.
Hansen, A.H. (1953) *A Guide to Keynes*, London: McGraw-Hill.
Harris, S.E. (1955) *John Maynard Keynes*, New York: Charles Scribner's Sons.
Hübler, A. (1990) 'On Metaphors Related to the Stock Market: Who Lives by Them?', in De Stasio, C., Gotti, M. and Bonadei, R. (eds), *La rappresentazione verbale e iconica: valori estetici e funzionali*, Milan: Guerini.
Kahn, R.F. (1984) *The Making of Keynes' General Theory*, Cambridge: Cambridge University Press.
Keynes, J.M. (1937) 'The General Theory of Employment', *Quarterly Journal of Economics*.
Klamer, A. and McCloskey, D. (1988) 'Economics in the Human Conversation' in Klamer (et al) (eds), *The Consequences of Economic Rhetoric*, Cambridge: Cambridge University Press.
Klamer, A., McCloskey, D. and Solow, R.M. (eds) (1988) *The Consequences of Economic Rhetoric*, Cambridge: Cambridge University Press.
Kuhn, T.S. (1970, 2nd edn) *The Structure of Scientific Revolutions*, Chicago: Chicago University Press.
Lakoff, G. and Johnson, G. (1980) *Metaphors We Live By*, Chicago: Chicago University Press.
Latsis, S.J. (ed.) (1976) *Method and Appraisal in Economics*, Cambridge: Cambridge University Press.
Leijonhufvud, A. (1968) *On Keynesian Economics and the Economics of Keynes*, Oxford: Oxford University Press.
Leijonhufvud, A. (1976) 'Schools, Revolutions and Research Programmes' in Latsis, S.J. (ed.), *Method and Appraisal in Economics*, Cambridge: Cambridge University Press.
Lekachman, R. (ed.) (1964) *Keynes' General Theory: Reports of Three Decades*, New York: St. Martin's Press.
Leontief, W. (1937) 'Implicit Theorizing: A Methodological Criticism of the Neo-Cambridge School', *Quarterly Journal of Economics*, vol. LI, repr. (1966) *Essays in Economics*, vol. I, Oxford: Basil Blackwell.
Malthus, T.R. (1827) *Definitions in Political Economy*, London.
Marschak, J. (1942) 'Identity and Stability in Economics: A Survey', *Econometrica*, **X**.

Marzola, A. (1988) 'Letterarietà e immaginario nel discorso economico di J.M. Keynes', paper presented to the seminar in Pavia 6 February 1988.

Merlini Barbaresi, L. (1988) *Markedness in English Discourse*, Parma: Zara.

Mirowski, P. (1988) 'Shall I Compare thee to a Minkowksi–Ricardo–Leontief–Metzler Matrix of the Mosak–Hicks Type?', in Klamer, A. (et al) (eds) *The Consequences of Economic Rhetoric*, Cambridge: Cambridge University Press.

Moggridge, D.E. (1976) *Keynes*, London: Macmillan.

Murad, A. (1966) *What Keynes Means*, London: Athena Publishing.

Musu, I. (1977) 'Disequilibrio, rigidità e teoria keynesiana' in *La teoria keyesiana quarant' anni dopo*, Milan: Giuffrè for the Italian Economic Society.

Naess, A. (1981, 2nd ed.) *Communication and Argument*, Oslo: Oslo University Press.

Patinkin, D. (1976) *Keynes' Monetary Thought*, Durham, N.C.: Duke University Press.

Patinkin, D. (1977) 'The Process of Writing "The General Theory": A Critical Survey' in Patinkin, D. and Clark-Leith, J. (eds), *Keynes, Cambridge and the General Theory*, London: Macmillan.

Patinkin, D. and Clark-Leith, J. (eds) (1977) *Keynes, Cambridge and the General Theory*, London: Macmillan.

Peirce, C.S. (1931) *Collected Papers*, Cambridge, Mass.: Harvard University Press.

Robinson E.A.G. (1964) 'Could there have been a "General Theory" without Keynes?', in Lekachman, R. (ed.) *Keynes' General Theory: Reports of Three Decades*, New York: St. Martin's Press.

Rossini-Favretti, R. (1988) 'L'argomentazione nella comunicazione e nell'epistemologia keynesiana', *Studi italiani di linguistica teorica e applicata*, **XVIII** (1).

Samuelson, P.A. (1964) 'The General Theory', in Lekachman, R. (ed.), *Keynes' General Theory: Reports of Three Decades*, New York: St. Martin's Press.

Samuelson, P.A. (1983) 'Lord Keynes and "The General Theory"', in Wood, J.C., *John Maynard Keynes: Critical Assessments*, vol. II, London: Croom Helm.

Schumpeter, J.A. (1952) *Ten Great Economists from Marx to Keynes*, London: Allen & Unwin.

Searle, J.R. (1969) *Speech Acts*, Cambridge: Cambridge University Press.

Sperber, D. and Wilson, D. (1986) *Relevance*, Oxford: Basil Blackwell.

Toulmin, S. (1958) *The Uses of Argument*, Cambridge: Cambridge University Press.

van Eemeren, F.H. and Grootendorst, R. (1984) *Speech Acts in Argumentative Discussions*, Dordrecht: Foris.

Vercelli, A. (1987) *Keynes dopo Lucas*, Rome: La Nuova Italia Scientifica.

Yeager, L.B. (1986) 'The Keynesian Heritage in Economics', in Burton, J. et al (eds) *Keynes's 'General Theory': Fifty Years On*, London: The Institute of Economic Affairs.

6. Rhetoric and Imagination in the Economic and Political Writings of J.M. Keynes

Alessandra Marzola

INTRODUCTION

Argument and Rhetoric in Economic Writing

The boundaries of classical rhetoric have been redefined and broadened by the new wave of studies in rhetoric which has been under way since the 1950s. In the new dispensation, the ways of organizing material and the techniques for setting it out which had been fully explored in Aristotelian rhetoric are no longer regarded as embellishments superadded to the discussion on purely persuasive and aesthetic grounds. Instead, they have come to be regarded as intrinsic to, and inherent in, the structuring of any type of argumentation. The promotion of rhetoric has been one unsurprising consequence of the crisis which has precipitated for Cartesian reason and for the criterion of indisputable certainty. Such a criterion has been put to use in underwriting a stark separation between the language of the sciences, which had been hallmarked by reference to evidence, and the language of other disciplines, such as philosophy, law and religion, which made room for pluralism and controvertible hypotheses. As Perelman notes:

> It is therefore clear if no space is left by the Cartesian ideal of universally applicable evident knowledge for rhetoric and dialectic, every time that a given subject is seen to fall outside the scope of knowledge, the value of rhetoric and dialectic is enhanced. One criticism of the idea of evidence which exemplifies the way in which evidence vanishes when we try to go beyond subjective intuition in trying to communicate by means of a language which never imposes itself, helps to show that the choice of a means of expression is, if not arbitrary, which it rarely is, at least the resultant of rhetorical and dialectical considerations. (Perelman 1981, p. 169)

Rhetoric and argumentation have been the natural mode in which to expound any thought whose self-evidence is not taken as given:

> Thus, all human reasoning about facts, decisions, beliefs, opinions and values are no longer thought of as obedient to the logic of an Absolute Reason, but are seen in their actual negotiations with emotional attachments, historical judgments and practical motivations. Seen in this way, persuasion irreversibly loses the aura of fraudulence which has accompanied it since the Golden Age of classical rhetoric ... and becomes one of the techniques of rational interaction, subject to doubts and revisions, and kept in check by a variety of extralogical circumstances. (Eco 1977, p. 345)

Despite being accepted in linguistic and rhetorical studies of the most far-flung disciplines, these premises have not been taken on board in the various subjects which have accorded themselves the status of sciences. Although the epistemological debate which has been revived by the neo-Positivist school has attracted wide notice, it is symptomatic that its implications for the meaning and function of rhetoric in the procedures of scientific discussion have been underestimated or entirely overlooked. It seems that, when it comes to the importance to be given both to writing and reading, the pragmatic attitude of the modern scientist towards language is in large measure influenced by the Cartesian principle of self-evidence.

The same goes, on the whole, for economic theory and for the critical reflections arising from it, which have been preponderantly concerned with the specifiable content of thoughts and with the demonstrative validity of arguments. It is only recently that the work of an economist, Donald M. McCloskey (1985), has focused on the importance of rhetoric and argumentation in economists' writings, even if its aims are less than clear, as has been shown elsewhere (Bellofiore 1988). It is not a matter of chance that among the many examples McCloskey gives, there is little mention of the writings of Keynes, an economist who shows, even to the casual observer, a theoretical and practical grasp of the problems of argumentation and rhetoric.

McCloskey's omission might be put down to the role which Keynes assigns to rhetoric, a role which, particularly in *The General Theory*, comes dangerously close to being indistinguishable from the analytic method which is there being put forward. Keynes's economic writing shows, contrary to what McCloskey might think, that the role of rhetoric is not that of persuading the intended recipients of the validity of *any* argument 'offering a vantage-point from which to admire and criticise radically different metaphors for economic life' (McCloskey 1985). Rather, for Keynes, the role of rhetoric is that of corroborating a very particular and innovative analytic method which is not different in kind from, but is point-for-point opposed to, the method of what he calls the 'classical' theory.

Rhetoric and Argument in Keynes

Keynes's unmistakable interest in and sensitivity to the problems of language can be accounted for by his intellectual background, which has been painstakingly explored (cf. Skidelski 1983). We may briefly recall that, in his most active years, Keynes was closely involved with the Bloomsbury Group which had embarked on intense theoretical speculation and narrative experimentation, aimed at replacing the out-worn notions about the relation between language and reality (cf. Bonadei 1988). And we ought not to forget the range of Keynes's interests and writings, which bears witness to his argumentative skill in adjusting his language to his intended audience, whether he is discuss-ing politics, economics or broader human affairs. But this undeniable flexibility has never been set alongside his specifically economic writ-ings in *The Treatise on Money* and *The General Theory*. In these works, he generally makes use of unformalized arguments and prefers ordi-nary language, as he himself explains and justifies. These features have caused some consternation and have given rise to efforts to reformulate and explain the complexities, frequently by reducing them to closed and systematic models, eliminating all the parts which break away from established expectations and immediate usefulness. In addition, the relevance of Keynes's political writings to his contributions to economics has been discounted, and the richness of their rhetorical and argumentative structure has been put down as a curiosity of the folklore of Keynes's strangely versatile talent (cf. Gotti 1988).

Many problems are raised and lines of enquiry opened by the start-ling way in which the importance of language is downgraded, both in economics in general and in the particularly telling case of Keynes. It has seemed worthwhile to engage on an account, for all that it is incomplete, of the rhetorical aspect of Keynes's political and economic writings. This may help to provide not only a new and perhaps enlight-ening reading of Keynes's specifically economic thought, but on a broader front, also a tentative re-examination of the methods which pervade economists' critical thought.

The Rhetoric of Persuasion and Analogical Thought

Argumentation, considered as a rhetoric of persuasion,[1] is a fundamental feature of Keynes's writing. In the two texts on which we shall focus, from different periods and aimed at different readerships, *The Economic Consequences of the Peace* and *The General Theory*, rhetoric is elaborated in different ways. But we can also see certain indicative similarities as well as the differences between what we might sum up as the discursive narrative style of *The Economic Consequences* and the expository treatment in *The General Theory* which respects the academic conventions. In both cases, the argumentative technique relies heavily on dissociations within a single thought so that, in trying to resolve a difficulty raised by a widely-held opinion, it becomes necessary to separate elements in such a way as to make space for a new organization of them (cf. Perelman 1981, p. 63).

Keynes's use of this argumentative strategy has methodological and semantic implications which we shall examine below. Suffice it for the present to note those which lead Perelman to say that the dissociative technique is typical of philosophical arguments. By distinguishing, relative to elements which are said to be the same, what is real from what is a mere appearance, we start to build up a philosophical account of reality which is in opposition to the common sense account (cf. Perelman loc. cit.).

The other feature which the two writings have in common is the frequent use of analogy and metaphor understood as a condensation which fuses range and domain. That is, starting from the analogy that *A* stands to *B* as *C* stands to *D*, the metaphor takes on the form of '*A* of *B*', '*C* of *B*', '*A* is *C*' (cf. Perelman 1981, p. 131). The large number of metaphors and analogies which make up the fabric of Keynes's argumentation draw attention to the presence of an analogical thought process which is as closely bound up with creative consciousness in the sciences as it is in the arts.[2] For, in both cases, creative thought is analogical in nature and has at its base a single process – the bringing together of objects and concepts which would not be brought together outside the particular rhetorical situation (cf. Lotman 1980, p. 1056).

Rhetoric and Textual Imagination

New prospects are opened up for the investigation of Keynes's writings by the fundamental role which rhetoric and argumentation play in them. If it is true that the rhetorical moves, the specific ways in which the text is ordered, are themselves really an 'authorised form of knowledge, or a way of putting knowledge which has been gained into crisis' (Eco 1977, p. 345), then it is reasonable to suppose that what we find actually said in a given text should, at least in part, be other than, different from or go beyond the author's intentions. A clear vision of the intended reader and the desire to persuade him produces writing which becomes a tool for knowledge-gathering for the writer himself. It unveils to him the links, associations and contradictions which would otherwise have been left hidden. Indeed, we find that the process of composition of Keynes's texts was one of repeated re-writing in response to a variety of readings by others.[3] This process tended to bring to the fore the manners appropriate to dialogue with various interlocutors. The dialogue here is a fruitful and open-ended exchange of views which does not tie criticism down to a pre-conceived system but gives it a voice on its own terms, even at the cost of breaking up the order and compactness of the exposition. Thus, what we find happening in Keynes as an economist is something which also happens to novelists and poets:

> The 'I' which writes, perhaps independently of the possibility of reading and rereading, draws on different and separate psychic sources from those of the thinking which is thought and of inner and outer speaking; these sources are different and separate, if not other, in respect of their greater organizational potential which drives towards goals which are partly known and partly unknown to the thinking 'I', to the speaker and to the writer himself. One who reads what he has himself written finds that he has gone beyond what he could have predicted, imagined or controlled. (Morpurgo 1987, p. 100)

In the Preface to *The General Theory*, Keynes stresses exactly this important function of language, noting its powers of generating sense, its autonomy of the thinker and more generally, brings out the difference and distance between what he had worked out in his mind and what his writing revealed:

> *This book has evolved into what is primarily* a study of the forces which determine changes in the scale of output and employment as a whole; and whilst *it* is found that money enters into the economic scheme in an essential and peculiar manner, technical monetary detail falls into the background. (*CW*, VII, p. xxii, emphases added)

The book has brought about its own evolution which is justified by its power and internal cohesion and which passes on the results thus gained both to the writer, and to the reader, who is invited to retrace with the author its route to knowledge: 'A monetary economy – *we* shall find – is essentially one in which changing views about the future are capable of influencing the quantity of employment and not merely its direction' (loc. cit., emphasis added). Thus, in the Preface to *The General Theory*, the intention to persuade which moulds all of Keynes's writings becomes an invitation to a precisely focused reading. Such a reading is to be understood as mimicking the writing, as an abandonment of our own most outworn conceptual structures and a plunge into a linguistic and rhetorical realm rich in traumatizing discoveries which are genuine attacks on established systems of thought: 'The *composition* of this book has been for the *author* a long struggle of escape and so must the *reading* of it be for most *readers* if the author's *assault* on them is to be successful, a *struggle* of escape from habitual modes of thought and expression' (*CW*, VII, p. xxiii, emphases added). In short, writing and reading are alike in being vehicles of an essential emancipation from 'habitual modes of thought and expression', from the conventional wisdom of a culture whose poles Keynes indicatively locates in the pair language–thought.

As an essayist, biographer, political commentator and economist, Keynes's undertaking follows a preparatory path through writing which mirrors the symmetrical liberation of the reader. As he himself claims, this journey is not so much the attainment of new goals as the gaining of the ability to leave behind the starting point, the safe womb of certainties: 'The difficulty lies, not in the new ideas, but in escaping from the old ones, which ramify, for those brought up as most of us have been, into every corner of our minds' (loc. cit.)

The transparency of what is asserted is altered by the convergent effects of the edges which jut beyond the thought of the writer and of the left-over meanings of the words which uncontrollably and autonomously direct the course which the discussion takes. Each in its own way, according to the intended readership and the style adopted, these form a complex and nuanced rhetoric rich in contradictions, often the battleground for conflicting trains of thought. The task of language is thus granted the freedom to create a space which goes beyond conscious reason and which reaches into matters and forces that run counter to conscious reason. A certain sort of perceptiveness and sensibility to matters of public concern – to the economic consequences of the peace and to the refutation of the 'classical theory' – is thus called into play and brings into view a new conceptual scheme which, taken with the logic of events and happenings, of axioms and postulates, contradicts and destabilizes them. In this way, rhetoric is shown up as the battleground of different conceptual schemes and, for that very reason, as the expression of an imagination. The imagination discloses itself whenever a conscious conceptual scheme indicates that it cannot use its overt logic to resolve all the possibilities of meaning, and when an alternative conceptual scheme is found interfering with the ostensible logic of the text (cf. Serpieri 1986, p. 25). It is in its production, its suspensions, its breakings off, its short circuits, that a piece of writing shines a light into an unsystematized and unstable cultural territory and allows us to gather the fruitful conflicts exposed by unforeseeable or barely foreseen and probed connections (cf. Eco 1977, p. 353).

The author's unconscious perception broadens the range of his rational reflections, and thanks to the creative power of rhetoric, gets to the core of the imagination both of the particular time and place and of the human archetype. This is the meaning of Keynes's emancipation. It is an exhausting labour which requires the author to face up to the results of his own writing and to draw from it new, and sometimes uncomfortable, further consequences. This is likewise what is required of the reader. It is a journey within the language itself which the Keynesians have ignored, a journey full of twists and turns, which gives greater prominence to the dark places, to the side lights and to the shifts in translucency, than it does to the search, not for new ideas, but for a method for breaking free from longstanding incrustations.

Both in politics and in economics, Keynes's persuasive strategy makes use of the resources of rhetoric in order to bring into focus the issues which are left unconsidered or marginalized by conscious knowledge, whether at the individual or the collective level, and by the institutions of economics themselves. Keynes's persuasion is the more effective when it is directed at still half-baked or latent opinions, at the imagination of the masses: 'The true voice of the new generation has not yet spoken, and silent opinion is not yet formed. To the formation of the general opinion of the future I dedicate this book' (*CW*, II, p. 189).

Thus, for Keynes, both in his writings in economics, such as *The General Theory*, and in politics, such as *The Economic Consequences of the Peace*, rhetorical creativity performs the important task of bringing to light the unconscious and repressed aspects of the views held, respectively, by professional economists and by the wider public. In the former work, language can be seen doing this work above all where the economic discussion is at its most tangled, in the most perplexed and disjointed passages. In the latter, it operates in the novel-like account which is given of the Versailles Conference of 1919.

Keynes's attentiveness to the psychological problems of society and to the unconscious forces at work in economic behaviour has long been recognized and is frequently attested in his writings.[4] In these discussions, Keynes scrutinizes what had hitherto not been taken seriously, the importance of unconscious factors in the formation of opinion. But it is worth stressing that the matters discussed are that much more important and valuable because of the rhetoric through which they are discussed. Thus, the 'psychology of society' is not visible only in the paragraphs which explicitly discuss it, but in the whole structure of the discussion and in the way in which it is discussed. We shall devote the forthcoming sections to the way in which Keynes discusses these matters, to his rhetorical techniques and to their possible implications for focusing on some specific aspects of the imagination of this time and place.

THE ECONOMIC CONSEQUENCES OF THE PEACE

After a tormented and frustrating membership of the Supreme Economic Council, Keynes returned from Paris to write *The Economic Consequences of the Peace*, a denunciation in seven chapters of the disastrous implications for Europe of the settlement. It was aimed at that part of the public which cared most for the future of Europe. In it, Keynes paints an economic and political portrait of the whole European scene. His language, free of the restraints of academic economics, takes on an openly polemical tone and a structure which resembles that of a novel. In the end, the Treaty of Versailles comes to be a pretext for a wide-ranging discussion which is rich in metaphor and resonance.

The 'Introductory' chapter sets out and summarizes the pamphlet's narrative preoccupations. These come to play the role of a prospectus for the discussion. The first part analyses the general situation in Europe and England. The second concerns the particularities of the Versailles Conference. These two parts form a historical sequence. But the language in which they are treated nevertheless indicates that they are to be treated on all fours with each other. In each case, what is underlined is a single contradiction, that between real change and illusory permanence. This contradiction is held to be at the root both of the mistakes which had led to the outbreak of war, and of the later mistakes which threatened to undermine the healing qualities of the peace. There are other, no less important, oppositions alongside the first: the real unity of the Continental states and the illusion of autonomy which each harboured, and England's real solidarity with the rest of Europe opposed to her indifference to the tragic destiny of the Continent. What Keynes stresses about the European situation is a generalized form of illusion, which his language likens to a sort of repression. It is illusory to treat contingent circumstances as if they were permanent and the outward forms of independence and isolation as if they did not make up an organically structured and interdependent whole.[5]

The structure and order of the discussion seems to assert a geographical differentiation among the various countries and between Europe and England, just as there is a chronological sequence from war to peace to the Versailles Conference. Nevertheless, other features of the rhetoric deny these and highlight the analogies and mirrorings in play. England is made to stand for the other side of the Europe-wide warlike coin. She is the sunny side of the stormy scenes at the Peace of Versailles, which in turn blows up and dramatizes the repressive desires of pre-war Europe. The linear sequence of events and of Keynes's reasoning turns into a trick done with mirrors which he sets up for his own ends. It is worth looking more closely at the rhetorical features which make this mirroring effective.

Europe: Home, Body and Theatre

Throughout the first chapter, the central metaphor which unifies the argument treats Europe as like a building, and as like a body which gradually changes into a stage on which the pantomime of the Versailles Peace Conference is played out. At the outset, the emphasis is on the illusory permanence which humans attribute to the most fleeting events. This is fleshed out with the image of a 'sandy and false foundation'; the foundation of a building which becomes the arena for political intrigues and ambitions, which are referred to as the devices and props of the theatre: 'We scheme for social improvement and dress our political platforms, pursue our animosities and particular ambitions ...' (*CW*, II, p. 1). The unstable foundations of the house in which we, 'the European family', all lived were overturned by the German people (loc. cit.). Likewise in England, a place which seems to be distinct and distant from the European tragedy, where the end of the war fostered illusions of increased well-being, doubtful projects were being undertaken whose involvement in the building metaphor is indicated by the verb 'to build': 'All classes alike thus build their plans: the rich to spend more and save less, the poor to spend more and to work less' (*CW*, II, p. 2). It is at the point at which England's separateness from Europe is at issue that the metaphor of the house turns into that of the body. As an assertion of organic interdependence, it points up the absurdity of England's political and economic isolation. The parts of the continental body whose future was at stake in the outcome of the war deluded themselves, once it was finished, that they could achieve a sort of independence, which is also the bullying of the defeated by the winners. Meanwhile England, allowed to get away with her actions because of her distance from the Continent, fails to recognize that she is a part of the same organism. 'England still stands outside Europe' says Keynes (loc. cit.), with the 'still' giving away his own view that even though the claim to be external to Europe has not been dropped, it has no grounds for being continued. The 'voiceless tremors' (loc. cit.) do not reach England from the parts of the body which are ill and guilty. They do not reach her because their dumbness is unable to cross the gap set up not merely by geography but by patterns of belief.

The European body has its nerve centre at the Versailles Conference. It becomes for its participants, such as Keynes, a place from which one cannot but see the structural unity of the European organism. 'Dreadful spectres', the shades of a body which is now dead, are haunting the house of the European family. The Versailles Conference thus becomes the site of evocations, and the scene of a tragedy which, without apportioning blame, drives to their conclusions the paradoxes and self-delusions of history. The oppositions between permanence and instability which had undermined the fabric of the building and the health of the body become oxymorons[6] which, by reducing the oppositions to a single contradictory whole, show their unreality and futility. The decisions taken at the Conference mingle 'significance and unreality' (*CW*, II, p. 3), 'importance and unimportance at the same time' (loc. cit.). Thus we are presented with a baroque stage on which the actors cannot even simulate being as they really are. Rather, they parade all their meretriciousness, and, like Woodrow Wilson and Clemenceau, they exhibit only masks: 'One could wonder if the extraordinary visages of Wilson and Clemenceau, with their fixed hue and unchanging characterization were really faces at all and not the tragic masks of some strange drama and puppet show' (*CW*, II, p. 3). In this shadow-theatre of catastrophes, language loses its capacity to grip onto the world. It is torn from fact and reality. It opens up the vacuousness and nullity of the cultural system on which the European house had been built: 'The decisions seemed charged with consequences to the future of human society, yet the air whispered that the word was not flesh, that it was futile, insignificant, of no effect, dissociated from events' (*CW*, II, p. 3). Keynes's use of the theatrical image and of its oxymoronic epitome allows him to bring to the fore the central paradox of the repression underlying the illusory belief in stability. It allows him to accentuate the deadly consequences of continuing to live under such an illusion. The hidden meaning of history, the truths rooted in its imagination, can only be revealed in terms of metaphor or of a fable which allows the analogies and continuities to show themselves, where mere journalism sees only difference and discontinuity.

Keynes's perspective, equidistant[7] between a neutral England and a sick Europe, is as much at home with the one as with the other. It encompasses the body of Europe with all the neutrality required to be able to find the most appropriate images for conveying its state.

'What is to Blame for the Instability?' ('The Psychology of Society')

It is one of the recurring motifs of Keynes's writings that the fact of instability is repressed by the illusory belief in permanence (cf. Minsky 1975). This motif is the argumentative and analytic core of the second chapter, 'Europe before the War'. In the section entitled 'The Psychology of Society' it becomes clear that our ability to give an analysis of the deep structure of society and to identify with its imaginative world depends on the way in which the discussion is organized. This is designed to generate varied and unexpected meanings which go well beyond what is immediately apparent in the linear sequence of the claims Keynes makes. To give some idea of the rhetorical power at work, we may look more closely at the central part of the section to which we have referred. Keynes emphasizes the central paradox of capitalism, that an improvement of general living conditions depends on the unequal distribution of wealth, by bringing the two notions together in a single claim: 'it was precisely the *inequality* of the distribution of wealth which made possible those vast accumulations of fixed wealth and of capital improvements which distinguished that age from others' (*CW*, II, p. 11, emphasis original). The expression 'capital improvements' lends itself to two interpretations. On the one hand, it is the 'increase of wealth'; and on the other, we can put the accent on the adjectival function of 'capital' meaning a substantial improvement. This ambiguity brings together the increase in the amount of capital with the improvement in living conditions and makes each of them all the more ironic for depending on the inequality of the distributions of wealth.

In the immediately following sentences, the correlation between collective welfare and the accumulation of wealth by a few privileged individuals is further highlighted. There, the point is made by a particular set of lexical and syntactic choices which conspire to enforce the effect of the illusoriness of progress: 'But like bees they saved and accumulated, not less to the advantage of the whole community because they themselves held narrower ends in prospect' (loc. cit.). Here, tucked into a subordinate clause, the advantage for society as a whole turns out to be the chance and unplanned result of the inborn drive to accumulate and to save. Keynes proceeds to show ever more clearly how this drive is a repressive superstructure, especially when he turns his gaze on the inseparability of inequality from the denial of freedom and pleasure which is implied by it.

> The immense accumulations of fixed capital which, to the great benefit of mankind, were built up during the half century before the war, could never have come about in a society where wealth was divided equitably. The railways of the world, which that age built as a monument to posterity, were, not less than the pyramids of Egypt, the work of labour which was not free to consume in immediate enjoyment the full equivalent of its efforts. (loc. cit.)

The accumulation of fixed capital and the building of the railways are set next to each other; the deep structure of each is stressed by the use of the single verb 'to build' which Keynes applies to the different categories of money and the railways.[8] By means of this lexical choice, Keynes attributes to money the aura of a monument built for posterity; and the accumulation of it corresponds to the same desire to overcome time and death which brought about the building of the pyramids. This is the deepest tactic of repression at the foundations of capitalism and of the puritan ethic:[9] the repressing of life and pleasure in favour of investment in material objects, an investment which derives from the death-wish.[10] This repression is one which Keynes's description brings to light when he outlines the process by which freedom is denied, describing the workforce as 'not free to consume in immediate enjoyment the full equivalent of its efforts'.[11]

In the essay *Economic Possibilities for our Grandchildren* (1930), Keynes further spells out the implications of the denial of the pleasure-principle as one of the presuppositions of capitalism. Here, Keynes insists on the pathological character of the desire to accumulate; he predicts a time when, as a result of the working out of economic processes, this repressed disorder will become a symptom which can no longer be avoided and which demands a drastic cure:

> We shall be able to rid ourselves of the pseudo-moral principles which have hag-ridden us for two hundred years by which we have exalted some of the most distasteful of human qualities into the position of the highest virtues. We shall be able to afford to dare to assess the money motive at its true value. The love of money as a possession – as distinguished from the love of money as a means to the enjoyments and realities of life – will be recognized for what it is, a somewhat disgusting morbidity, one of those semi-criminal, semi-pathological propensities which one hands over with a shudder to the specialists of mental disease. (*CW*, IX, p. 370)

Whereas in the 1930 piece, given its different historical context, Keynes can denounce the capitalist saving disease as a death-wish which had then been revealed as such by historical circumstance, in *The Economic Consequences of the Peace*, his denunciation of the illness which is the object of repression crops up in the midst of a rhetorical compromise, as a flaw in the smooth surface of the argument which itself instantiates the repression.

The double bluff on which capitalism is founded involves a double repression. First, the guilt at distributive inequality is repressed by the denial of immediate gratification; and second, the death-wish is repressed by the building of monuments which challenge our transience. The historically contingent guilt of inequality thus fuses with an archetypal guilt dating from the founding of individualistic society and is a Faustian guilt at the yearning for immortality.[12] This archetype is underlined by the symmetry between the postures of the working class and of the capitalists. The symmetry is expressed paratactically[13] and manifests the determinative power of unconscious forces to hold up social conflict:

> Thus this remarkable system depended for its growth on a double bluff or deception. On the one hand the labouring classes accepted from ignorance

or powerlessness or were compelled, persuaded, or cajoled by custom, convention and authority and the well-established order of society into accepting a situation in which they could call their own very little of the cake that they and nature and the capitalists were co-operating to produce. And on the other hand the capitalist classes were allowed to call the best part of the cake theirs and were theoretically free to consume it, on the tacit underlying condition that they consumed very little of it in practice. (*CW*, II, p. 12)

By use of a symmetrical form and rhetoric, the deep similarities between the working class and the capitalists are revealed. Each is introduced by the same adverb ('on the one hand', 'on the other hand') and each is the subject of a passive construction ('were persuaded', 'were allowed'). But the clearest similarity is brought out by the image of the cake – representing the products of industry – which cannot be eaten by either party and which is only nominally owned by anyone. Ownership is in each case reduced to the capacity for a verbal designation: 'a situation in which they could call their own very little of the cake' as against 'The capitalist class were allowed to call the best part of the cake theirs'. The emphasizing of the fact that ownership is merely nominal, places the stress on the psychoanalytic roots of the relation between society at large and money. It underlines money's symbolic power which arises, not from the actual amount of capital one owns, but from the purely formal fact of owning it. The capitalist and the worker are at one in the repressive context in which this sort of power is represented by the drive to save, by the puritanical religion of non-consumption. The deep unity of the two classes is reinforced at the end of the section. Here, Keynes identifies the fact of the war as the precipitating cause, as well as a symptom, of the betrayal of the trick, the site at which the repression returns:

The war has disclosed the possibility of consumption to all and the vanity of abstinence to many. Thus the bluff is discovered: the labouring classes may no longer be willing to forgo so largely and the capitalist classes, no longer confident of the future, may seek to enjoy more fully their liberties of consumption so long as they last, and thus precipitate the hour of their confiscation. (*CW*, II, p. 13)

The religion of non-consumption and the virtuous duty of saving show up the other side of the coin, its irrational side:

And so the cake increased, but to what end it was not clearly contemplated. Individuals would be exhorted not so much to abstain as to defer, to cultivate the pleasures of security and anticipation. Saving was for old age or for your children, but this was only in theory – the virtue of the cake was that it was never to be consumed, neither by you nor by your children after you. (*CW*, II, p. 12)

But, in the second part of his discussion, Keynes is concerned to show that the repressive manoeuvre is not arbitrary, by outlining the logic which underpins it. To do so, the writing adopts the viewpoint of society as a whole which bears with it the notion of the 'future in the past', the time of a possible future realization of the goods accumulated. By the introduction into the writing of the motives underlying the notion of progress accepted in his time and place, there arises within the section an ironic contrast with the author's own views. Nevertheless, it is while Keynes appears to be legitimizing and justifying the repressive choices which Victorianism had made that his writing, almost incidentally, displays its deep contradictions. Thus, the geometrical growth of population which Malthus had predicted displays telling similarities with the sort of growth we find in compound interest:

> If only the cake were not cut but was allowed to grow in the geometrical proportion predicted by Malthus of population, but not less true of compound interest, perhaps a day might come where there would at last be enough to go round, and then posterity would enter into the enjoyment of *our* labours. In that day overwork, overcrowding, and underfeeding would come to an end, and men, secure of the comforts and necessities of body, could proceed to the nobler exercises of their faculties. One geometrical ratio might cancel another, and the nineteenth century was able to forget the fertility of the species in a contemplation of the dizzy virtues of compound interest. (*CW*, II, pp. 12–13, emphasis original)

Thus, the similarity between the value attached to the accumulation of money and the accumulation of offspring is given away by the replacement of the one by the other. Fertility's role is usurped, in the telling phrase about the 'dizzy virtues' of compound interest, by the virtue of saving and by the pleasure of accumulation for its own sake with its own 'dizzy' irrationality, each of which has its own drive to geometrical growth. And in concluding the section, Keynes observes the pathological psychology which supports capitalism and the notion of progress:

> I seek only to point out that the principle of accumulation based on inequality was a vital part of the pre-war order of society and progress as we then understood it, and to emphasize that this principle depended on unstable psychological conditions which it may be impossible to recreate. It was not

natural for a population of whom so few enjoyed the comforts of life, to
accumulate so hugely. (*CW*, II, p. 13)

From society's point of view, saving and accumulation pointed to the
creation of a future based on equality. But it is only in the interests of
historical accuracy that Keynes adopts this point of view which runs
directly counter to the specification which he several times supplies in
the course of the section, of the paradox of capitalism.

The way in which the section is organized helps to show how the
system which Keynes decries as paradoxical was experienced as a
living undertaking which would lead to an improvement in collective
welfare. From this, we can make better sense of the clash between the
illusion of equality as the mould in which progress is cast, and the need
for inequality as the precondition of individual accumulation. The clash
can be traced in the way the object and process of repression are
expressed in correlated terms which are sequentially set out in the
development of the section. The contrast between illusory permanence
and real instability is spelt out in this section by setting progress–
accumulation–saving–virtue–non-consumption (all illusory); against
social conflict–inequality–consumption–sin–guilt (all real).

THE GENERAL THEORY

The State of Long-Term Expectation

The discussion of 'The Psychology of Society' is connected in the
development of Keynes's thought with Chapter 12 of *The General
Theory*, entitled 'The State of Long-Term Expectation'. There is, as
Keynes wished to emphasize, something anomalous about the setting
of this chapter in the midst of a specialist discussion of considerable
theoretical importance which is aimed specifically at economists. It
develops 'on a different level of abstraction' (*CW*, VII, p. 149) the
issues considered in 'The Psychology of Society' and other parts of
The Economic Consequences of the Peace, concerning the psychological behaviour of individuals and society as a whole in the face of
unpredictability. So far forth, it considers a topic which does not figure
in orthodox economics.

The eight sections of the chapter divide into two parts. The first
considers the motives of individual economic behaviour; the second

encompasses the influence of collective reactions to the state of the Stock Exchanges of New York and London. 'Long-term expectation' is picked out as the state of confidence in future events which is based hardly at all on rational calculation of probabilities; rather, that state derives from psychological factors such as the tendency to project the current state of affairs into the future, and the tendency to optimism and activity which is encouraged by the objective absence of rational grounds for precise evaluation of the state of the market.

Market operators who, instead of trying to identify what stocks will really be worth, set out to 'beat the gun' (*CW*, VII, p. 155) on the fluctuations in expectations, thus exploiting and further worsening the situation. This sort of speculative activity exacerbates the irrationality of a type of human behaviour which is of itself positive. This is the urge to act in the confidence that the present state of things will continue into the future and not get worse. Indeed, the conduct of the Stock Exchanges is run by an implicit convention on that sort of confidence. Even though its aim is to be a guarantee of the security and tranquillity of the individual investor, the convention derives in reality from his insecurity and from his need for continuity. Thus in the same way as, in *The Economic Consequences of the Peace*, the war showed up the uncertainties and instabilities which were hidden in time of peace, so the convention of continuity, instead of overcoming the precariousness of individuals' knowledge, magnifies its effects and brings into view the instabilites inherent in it.

The conflict between individual and collective investment is limited by the fact that the convention is generally believed in, and not by any process intrinsic to the process itself. Under the guise of an implicit and tacit agreement, the importance of the convention extends to include the conventional behaviour of legitimate operators in the share market who guide their transactions by long-term predictions. Within the share market, the collective as a whole dictates the laws of the behaviour of individuals. These are laws by which each guides his own actions and which he has an interest in seeing strengthened.

As we can see from this brief résumé, Keynes does not use this chapter for persuasion. Instead, his line of thought brings to the fore a set of problems expressed highly metaphorically, in the exposition of which he repeatedly introduces rhetorical figures of opposition and iteration. These figures carry clashing meanings indicating a fault-line between two neighbouring conceptual schemes. In particular, iteration of terms is used to indicate the continuity between apparently different elements, or the reprise of a certain set of presuppositions. For example, the precariousness of knowledge is taken up and studied from various points of view, including in terms of the precariousness of the convention which is designed to overcome the precariousness of knowledge. By exploring the semantic field of the arbitrary and the precarious, of surprising and unpredictable change, Keynes brings out the similarities between the sort of knowledge which underlies individual prediction and expectation, and the sort of knowledge which is operative in setting up the convention. That very knowledge grows and fixes the fact of arbitrariness within a system which makes use of it as an index for speculation:

> But it is not surprising that a convention, in an absolute view of things so *arbitrary*, should have its weak points. It is its *precariousness* which creates no small part of our contemporary problem of securing sufficient investment. (*CW*, VII, p. 13, emphases added).

> *Day-to-day fluctuations* in the profits of existing investments, which are obviously of an *ephemeral and non-significant character*, tend to have an altogether excessive, and even an absurd influence on the market. ... A conventional valuation which is established as the outcome of the mass psychology of a large number of ignorant individuals is liable to *change violently* as the result of a *sudden fluctuation* of opinion ... since there will be no strong roots of *conviction* to hold it steady. (*CW*, VII, pp. 153–4, emphases added)

In the course of the argument, the structural indivisibility of individual investments and the convention, on which the mechanism of collective investments is based, turns out to be a symptom of a serious economic pathology. Its presence is emphasized by the trope of epistrophe, in a repeated and rich series of dissociative or binary oppositions which systematically set the irrational investment choices of market operators up against the healthy good sense of the policies which they spurn. The writing turns the choices into repressive symptoms and in each case, picks out what is being repressed, as follows:

(a)   The genuine prediction of those who are choosing for themselves and of 'practical men' (as against the predictions of economists and those based on the convention)

> The *state of confidence*, as they term it, is a matter to which *practical men* always pay the closest and most anxious attention. But economists have not analysed it carefully and have been content, as a rule,

> to discuss it in general terms. (*CW*, VII, pp. 148–9, second emphasis added)

> Thus certain classes of investment are governed by *the average expectation* of those who deal on the Stock Exchange as revealed in the prices of shares, rather than by the *genuine expectations* of the professional entrepreneur. (*CW*, VII, p. 151, emphases added)

> so that each competitor has to pick, *not the faces which he himself finds prettiest*, but *those which he thinks likeliest to catch the fancy of the other competitors.* (*CW*, VII, p. 156, emphases added)

(b)   Long-term expection and social goals (as against short-term expectation and individual goals)

> For most of these persons are, in fact, largely concerned, not with making superior long-term forecasts of the probable yield of an investment over its whole life, *but with foreseeing changes in the conventional basis of valuation a short time ahead* of the general public. (*CW*, VII, p. 154)

> *The social object* of skilled investment should be to defeat the dark forces of time and ignorance which envelop our future. *The actual private object* of the most skilled investment is 'to beat the gun', as the Americans so well express it ... . (*CW*, VII, p. 155, emphases added)

(c)   The (conventional) assumption that the future will resemble the present (as against the actual belief that the present state of affairs will remain unaltered)

> The essence of this convention ... lies in assuming that *the existing state of affairs will continue indefinitely. ... This does not mean that we really believe that the existing state of affairs will continue indefinitely.* (*CW*, VII, p. 152 emphasis added).

In short, Keynes points out the sickness of a convention which represses social goals and long-term valuations in favour of short-term profit deriving from a game of predicting predictions. Nevertheless, in the seventh section of the chapter, Keynes does justice to the strength of the entrepreneurial spirit which, at bottom, has the same features; but those features only become pathological when perverted by rampant speculation. The hope for a future which resembles the present, and the drive to make short-term predictions, both seem to Keynes to be positive qualities, 'animal spirits' which, outside the convention and outside the sphere of individual choice, and when supplemented with a reasonable amount of predictive rationality, turn out to be necessary for the growth and development of business. But even in the light of this judgement, the argument continues to display a binary form. The freight of death and inertia which is thus thrown up is further repressed, for all that that is providential in this case, and reaffirmed in the setting out of the very manoeuvre by which it is repressed.

The 'animal spirits' whose virtues Keynes praises have all the features of a will to produce and to invest. And this is strikingly similar to the Victorian notion of progress discussed in *The Economic Consequences of the Peace*, and to the desire to increase the size of the cake without ever eating it. In this way, what prompts action is an option which takes the place of the complementary and negated inaction.

> Most, probably, of our decisions to do something positive, ... can only be taken as a result of animal spirits – of a spontaneous urge to *action rather than inaction*, and not as the outcome of a weighted average of quantitative benefits multiplied by quantitative probabilities. (*CW*, VII, p. 161, emphasis added)

Calculation and mathematical prediction are set aside in so far as they may stifle the pioneering spirit of a vigorous victor who, if he is to carry his project to term, must repress the acknowledgement of his own mortality:

> But individual initiative will only be adequate when reasonable calculation is supplemented and supported by animal spirits, so that the thought of ultimate loss which often overtakes pioneers, as experience undoubtedly tells us and them, is put aside as a healthy man puts aside the expectation of death. (*CW*, VII, p. 162)

Relative to the pathological and paradoxical structure of speculation in the share market, the specific features of an optimistic outlook seem to be purely physiological. But they too are not free from a certain disease which, in this case, subserves the individual's survival. Thus, it is necessary to strike a fine balance between individual enterprise and collective and speculative investment. This is to be achieved by controlling the market so as to reduce speculation to the status of the exceptional and anomalous, a bubble on the calm sea of private initiative: 'Speculators may do no harm as bubbles on a steady stream of enterprise. But the position is serious when enterprise becomes the bubble on a whirlpool of speculation' (*CW*, VII, p. 159). In *The Economic Consequences of the Peace*, the Victorian disease of progress, the religion of non-consumption and of abstinence, the death-wish, have been unveiled by the war. Here, they show themselves in speculation; but they can also be seen to have their uses in the restricted sphere of individual initiative. In Keynes's most purely economic thought, the dialectic between individual and collective investment follows the path of a far-sighted and wakeful interaction between repression and what is repressed. And this expresses itself in the need to prevent what is repressed from staging a return in the whirlpool of speculation.

The General Theory as the Portrait of an Economist

The rhetorical excursus of Chapter XII of the *General Theory* arises from the call to focus on the complications and psychological aspects of, rather than on the solutions to, a particular problem. The economic discussion in which the chapter is embedded is one which, while it also deploys normal rhetorical and argumentative techniques (cf. Rossini-Favretti 1988, Gotti 1988), is not structured to follow a single line of thought. The form which Keynes adopts is, in large measure, a reflection of the polemical manner in which he builds up his positive theory. This manner itself is one feature which, in the light of what we find in the *Treatise on Probability*, can be seen to have a clear value in the process of knowledge gathering. Rossini-Favretti observes that the writer shows forth the procedures employed in enquiry by means of a set of communicative acts which mark the stages of the growth of knowledge. These stages make up part of a non-Positivist model of knowledge, in which the classical theory is set up as a rival, and is used as a framework and reference-point in the presentation of the 'new' facts, which are picked out by the new theory (Rossini-Favretti 1988, p. 28).

More than any other text in economics, *The General Theory* explicitly sets itself up, from the very first chapter, as a process of emancipation from the classical theory. It represents an essential stage in the intellectual journey of Keynes as an economist. In it, the theory comes to be formulated by moulding itself in the language which gives the theory its bulk. The dispute with the classical theory follows the path of an indispensable dialectic with parent-figures. Nevertheless, there is none of the upward, linear progression which we find in the conquest which, buoyed up by optimism, Robinson Crusoe makes of a new world. Rather, the rehearsal of the classical theory follows in the footsteps of the reformulation of the language of his father and of the institutions which Stephen Dedalus shows us in Joyce's *Portrait of the Artist as a Young Man*.[14] In each case, we find a painstaking fabrication which comes about by a series of tentative underminings and then fragmentary rebuildings using the very materials from which the inherited structure had been constructed but which had become unserviceable because ill-fitted to the world of experience and everyday reality. On the one hand, Stephen Dedalus recounts the concrete and real steps, from the circuitous and erratic dismemberment of his real self to the construction of an artistic subject. On the other, Keynes's *alter ego* tells of the movement from the dismemberment of himself as classical theorist to the construction of the *General Theory*; in this way he exhibits the gaps in our knowledge, taking apart and fitting back together the pieces of a mosaic which is the picture both of the economy and of the economist himself. By holding up the flow of the argument and singling out particular points, Keynes shows himself willing to go back over the stages of his own liberation, which map onto the construction of the new theory, by recounting their workings in a sort of methodological autobiography. This process is integral to a proper understanding of the theory itself.

Just as in Joyce's *Portrait*, so in the *General Theory*, the process which leads to the creation of an author takes place in the act of writing, a slow-motion activity in which it sometimes happens that the narrator and the fictional character become one and the same (cf. Riquelme 1983, p. 51).

Viewed in this way, as an empirical investigation into method, the lack of organic unity in the flow of thought, the digressions, the spiralling evolution of the discussion, the repeated picking up and dropping of a single theme, can all be seen as having the valency of a basic methodological demonstration. Keynes himself draws attention to his heretical style of argumentation and to its strangeness relative to the traditional sort of persuasion in economics. At the end of Chapter III, he embarks on a digression on the rhetorical reasons for the success of Ricardian theory. Keynes distances himself from these argumentative strategies. But he carefully lists them both to emphasize the close link between rhetoric and economics and to elucidate a model which is left entirely aside in the writing of *The General Theory*:

> The completeness of the Ricardian victory is something of a curiosity and a
> mystery. It must have been due to a complex of suitabilities in the doctrine

to the environment into which it was projected. That it reached conclusions quite different from what the ordinary uninstructed person would expect, added, I suppose to its intellectual prestige. That its teaching, translated into practice, was austere and often unpalatable, lent it virtue. That it was adapted to carry a vast and consistent logical superstructure, gave it beauty. That it could explain much social injustice and apparent cruelty as an inevitable accident in the scheme of progress, and that the attempt to change such things was likely on the whole to do more harm than good, commended it to authority. That it afforded a measure of justification to the free activities of the individual capitalist, attracted to it the support of the dominant social force behind authority. (*CW*, VII, pp. 32–3)

In *The General Theory*, then, we do not find that unassailable formal consistency which, in Ricardo, helps to justify social injustices by fitting them into the classification of 'inevitable accidents'. Stripped of the intellectual prestige, of the beauty and strength of the Ricardian construction, Keynes's theory makes its appeal to those 'professional economists' who are ready not to forget the common sense of the man in the street, and are prepared to give up the comfortable *Candide* role of ignoring the way the world is and cultivating their gardens.

In this digression about Ricardo's rhetoric, Keynes reinforces the similar remarks he had made in the 'Preface'; and he brings out the repressional function of the classical theory as well, implicitly, as the role which he attributes to his own general theory as a lifting of the repression: 'It may well be that the classical theory represents the way in which we would like our economy to behave. But to assume that it actually does so it to assume our difficulties away' (*CW*, VII, p. 34).

Just like Stephen Dedalus's, Keynes's route as an economist is therefore that of the search for a truth which seems to have been obscured by the language and method of tradition. And, just like the artist's, the economist's growth takes place away from the *logos* of the father, but close to the maternal placenta:

> The sense of the soul's development as like that of an embryo not only helped Joyce to the book's imagery, but also encouraged him to work and rework the original elements in the process of gestation. Stephen's growth proceeds in waves, in accretions of flesh, in particularizations of needs and desires, around and around but always ultimately forward. (Ellmann (rev. edn 1959) 1982, p. 297)

The first three chapters of *The General Theory* give us an example of this toil, a first taste of a method which is at once constructive and deconstructive, the first strokes in a portrait of the economist.

Order and Hierarchy in Argument: Linearity and Circularity

The dissociation of ideas provides the prime instance of the rhetorical figure embodying the simultaneous processes of dismemberment of the classical theory and construction of the general theory. It has been pointed out that this trope is in large measure based on the basic separation of appearance and reality. It comes into operation in the face of the contrarieties which ordinary thought encounters, whenever we are not content to avoid the difficulty by pretending not to see it, but wish to achieve an intellectually satisfying resolution and to re-establish the coherence of our vision of reality (cf. Perelman 1981, p. 137).

In the first three chapters of *The General Theory*, the dissociation of ideas is the principal trope employed. Indeed, from the very first chapter, *The General Theory* is put forward as the axis of reality or, in Perelman's account, as the second (normative and explanatory) term relative to the classical theory which is the first term as the axis of (mere) appearance. The second term supplies a criterion, a rule which allows us to distinguish, among the facets of the first term, those that are in good order from those that are not. The second term is not something simply given; it is rather a construction which determines, in the dissociation of the first term, a rule by which its many aspects can be ranked and by which to judge those which are illusory, misleading or (merely) apparent (cf. Perelman 1981, p. 138).

Keynes's case fits Perelman's account perfectly, especially as regards the idea that the norms arise from a process of construction rather than from one of definition. The very naming of the theory as 'general', the birth certificate of the new project, does not come about in a vacuum but from the desire to escape from and be emancipated from the classical theory:

> I have called this book the General Theory of Employment, Interest and Money, placing the emphasis on the prefix General. The object of such a title is to contrast the character of my arguments and conclusions with those of the classical theory of the subject, upon which I was brought up and which dominates the economic thought, both practical and theoretical, of the academic and governing class of this generation, as it has for a hundred years past. (*CW*, VII, p. 3)

Immediately following this passage, Keynes specifies the nature of the target of the oppositional and polemical aim which, by putting it as the opening of the book, he thus roundly advertises. 'General' is a reaction and reply to the fact that the classical theory applies 'only to a special case' and only under conditions which do not reflect genuine economic reality. The opposition between the general and the particular sets in train Keynes's project. It sets that project up as the search for a truth which is not merely local but general, not limited but unrestricted.

In Chapter II, Keynes starts by considering the basic postulates of the inherited wisdom, and he sets himself the task of examining their presuppositions, a murkier matter than is commonly thought. The complex conceptual background shaping the forefathers' knowledge is treated as the object of the enquiry and as the material out of which to build the new theory:

> But the pure theory of what determines the *actual employment* of the available resources has seldom been examined in great detail. ... I mean not that the topic has been overlooked, but that the fundamental theory underlying it has been deemed so simple and obvious that it has received, at the most, a bare mention. (*CW*, VII, pp. 4–5, emphasis original)

In drawing attention to the gaps which open up in the postulates, Keynes takes care to explain their genesis by reference to the general axis of the (merely) apparent with which the classical theory is associated. Appearance, and the limited applicability which is its symptom, feeds on 'false', 'illicit' and, above all, 'tacit' assumptions succouring a picture of the economy which fails to reflect its complexity:

> In other words, it may be the case that within a certain range the demand of labour is for a minimum money-wage and not for a minimum real wage. The classical school have tacitly assumed that this would involve no significant change in their theory. But this is not so. For if the supply of labour is not a function of real wages as its sole variable, their whole argument breaks down entirely and leaves the question of what the actual employment will be quite indeterminate. (*CW*, VII, p. 8)

Moreover, the falsity and illicitness of the presuppositions can be attributed to an error of perception, to an optical illusion which can be understood as a repression of complexity:

> Those who think in this way are deceived, nevertheless, by an optical illusion, which makes two essentially different activities appear to be the same. They are fallaciously supposing that there is a nexus which unites decisions to abstain from present consumption with decisions to provide for future consumption; whereas the motives which determine the latter are

not linked in any simple way with the motives which determine the former. (*CW*, VII, p. 21)

The contents and aims of *The General Theory* are presented as answering to the felt need to respond to the classical theory's silences, to fill the gaps which have opened up and to correct for the 'illicit assumptions'. It is thus the spirit of refutation which sets out the path which the enquiry will follow:

> In assuming that the wage bargain determines the real wage the classical school have slipped in an illicit assumption. For there may be *no* method available to labour as a whole whereby it can bring the wage–goods equivalent of the general level of money-wages into conformity with the marginal disutility of the current volume of employment. There may exist no expedient by which labour as a whole can reduce its *real* wage to a given figure by making revised *money* bargains with the entrepreneurs. This will be our contention. We shall endeavour to show that primarily it is certain other forces which determine the general level of real wages. The attempt to elucidate this problem will be one of our main themes. We shall argue that there has been a fundamental misunderstanding of how in this respect the economy in which we actually live works. (*CW*, VII, p. 13 emphases original)

Keynes employs the conflict thus set up to work out the epistemological significance of his method in terms of the oppositions of licit with illicit, true with false, explicit with tacit, true perception with optical illusion, complex with simple. What emerges is a search for truth and complexity by means of a process of unmasking and destabilization, by an enquiry into the repressive drives at work in economics.

Nevertheless, Keynes does not fill in the gaps in our knowledge in a systematic way. Rather, he sets himself to the business of specifying exactly what they consist in and, by explaining their origins, of narrating how they are to be uncovered. Thus we find in Chapter II an outline of a critical rereading of the foundations of the classical theory and a snapshot of Keynes's initial comments on it. These summary materials are set down in a sort of diary form, and they accompany the reader on a journey of knowledge gathering, which Keynes had completed by the time that *The General Theory* came to be written down. The digressive and fragmented path which the reader has to follow often gives rise to frustration, impatience and irritation, even though the reader is often reminded that the author has a complete picture of the theory's overall structure: 'The theory of wages in relation to employment, to which we are here leading up, cannot be fully elucidated, however, until chapter 19 and its Appendix have been reached' (*CW*, VII, p. 18). There is an appearance of rigid logic in the first three chapters: the formulation of the problem in the first; the refutation of the commonly accepted theory in the second; and the presentation of the alternative in the third (cf. Rossini-Favretti 1988). But in fact, this appearance is gainsaid by a different, circular, logic. For in the second chapter, the refutation of the classical theory makes way for a sketch of the principal points of the general theory; and in the third, the exposition of the general theory continues to rest on attacks against the classical theory. At the very outset of that chapter, the need for a new language of economics is understandably justified as the filling up of a gap in our knowledge: 'We need, to start with, a few terms which will be defined precisely later' (*CW*, VII, p. 23). Almost as soon as it has been formulated, the principle of effective demand, which carries a heavy load in the new theory, is compared with the classical theory's very different claim, whose misleading consequences are demolished in detail. The range and importance of the new theory's application is made clear by the analysis of the gaps in the classical theory, here identified with Say's law. The space to be filled is much vaster than that which Keynes's provisional formulations of his theory had hitherto covered. The specification of the principle of effective demand can therefore be seen as only a first skeletal sketch for the setting-out of the essential economic discussion which is called for by the shortcomings of the classical theory:

> Thus Say's law, that the aggregate demand price of output as a whole is equal to its aggregate supply price for all volumes of output, is equivalent to the proposition that there is no obstacle to full employment. If, however, this is not the true law relating aggregate demand and supply functions, there is a vitally important chapter of economic theory which remains to be written and without which all discussions concerning the volume of aggregate employment are futile. (*CW*, VII, p. 26)

The summary pre-empting of the contents of *The General Theory* which we find in the second section of Chapter II seems to be striving to fill in this basic gap and to write the 'vitally important chapter' straight away. But once again, in the very act of providing the account of its first version as a synopsis of the whole, Keynes seems to want to give greater prominence to the way in which his ideas were formed than to the theoretical contribution which they make. For all that its implications are set out in full, the picture which we are offered is an incomplete and partial result, as provisional as the assessments which have been arrived at. All the same, it seems that this partialness itself allows us to focus very clearly on the ground which is still to be covered. As the gaps come to be filled, the terrain still to be explored seems to stretch away unendingly: 'Thus the analysis of the propensity to consume, the definition of the marginal efficiency of capital and the theory of the rate of interest are the three main gaps in our knowledge which it will be necessary to fill' (*CW*, VII, p. 31). But Keynes does not give up on the vision of bringing the process of analysis to an end. He aims to bear witness to his global and systematized understanding of what is going on at the same time as pointing out the stages of the ripening of his method. He does not bar himself from jumping ahead to the story's happy ending and to the orderly rearrangement of the tiles taken from the inherited mosaic:

> When this has been accomplished, we shall find that the theory of prices falls into its proper place as a matter which is subsidiary to our general theory. We shall discover, however, that money plays an essential part in our theory of the rate of interest; and we shall attempt to disentangle the peculiar characteristics of money which distinguish it from other things. (*CW*, VII, pp. 31–2)

CONCLUSION

By looking more closely not only at the lexical choices and juxtapositions, but also at the overall structure of the ordering of claims and arguments, we have tried to show how linearity and circularity, sequentialness and repetition co-exist in Keynes's writing.

This twin-track movement is a striking feature of *The General Theory* and may account for the disquiet felt by economists reading it. But it is also impressive evidence of the innovative contribution which Keynes's rhetoric makes to his writing. For it is a faithful transcription of a method which amounts to the process of the formation of an idea. Keynes's goals were to throw light on obscure matters, to discover the complexity behind apparent simplicity, by means of a dialectical confrontation and to allow the release of what economists had repressed. With such goals, the twists and turns of the discussion, whether in terms of the linguistic texture and composition or in terms of the overall architectonic, come to be as important as the results which are achieved.

Thus, Keynes's economic and political writings present us with a picture of the greatest interest. It is an example of the interaction between reflection on words and innovative theory-building. It is the portrait of an economist, as well as of an economic theory suffused with the sap of cultural growths which drew much of their nourishment from the theorizing and experimentation of the Modernist avant-garde. Keynes's most significant contribution lies in his having proposed a *method* of thinking and writing which was the same as the method about which Virginia Woolf quizzed herself at about the same time in the following thought, which can also be applied to Keynes:

> But it is possible to press a little further and wonder whether we may not refer our sense of being to a bright yet narrow room confined and shut in, rather than enlarged and set free, to some limitations imposed by the method as well as by the mind. Is it the method that inhibits the creative power? Is it due to the method that we feel neither jovial nor magnanimous, but centred in a self which, in spite of its tremor of susceptibility, never embraces or creates what is outside itself and beyond? Does the emphasis laid, perhaps didactically, upon indecency contribute to the effect of something angular and isolated? Or is it merely that in any effort of such originality it is much easier, for contemporaries especially, to feel what it lacks than to name what it gives? In any case, it is a mistake to stand outside examining 'methods'. (Woolf 1919, p. 266)

NOTES

1. In the new extension of classical rhetoric, argumentation and rhetoric are inseparable. Perelman's comments on this matter are illuminating:

    > The new rhetoric, unlike that of classical times, concerns discourses directed at any sort of audience, whether it be a crowd gathered in a public square or a meeting of specialists, whether it be a single individual or the whole of mankind. The new rhetoric sets itself to take into account also the arguments which a person deploys in thinking things out for himself. Given that its subject-matter is the study of non-demonstrative reasoning, the analysis of arguments – not restricted to formally valid inferences or to more or less mechanical calculation – the theory of argumentation understood as a new rhetoric (or a new dialectic) covers the whole range of uses of language for the purposes of persuasion *whatever audience they are aimed at and whatever issue they deal with.* (Perelman 1981, pp. 16–17).

2. Hence, Keynes makes creative use of rhetorical figures and, for that very reason, they do not 'serve to embellish a pre-existing content, but help to delineate a distinctive content' (Eco 1977, p. 345).

3. In their biographies of Keynes, both Harrod and Skidelsky note his habitual practice of first giving his latest writings to some of his economist colleagues for scrutiny and discussion before sending them for publication. This was, in any case, a matter of course in Keynes's milieu, and typical of the Apostles and of Bloomsbury itself (see Harrod 1951, Skidelsky 1983).

4. Keynes's awareness of the psychological problems of society, underwritten by the clear influence of Freud's thought and writing on the Bloomsbury Group (see also Rossana Bonadei's contribution to the present volume), is most prominently related to the parts of *The General Theory*, such as Chapter 12, which attribute to the psychology of society a determining role in long-term expectations. But we also find it elsewhere. In particular, in *The Economic Consequences of the Peace* and the *Essays in Persuasion*, there are frequent observations on and evaluations of the psychoanalytic structure of puritanism understood as an underlying structure of capitalism (see Winslow 1986).

5. In her contribution to the present volume and in her earlier (1988) work, Anna Carabelli has set out in detail the importance of the concept of organic interdependence in Keynes's thought.

6. 'Oxymoron', from the Greek for 'pointedly foolish', denotes a condensed paradox 'combining in one expression two terms that are ordinarily contradictory, and whose exceptional coincidence is therefore arresting' (*Fowler's Modern English Usage* s.v.), e.g John Milton's 'darkness visible', or G.M. Hopkin's 'swift, slow, sweet, sour, adazzle, dim'.

7. To bring out a similar distance of perspective from England and from the scene in Paris, Keynes uses the one expression, 'an occasional visit', to refer both to his attendance at the decision-making of the Big Four and to his visits to London: 'For one who spent in Paris the greater part of the six months which succeeded the armistice an occasional visit to London was a strange experience' (*CW*, II, p. 2); cf. 'In Paris, where those connected with the Supreme Economic Council received almost hourly reports of the misery, disorder and decaying organisation of all Central and Eastern Europe, Allied and Enemy alike, and learnt from the lips of the financial representatives of Germany and Austria unanswerable evidence of the terrible exhaustion of their countries, an occasional visit to the hot, dry room in the President's house where the Four fulfilled their destinies in empty and arid intrigue, only added to the sense of nightmare (*CW*, II, pp. 3–4).

8. Even if 'the immense accumulation of fixed wealth' and 'the railways of the world' are, grammatically speaking, respectively the subject and the direct object of the sentence, they are, from the point of view of stylistic organization, both subjects.

9. The connections between capitalism and puritanism which Keynes is here anticipating were later worked out in full by Weber in his now standard work on the protestant ethic and the spirit of capitalism (first pub. 1904–5, available in book form 1921); by Tawney (lectures delivered 1922, available in book form 1926); and subsequently by Christopher Hill (1961, 1974).

10. In an interesting work on the psychoanalytic meaning of history which is still up to date, Norman Brown describes the psycholanalytic structures of protestantism and of the puritanism which followed it, and specifies them in terms of the anal character of the culture. On Brown's reading, which makes frequent reference to Freud's studies on the anal character of attachment to money, the Lutheran phase of protestanism which was marked by contempt for and moral condemnation of money, represented a return of anal repression. Protestantism converted the return of what had been repressed into a further repression which legitimates saving and wealth in terms of their being a sign of God's Election. Developing Freud's essay *Beyond the Pleasure Principle* (1920), Brown puts particular stress on the relation

222   *John Maynard Keynes: Language and Method*

between the anal character of protestantism and the death wish, and he emphasizes that the relation is most visible in civilized man's attempts to defeat death by the construction of works, by the accumulation of stones which reveals a libidinous investment, and by an emotional attachment to inorganic matter which is the symbolic place-holder for excrement. But the flight from death by means of investment in objects which are incapable of dying is itself the most striking sign – or, rather, the symptom – of the denial of the pleasure principle and the triumph of the death instinct. It is not a matter of chance that, in discussing this central part of the argument, Brown makes repeated reference to Keynes's *Economic Consequence of the Peace* and the *Essays in Persuasion*, and he gives Keynes due credit for intuiting the connection between capitalist society and the death instinct (Brown 1959, p. 321).

11. In this case, Keynes is adopting a rhetoric of 'litotes' – from the Greek for 'plainness' or 'simplicity', meaning 'the particular kind of rhetorical understatement in which for the positive notion required is substituted its opposite with a negative' (*Fowler's Modern English Usage* s.v.), e.g. 'not bad' meaning 'excellent', or the Bible's 'I praise you not' to indicate emphatic blame. See also Freud, *On Negation* (1935).

12. *The Economic Consequences of the Peace* thus becomes one of the primary texts for the expression of the imagination of Keynes's times. The writing of it borrows from the techniques of literary narrative and employs a rhetoric which condenses in a single compromise both what can be said and advocated in public and what is to be found only in the collective unconscious. The idea that rhetoric represents a compromise comes from Freud whose *Jokes and their Relation to the Unconscious* (1905) has become a standard reference point for subsequent psychoanalytically-inclined literary studies (cf. Orlando 1972). There, Freud finds that the techniques of condensation and displacement which are in evidence in the rhetoric of joke-making operate a compromise between elements which are socially acceptable and others which are transgressive.

13. 'Parataxis', from the Greek for 'placing side by side', means 'the placing of propositions or clauses one after another, without indicating by connecting words the relation (of co-ordination or subordination) between them' (*Oxford English Dictionary* s.v.), e.g. 'He's a sly one. He'll go far'.

14. Joyce wrote the *Portrait of the Artist as a Young Man* between 1905 and 1911, and published it in 1916.

REFERENCES

Bellofiore, R. (1988) 'Retorica ed economia. Su alcuni sviluppi recenti della filosofia della scienza economica e il loro rapporto con il metodo di Keynes', *Economia Politica*, V (3).

Bonadei, R. (1988) 'John Maynard Keynes: la costruzione di un metodo' *Il Piccolo Hans*, **59**.

Brown, N. (1959) *Life against Death*, Middletown, Conn.: Weslyan University Press.

Carabelli, A.M. (1988) *On Keynes's Method*, London: Macmillan.

Eco, U. (1977) *A Theory of Semiotics*, London: Macmillan.

Ellman (1982) (2nd ed.) *James Joyce*, Oxford: Oxford University Press.

Freud, S. (1905) *Jokes and their Relation to the Unconscious*, in Strachey, J. (ed.), Standard Edition, vol. 8, London: Hogarth Press.

Freud, S. (1908) *Character and Anal Erotism*, Standard Edition, vol. 9, London: Hogarth Press.
Freud, S. (1920) *Beyond the Pleasure Principle*, Standard Edition, vol. 18, London: Hogarth Press.
Freud, S. (1935) *Negation*, Standard Edition, vol. 19, London: Hogarth Press.
Gotti, M. (1988) 'Il modello argomentativo di J.M. Keynes nella *General Theory*', *Quaderni del Dipartimento di Linguistica e Letterature Comparate*, **4**, Bergamo: Università degli Studi.
Harrod, R. (1951) *The Life of J.M. Keynes*, London: Macmillan.
Hill, C. (1961) 'Protestantism and the Rise of Capitalism', in *Essays in the Economic and Social History of Tudor and Stuart History* (in honour of R.H. Tawney), Cambridge: Cambridge University Press.
Hill, C. (1974) *Change and Continuity in 17th Century England*, London: Harmondsworth.
Joyce, J. (1916) *A Portrait of the Artist as a Young Man*, London: Granada.
Lotman, J. (1980) 'Retorica', article in *Encyclopaedia*, Turin: Einaudi.
McCloskey, D.N. (1985) *The Rhetoric of Economics*, Wisconsin: Wisconsin University Press.
Minsky, H.P. (1975) *John Maynard Keynes*, New York: Columbia University Press.
Morpurgo, E. (1988) *Fra tempo e parola. Figure del dialogo psicoanalitico*, Milan: Franco Angeli.
Orlando, F. (1972) *Per una teoria freudiana della letteratura*, Turin: Einaudi.
Perelman, C. (1981) *Il dominio retorico. Retorica e Argomentazione*, Turin: Einaudi.
Riquelme, J.P. (1983) *Teller and Tale in Joyce's Fiction, Oscillating Perspectives*, Princeton: Princeton University Press.
Rossini-Favretti, R. (1988) 'L'argomentazione nella comunicazione e nell'epistemologia keynesiana', *Studi Italiani di Linguistica Teorica ed Applicata*, **XVIII** (1).
Serpieri, A. (1986) *Retorica e immaginario. Le forme del discorso*, Parma: Pratiche.
Skidelsky, J. (1983) *John Maynard Keynes. Hopes Betrayed*, London: Macmillan.
Tawney, R.H. (1926) *Religion and the Rise of Capitalism*, London: Macmillan.
Weber, M. (1930, English trans. of 1921) *The Protestant Ethic and the Rise of Capitalism*, London: Macmillan.
Winslow, R.J. (1986) 'Keynes and Freud. Psychoanalysis and Keynes's account of the "animal spirits" of capitalism' *Social Research*, **53** (4).
Woolf, V. (1919) 'Modern Fiction' in Woolf, L. (ed.), *Collected Essays*, London: Hogarth Press.

7. The Case of Keynes: Economics from Rhetoric to Critique[1]

Riccardo Bellofiore

> The question whether truth about the objective world is attained by human thinking – is not a question of theory, but a *practical* question. In practice must man prove the truth, that is reality and power, this worldliness of his thinking. The dispute over the reality or non-reality of thinking – that is isolated from practice – is a purely *scholastic* question. (Karl Marx, 'Theses on Feuerbach' II, tr. by Wal Suchting)

INTRODUCTION

In recent years, interest in the linguistic, literary and rhetorical aspects of economics has been growing, if only at the more critical margins of the profession. This interest can be accounted for in many ways, from the reconsideration of the epistemological bases of the subject, to the undoubted success of McCloskey's book in provoking useful debate. The investigation which makes up the present book, for all that it centres on the specific case of Keynes, has been predicated on the basic thought that language 'counts' in at least two senses. First, it counts in the sense that a writer's method in economics cannot be distinguished from the form which the resultant writing takes, if those results are viewed in terms of the art of persuasion, rather than those of the faithful representation of the external world. And second, there is the deeper sense that the very conceptual schemes, the substance and content of the models which economists put forward, cannot be separated from the explicit and implicit 'argumentation' which carries them.

In Chapter 3 of this volume, I tried to show in what way interest in the rhetorical aspects of economics does not amount to a unified research programme in opposition to the tradition underwritten by neo-Positivism and Falsificationism. Rather, it is a symptom of the crisis which those epistemological proposals are undergoing. Or it is the arena in which divergent lines of thought come together in a world which is now irreversibly post-Positivist. Viewed in this way, it seemed worthwhile to highlight an apparent divergence between the recommendations which McCloskey's makes and the manner in which Keynes 'persuaded'. The former locates the whole of the 'conversation' among economists in a post-modern world, in which talk itself exhausts the activity of research and in which truth is merely a matter of convention. Keynes, on the other hand, can avoid the hard choice between science as representation and as mere talk, because he aims at a vision of it as intervention, as a practical reshaping of the world. On this vision, it is impossible to abstract the 'subjective' aspects from the act of knowing or from the 'object' known; hence, it is not possible to verify or falsify *The General Theory of Employment* without acting.

Alessandra Marzola's contribution allows me an opening to draw some threads together so as to make some claims which are, at once, both very modest and too ambitious. On the one hand, I would like to offer a wholly personal summing up of the way that thought about the rhetoric of economics has developed since Chapter 2 of this book was written. On the other hand, taking inspiration from the perspective taken up by the literary scholars represented in this volume, I would like to try to show what uses, other than those proposed by McCloskey, attention to the 'text' can be put to in considering the ways that economic thought is embodied. In short, the text is a crucial stage in a broader cognitive process which however, includes – in a sense to be defined – extralinguistic elements whose contradictions the text reflects and elaborates and even distorts. Rhetorical and linguistic investigations seem to me usefully to refer us beyond the text, to things which can only be seen by going through the ambiguities and stratifications of the economist's writing without putting these down to the mere contingencies of purely ornamental style.

The modesty of the proposal, then, is that little of what I shall say will be original, but will derive – I hope not too inaccurately – from what others, especially my co-authors in this volume, have said. The excess of ambition lies in the fact that in drawing my conclusions, for all that they are still too inchoate and unargued, I shall refer to writers and disciplines which are far not only from economics, but from my own speciality.

Barbarians in the Senior Common Room

The articulation which Donald McCloskey and other writers of the same stamp, such as Arjo Klamer, have given to a Rhetoric of economics has given rise to an enviable harvest of discussions, conferences, and collections of articles on the theme. I shall not undertake a detailed review of this material, although I have appended some references to the end of this chapter. Instead, I would like to bring out some of the areas in which the recent discussions seem to me to have been enlightening or to have raised fresh problems.

There are three basic issues: a greater clarification of the intellectual background of the rhetorical approach to economics; the alliances which can be set up with other disciplines; and the reply to criticisms which have been levelled, often with ferocity and not always with a sense of fair play, at the new enterprise.

We may begin with the new genealogy put forward by the supporters of rhetoric. This is a wholesale history of thought (in the West). The first point of reference is, unsurprisingly, Greek and Roman rhetoric, running from the Sophists, taken as an undifferentiated group, to Cicero and Quintilian, who all emphasize the inseparability of argumentation and knowledge, of ethics and truth. Plato is viewed as responsible for demonizing the Sophists, and as the founder of the anti-rhetorical project in philosophy of privileging the True over the Good, a privilege which is widened and reaffirmed by Aristotle, even though he was himself the author of his own *Rhetoric*. Descartes and Kant countersign the definitive condemnation of rhetoric in recent centuries. On the one hand (Descartes), philosophy is seen as the handmaiden of the sciences and is reduced to the visual metaphor of the mirror of nature; and on the other hand (Kant), the liberating project of the Enlightenment is founded on a notion of Reason which has been deplored by its critics as totalizing and authoritarian.

It is said that the rebirth of rhetoric in the present century is marked by the many voices raised against scientism and rationalism. The list here is long and made up mostly of philosophers and philosophers of science. In the former group, suffice it to drop the names of such continental figures as Nietzsche, Heidegger, Wittgenstein, Gadamer, and Habermas, leading to such theoreticians of the post-modern as Foucault and Derrida, as well as, in the anglophone world, Dewey, Rorty and MacIntyre. In the latter grouping we may freely point to the dissidents from Logical Empiricism and Falsificationism: from Kuhn to Toulmin and from Feyerabend to Mary Hesse. The variety within such a list is striking and raises a problem which seems not to have worried the supporters of rhetoric, at least in economics. The problem, in its most basic form, is that all that the writers cited have in common is, at best, a shared discontent with scientism. It would be much more difficult to realign them according to their different attitudes towards, for example, the Enlightenment.

But we might ask whether these thinkers can be taken together as the founding fathers of the new rhetorical stand simply because they join both (*i*) in attacking the subject–object dichotomy which underlies the metaphor of science as representative; and (*ii*) in paying attention to the communicative and collaborative nature of knowledge-gathering. It is hardly likely that many of the others named would accept Derrida's claim that there is nothing outside the text; Habermas is certainly more an opponent than fellow-traveller of Heidegger or of the post-modernists; what Wittgenstein and Rorty share is anti-foundationalism, but the former would not have thought that there was much sense to be found in the latter's relativism; and Mary Hesse would seem rather too moderate to Feyerabend. Thus, what seems to me to lie behind the making out of a genealogy of this sort is, paradoxically, a defensive attitude which arises from a judgement which is, in my view, mistaken. The judgement is that, without these thinkers, Positivism and Falsificationism would be still alive and thriving. The attitude which follows from this judgement is that what has to be done, for the time being, is spread doubts rather than build alternatives.

Against this view, I maintain that we ought to take on board the fact that we are already *beyond* Positivism. Going about denying Positivism is bad rhetoric. To hold, quite properly, that the metaphor of knowledge as a sort of sight or vision is a bad metaphor, is insufficient to persuade anyone of the alternative metaphor: that knowledge is a sort of speech or talking. Other metaphors are possible; conflicts within post-Positivism are possible. For my part, I have already hinted, and shall spell out shortly, that knowledge is more like a sort of agency or activity, in which we find both linguistic and extralinguistic elements.

In economics, there is some justification for the defensive strategy which turns every expression of discontent with general and prescriptive methodology into support for rhetoric. McCloskey rightly stresses how here the fascination of writing about methodology has continued to be powerful, as can be seen from the late arrival on the scene of the philosophy of science. All the same, McCloskey oversimplifies in identifying as Positivist or Falsificationist the positions of most of the epistemologists of economics, who have tended to be spread along the axis which runs from Laudan to Lakatos and Kuhn.

From this point of view, the rhetoric of economics can be understood as a proposal to bring the academic or research community up to date. It is in this light that we can understand the many interdisciplinary initiatives which have been taken by McCloskey. The longstanding alliances with the natural sciences (physics) and with the exact sciences (mathematics) have been abandoned. Economics is coming to be seen no longer as the 'hardest' of the social sciences, to use one of the epithets often complacently applied with implicit, but clear, 'masculine' undertones. The rhetoric of economics has exerted itself to restore relations and to set up new alliances with other departments. Naturally enough, this began with literary and historical studies, as well as with anthropology and sociology. Subsequently, it has been happening in relation to the study of law and political science, and understandably, there has been a preference for those branches of philosophy which are of a hermeneutical rather than an analytical bent.

This effort is aimed at two goals. The first is the re-education, by means of 'conversation' with other types of intellectual, of the sort of economists who have become conceited and isolated, who have been barbarized by pride and ignorance, to the point where they have no idea what is going on even in closely neighbouring disciplines. The second is the goal of refining the rhetorical project itself. Such a refinement, we may say immediately, ought to be understood as part of the meta-theory of the human and social sciences. The meta-theory picks out the features common to these different disciplines as their 'narrative' character and their aiming at 'understanding' rather than at 'explanation'. At the same time, rhetoric prompts a closer analysis not so much of how in the abstract, to prove the truth and certainty of a given proposition, but rather of how, in particular cases, one's peers come to be persuaded. The result is an invitation to enquire into the ways in which, in the various disciplines, a truth comes to be established 'locally', by the agreement of the 'learned'.

But even here, not everything goes its way. Rhetoric, both in economics and elsewhere, wants both too much and too little. In so far as it is a meta-theory, the attention which it gives to the textual and communicative features of its subject matter may point at either of two conclusions. On the one hand, it might encourage the replacement of the 'physical' model of science by the 'literary' or 'hermeneutical' model. On the other, it might be drawing attention to the fact that rhetorical ploys are inevitably to be found in every discipline, including the natural and exact sciences. The former alternative, which we find hinted at here and there, is a strong claim which is, at least potentially, capable of resulting in genuine discoveries on the basis of the analogy between such activities, which at first sight seem very distant, as knowledge-gathering and story-telling. However, under criticism, McCloskey and Klamer react by explicitly and unequivocally disowning any totalizing aims for the rhetorical project. As a result, they seem to be pushed into accepting the second alternative, which notes the presence of rhetorical features in the social sciences but which risks falling into the banality of the commonplace. For it would be easy, under such circumstances, to say, 'Yes, it's true, thank you for reminding us of the rhetorical trimmings in economics and of the need to write better; now let's move on to something else'. Again, we find that the interesting discussions come *after* we have recognized that economics, like every other science, is *also* persuasive argumentation.

Indeed, there is something peculiar about the reaction of, especially McCloskey, but also of Klamer, to the criticisms levelled at the rhetoric of economics. They are happy to accept the agreement of those who have no difficulty with the presence of the rhetorical features of economics; and yet they ignore the limitations and reservations which are expressed. In any case, such agreement is much more common among philosophers and literary scholars, among anthropologists and social scientists than it is among economists, although such important figures as Tobin and Solow have been ready to show an interest in the issue. Among philosophers of economics the opposition to rhetoric has been fierce and very clear cut. The replies which McCloskey and Klamer have offered make up another interesting aspect of more recent discussion. It is worth offering a sketch of what has been going on.

The most common objections can be taken all together as the idea that the Rhetoric of economics risks falling into irrationalism, that it is following the fashion of deconstructionism by denying the notion of truth, leading to the denial of the empirical side of knowledge, and replacing demonstrative procedures with mere oratory.

It has not proved hard to take the sting out of attacks like this, in so far as they are put forward from within an out-dated way of viewing things. According to McCloskey and Klamer, far from denying reason, or the central notions of realism, rhetoric encourages us to accept a

pluralist model of 'local' reasons and to relocate realism in the philosopher's or scientist's personal, and altogether legitimate metaphysics. As
just one of many of the 'sources' of the rhetoric of economics,
deconstructionism does not in any way prevent a researcher from pursuing empirical enquiries if that is what he wants to do; rather, it sets
itself up against a particular empiricist ideology of the relation between
the scientist as isolated and the world as external to him. In this way,
the rhetoric of economics denies neither the notion of truth nor the
existence of 'guarantees' of knowledge. Rather, it gives an account of
them in terms of agreement, context and ethics: what is true is what
persuades the 'good' scientist here and now; it is what is accepted as
true in debate with the other participants to the specific 'conversation',
to which a given claim is a contribution and which is in accord with the
standards that are accepted there. The 'goodness' of the scientist to
which we have referred is important: we are directed to think not just of
professional expertise, but more significantly of a specific moral quality.

Once again however, I am not convinced. At bottom, the reason
remains the same. The rhetoric of economics reduces the whole of
knowledge to 'conversation', to an exclusively textual and linguistic
dimension. On this point, we can make out a difference between
McCloskey and Klamer. The former wishes to wake economists up to
the ways in which they actually persuade, and to get them to leave
behind the hampering and damaging 'methodologistic' conceptual
schemes. The latter, on the other hand, aims to 'fill in' the missing links
in economists' texts, to bring out the implicit presuppositions which, in
so far as they are implicit, are assumed but never discussed; the point
of doing this is to bring into the open the things which are too easily
taken for granted. Thus, while McCloskey is at home with the neoclassical orthodoxy and with the traditional economic science whose success he stresses but whose self-image he criticizes, Klamer finds alien
to him the basic assumption of the dominant theory, viz., that we are
living in the best of all possible worlds.

But in each case, the strength of the rhetoric of economics resides in
its attack on every remaining scrap of 'objectivism', and equally, its
weakness is in denying the role of the extra-linguistic aspects in knowledge gathering. These are, so to speak, its ineliminable 'before' and
'after' if knowledge is to be understood as a part of human activity, and
if science is to be seen as an identifiable practice which involves, in
appropriate ways, a stage of experiment or experience. Throwing in a

gesture at ethics is no way to escape from conventionalism and relativism: for who is to decide the 'goodness' of the scientist? Is it not the case, as we may agree with Popper, that the raising of doubts about and criticisms of established knowledge is the objective of self-reflection, whether that self-reflection is to be regarded as 'epistemological' or as 'rhetorical'?

DE GUSTIBUS NON EST DISPUTANDUM?

Despite the interest of the proposal to widen the focus of the human and social sciences, and – why not? – to enrich the store of metaphors and analogies which economists employ in their thinking, something is still awry with the rhetoric of economics. It seems to me that alternative ways of thinking about the matter can emerge from the present discussion of Keynes and especially from the parts which look more closely at features of his use of language. From within this interdisciplinary project, I would like to draw a proposal for further inquiry which I hope is promising.

It is worthwhile beginning with some of the assessments to which Alessandra Marzola has given clear voice. In Keynes, rhetoric and language perform two fundamental tasks. On the one hand, Keynes's political and economic rhetoric brings to light the unconscious side, the hidden presuppositions, of social and economic processes, which find no place in the terms which the 'classical' theory uses. On the other hand, Keynes's language is the site at which unexpected discoveries are made, truths which not even the author had predicted; these discoveries take on an autonomous role in the conduct of knowledge gathering, and remains at least partially latent in the text which produces them. In this way, we are brought to see society's own self-contradictions, its partially false theoretical self-image; the opposition between a surface logic of conventions and a hidden logic of crisis; and the continuing and never-settled struggle to get rid of the old certainties and the 'old habits of thought which ramify into every corner of our minds'.

I would like to take this line of thought a little further by bringing it into contact with my earlier discussion of the rhetoric of economics. That is, I would like to see whether Keynes's case can be read as a different way of dealing with the question of the 'scientificness' of political economy. Keynes's line of thought treats the objective and literary aspects of theory as two complementary aspects which can be brought together only if the scientific endeavour simultaneously demands an attitude at once critical and self-critical. With this end in view, I would like to make a fairly bold suggestion about how Keynes's position can be illuminated by a fresh metaphor: that of psychoanalytic practice. For reasons of space and the limits of my own acquaintance with the relevant literature, I shall refer to only two texts which I have found particularly stimulating. One is an article by Paul Ricoeur, 'Psychoanalysis and Science' which takes up and develops the conclusions of his *Freud and Philosophy: An Essay on Interpretation*. The other is Giovanni Jervis' book *La psicoanalisi come esercizio critico*.

Ricoeur examines three related questions. What are we to make of the notion of 'fact' in psychoanalysis? What is the relation in this discipline which holds between theory and the experience of analysis? What form does the procedure of 'proof' take in this case? In Ricoeur's view, the notion of a psychoanalytic fact must set aside the impossibility of accounting for behaviour independently of the language which 'reports' and describes that behaviour. A psychoanalytic 'fact' is an event which is intrinsically linked to the inter-subjective realm, to the concrete relation with another, with the analyst. Such a 'fact' presupposes a psychic world which is just as real as the material world, although it is frequently in conflict with this latter. And it is capable of being regarded as important only in so far as it has within itself the potential to figure in an alternative account of behaviour, an account which differs from that which was being built up. In this way, the psyche is as much a text to be decoded as a text to be reconstructed. But we should bear in mind that it is a text which can be decoded and reconstructed only because psychoanalytic theory grants to the pre- or extra-linguistic drives the status of a 'mechanism of deformation' which reveals itself under its own colours in the exchange between analyst and analysand. On these grounds, theory and therapy are indistinguishable in the psychoanalytic method. There is already written into the 'practical' relation between the two people involved in an analysis a sort of 'manipulation'. It is on this manipulation that psychoanalytic 'facts' depend, as do claims to truth and the procedures for their verification and falsification. It is not profitable to follow Ricoeur beyond this point. Indeed, I would like to distance myself from the later moves he makes at the end of the paper where he defines truth in psychoanalysis, and relapses into a thoroughly narrative approach. There would be nothing to psychoanalytic truth but the regaining of the ability to 'speak truly' in intersubjective exchanges with the other. Thus, it is identical

with being able to provide an intelligible 'case history' out of fragments which were thrown up one by one and in no order.

Before moving on, it is worth noticing, without pressing the similarity too far, the correspondences between what Ricoeur has to say and
Keynes's method. The notion of inter-subjectivity brings to mind
Keynes's notion of the holistic character of economic knowledge. The
role given to beliefs and expectations correspond, in economics, to the
impossibility of rigidly separating 'subjective' impulses from 'objective' behaviours. Thus, in specifiable circumstances when speculation
is rife, we witness the victory of a hidden reality over the surface
reality. The old theory – the old 'story' – is replaced by a new theory –
new 'story' – which, because it is more general, takes on board what
the old theory had to treat as anomalous. And lastly, the link which
analysis makes between theory and treatment has its most satisfactory
counterpart in Keynes's vision of the inseparability of political economy
from economic policy.

In his most recent book, Jervis explicitly takes stock of the
hermeneutic interpretation of psychoanalysis. Ricoeur is praised for
having stressed the desacralizing character of Freudian theory. This is
the respect in which the theory fosters suspicion both towards interpretation, considered as a restoration of meaning, and towards a self-
deceiving critical understanding, one which is unsuspicious of itself.
However, Jervis rightly makes the point that Ricoeur's argumentation
hangs crucially on purely linguistic considerations. More specifically,
Jervis observes that Ricoeur returns to the idea of a *text* as the privileged reference-point, rather than to that of interpersonal relations; he
therefore improperly underestimates the extralinguistic and paralinguistic
elements in the production of meaning as part of the complexity of
everyday life (cf. Jervis 1989, p. 160). Following Gadamer, Jervis takes
it that 'to understand a text is to grasp the question to which it is an
answer and the answer which it demands' (ibid.)

Lacking Ricoeur's richness and ambiguity, hermeneuticism takes his
rigidly textualist conclusions to their extreme; and, viewed in this way,
it must be straightforwardly forsworn. On the one hand, hermeneuticism
flattens out the business of interpretation because, if it is understood on
the standard hermeneutic model, as the decoding and interpreting of an
ambiguous text, a psychoanalytic investigation can easily boil down to
a simple and relatively banal exploration of obscurities and gaps. This
in contrast with what we find in Freud: the discovery of senses which
had been denied or excluded (cf. Jervis 1989, p. 161). On the other

hand, hermeneuticism favours conventionalism in interpretation, because it turns psychoanalytic interpretation into an interpretative *creation* which therefore produces what has been called an excessive emphasis on the constructive nature of the narrative. And this can lead to our losing sight of the fact that somewhere there exists a reality which is to be 'read' and not only to be 'written' (cf. Jervis 1989, p. 162).

Thus for Jervis, Freud's reference to the drives as the real, extra-linguistic foundation of the subjective world is essential to the psychoanalytic endeavour. Jervis further develops in this direction Ricoeur's most suggestive thought about the drives as lying at the base of deforming mechanisms whose influence is felt *through* the text of the *concrete* analytic dialogue. Despite the weaknesses of the first formulation of the theory of the drives, the critical undertaking of psychoanalysis is nevertheless bound up with the subject matter which that theory is aimed at expressing. That is to say, it seeks to reduce, in a materialistic mode so to speak, mind to matter, and the text to what lies outside the text.

I hope that it is now clear how the foregoing digression can come in useful in thinking about the rhetoric of economics, and about Keynes as a 'case' with respect to the relation between language and theory. It seems to me that what the movement in favour of the rhetoric of economics can be accused of is a rerun of the mistake which hermeneuticism makes. This is the mistake of restricting the focus to wishing to 'restore the integral, unmutilated and unfalsified text' without being able to explain the 'very mechanisms that distort the text' (Ricoeur 1981). Hermeneuticism gives itself the job, which Jervis describes as 'relatively banal', of bringing out and clarifying what is obscure and of exhibiting what is incomplete. At the same time, it declines to offer any reconstruction which *explains* or *overturns* by referring to what is *beyond* and *prior to* subjective consciousness.

As Alessandra Marzola (see Marzola, contribution in this volume, p. 197) reminds us, Keynes engages us in a procedure closely resembling the task from which Hermeneuticism stands aloof. Keynes's texts and lines of argument are typified both by his 'abandonment of our own most outworn conceptual structures' and by his 'plunge into a linguistic and rhetorical realm rich in traumatizing discoveries which are genuine attacks on established systems of thought'. This is a proposal which destabilizes the very self of the author because it aims not so much at 'reaching new goals' as at 'gaining the strength to leave the point of departure, the origin, the safe womb of certitudes'.

By way of conclusion, it seems that we are in a position to float the idea that the power of Keynes's language is an aspect of a project which is at once strongly scientific and strongly political; it is a project which leaves room within a single narrative weave for what is obscure and hidden in reality. In other words, following Jervis, I take it that the core of Keynes's message is the discovery of senses which had been denied or excluded by the neoclassical orthodoxy. The very thing which classical theory had haughtily dismissed – money – comes to occupy centre stage. Money itself is the concrete origin of the 'mechanisms of deformation' which periodically crop up and outstrip economists' story-telling and society's psychology. As a result, investigations into what ought to be the economists' most commonplace topics, accumulation and crisis, have been rendered difficult, if not impossible. Such topics are too easily set aside in normal circumstances in favour of discussions of scarcity, rational choice, reproducibility and balanced growth, which are the tranquillizing language games of the profession.

A new theory, such as Keynes's, can make us aware of what has been left out of economists' story-telling because it submits itself to being put to the test by manipulating reality, thus testing its ability to *transform* the world. It takes up the challenge to make language susceptible to the world 'out there', which is inseparable both from the psychology of agents in the market and from the subjectivity of the economist. Knowledge, rather than being a sort of vision or a sort of talk, is probably most of all a sort of activity in which the communication of one person with another, and the bringing about of practical change can hardly be distinguished. As for Freud, so for Keynes, the project counts far more here than does the form he gave to the theory. In my view, this is an attitude which we would do well to revive today, in the midst of our epistemological crisis, even if Keynes's own formulation of it is less than ideal. Our efforts should be directed more at analytical developments within this method, than at providing a philological reconstruction of Keynes's writings.

At least from the point of view of the rhetoric of economics, it might seem paradoxical that we have been led by an investigation of Keynes, which was of literary inspiration, to a result about knowledge as critique and as transformation. Indeed, what is at issue is a strong claim in favour of a critical science and a radicalized Enlightenment, both positions which today seem definitely unfashionable. It seems to me, however, that such a result might represent a partial but useful beachhead for further research which is prepared to take seriously the limitations of language, without being trapped by them.

NOTE

1. This chapter is a comment on A. Marzola (Chapter 6). It develops a short paper presented to the seminar on Keynes's language and method held at the University of Bergamo, 23 June 1989.

REFERENCES

Jervis, G. (1989) *La psicoanalisi come esercizio critico*, Milan: Garzanti.

Klamer, A. (1987a) 'As if Economists and Their Subjects Were Rational', in Nelson, J., Megill, A. and McCloskey, D. (eds), *The Rhetoric of the Human Sciences*, Madison: Wisconsin University Press.

Klamer, A. (1987b) 'A Rhetorical Interpretation of a Panel Discussion on Keynes', in Samuels, W. (ed.), *Research in the History of Economic Thought and Methodology*, JAI Press.

Klamer, A. (1988a) 'Economics as Discourse', in De Marchi, N. (ed.), *The Popperian Legacy*, Cambridge: Cambridge University Press.

Klamer, A. (1988b) 'Negotiating a New Conversation about Economics' in Klamer, A, McCloskey, D. and Solow, R. (eds) *The Consequences of Economic Rhetoric*, Cambridge: Cambridge University Press.

Klamer, A., McCloskey, D. and Solow, R. (eds) (1988) *The Consequences of Economic Rhetoric*, Cambridge: Cambridge University Press.

McCloskey, D. (1983) 'The Rhetoric of Economics', *Journal of Economic Literature*, June.

McCloskey, D. (1985) *The Rhetoric of Economics*, Madison: University of Wisconsin Press.

McCloskey, D. (1987a) 'Rhetoric', *The New Palgrave*, London: Macmillan.

McCloskey, D. (1987b) 'Towards a Rhetoric of Economics', in Winston, G.C. and Teichgraber, R.F. (eds) *The Boundaries of Economics*, Cambridge: Cambridge University Press.

McCloskey, D. (1988) 'Thick and Thin Methodologies in the History of Economic Thought' in De Marchi, N. (ed.) *The Popperian Legacy*, Cambridge: Cambridge University Press.

McCloskey, D. (1989) 'Formalism in Economics, Rhetorically Speaking', *Ricerche Economiche* (1–2).

McCloskey, D. (1990a) 'Storytelling in Economics', in Lavoie, D.C. (ed.), *Hermeneutics in Economics*, London: Routledge and Kegan Paul.

McCloskey, D. (1990b) 'Why I am no Longer a Positivist', forthcoming.

McCloskey, D. and Megill, A. (1987) 'The Rhetoric of History', in Nelson, J., Megill, A. and McCloskey, D. (eds), *The Rhetoric of the Human Sciences*, Madison: Wisconsin University Press.

Nelson, J., Megill, A. and McCloskey, D. (eds) (1987) *The Rhetoric of the Human Sciences*, Madison: Wisconsin University Press.

Ricoeur, P. (1981) 'The Question of Proof in Freud Psychoanalytic Writing', in *Hermeneutics and the Social Sciences*, Cambridge: Cambridge University Press.

Index

Adorno, T. 94
Against method (Feyerabend) 85
agnosticism 20, 21–2, 24, 29, 30, 52
Agnostic's apology (Stephen) 22, 69
Allocution (Keynes) 146
analogy, use of 27–8, 29, 30, 32, 89,
    195, 200
analytical appproach
    General theory translated into 121
    Keynes and 44–5, 51, 118, 141,
        143, 147, 150, 184–5
    Malthus and 146–7
    recent criticisms of 2, 226–7
    Russell and 38–9
    Wittgenstein and 41, 147
Annan, N. 69
anti-foundationalism 82, 92–3, 95,
    96–7, 115, 125, 227
anti-methodology 86, 88, 94, 114, 121
anti-realism 93
Apostles 7, 19–21, 24, 35, 37, 221
appearance
    and reality 215–17
arts
    Bloomsbury group and 47
Asimakopoulos, A. 150
atomic hypothesis 141, 150, 163,
    164, 184, 189
Austin, J.L. 187
axiom of parallels 141

Baptism 23
Bausor, R. 150
Becker, G.S. 89
beliefs, role of 43–4
Bell, C. 13, 36, 46, 47, 69, 70
Bell, Q. 69
Bellofiore, R. 6, 7, 8, 10, 32, 69, 105,
    144, 188, 193

Berman, M. 96
Bernoulli's principle 141, 147, 149
Beveridge, W. 161–2, 171
Blaug, M. 76, 168
Bloomsbury Group
    Freud and 60–63, 70, 221
    Keynes and 6, 7, 14, 20, 29, 32,
        36–7, 46–8, 194, 221
    political involvement of 70
    studies of 69
Boland, L. 76, 149
Bonadei, R. 6, 7, 145, 150, 194, 221
Brenan, G. 20
Brothwell, J. 150
Brown, N. 221–2
Brown-Collier, E. 150
Bryce, R.B. 176
Buckley, J.K. 68

Caldwell, B. 76
Cambridge
    clubs and societies 19–20, 29, 69
        see also Apostles
    epistemology 33–46, 174
Cambridge economic handbooks 157
Cannon, W.F. 69
Cantor, N.F. 68
capital
    accumulation 10, 202–7
        protestant ethic and 54, 203–6,
            221–2
    aggregate 89
    marginal efficiency of 178, 219
    prospective yield on 119
Capital (Marx) 4–5
Carabelli, A. 5, 6, 8, 24, 38, 69, 76,
    141, 143, 144, 145, 146, 147,
    150, 186–7, 221
Cartesian project 91, 192–3

oxymoron 201, 221

parataxis 204, 222
Parsons, D.W. 146
Patinkin, D. 159, 171, 180, 187, 188
Peirce C.S. 124, 182–3
Perelman, C. 192, 195, 215, 220
permanence, illusion of
   in Europe 199–202
   and psychology of society 202–7
Pesaran, H. 76
Phaedrus 122
Phillips, H. 68
Philosophical investigations
   (Wittgenstein) 44, 45, 67
philosophy
   Cartesian project 91, 192–3
   and causality 41–2, 45
   of language 40, 43
   of science 40, 76, 78, 81, 84, 88,
      91
   Wittgenstein on 40–42, 44, 45, 46,
      67, 115–16
Pigou, A.C. 128, 131, 135, 147, 150,
   169
Pirsig, R.M. 122–4
Platonism 145
Polanyi, K. 89
Popper, K.R. 77, 78, 82, 83–5, 86,
   96, 231
Portrait of the artist as a young man
   (Joyce) 213, 222
positivism 81–2, 84, 86–7, 90, 92,
   227, 228
   see also modernism
Post-Impressionist Exhibition (1910)
   47
post-modernism 92, 93–4, 95
   see also post-positivism
post-positivism 76, 77, 93, 225
   see also post-modernism
*Poverty in plenty: is the economic
   system self-adjusting?* (Keynes)
   101–2, 130, 131, 133
pragmatism 43, 122–4
   in *General theory* 120–21, 122, 123
prices, theory of 171, 219
Prigogine, I. 145

Principa ethica (Moore) 34–7, 46,
   47–8
Principa mathematica (Russell) 34,
   39, 46
Principles of economics (Marshall)
   157, 159, 174
probability
   Bernoulli's principle 141, 147, 149
   Keynes on 25–6, 27, 32, 33, 42,
      55, 69, 109, 110–12, 113,
      119–20, 131, 132–3, 141,
      142, 143, 144–5, 147, 149–50
   Moore on 52, 55
   Wittgenstein on 42, 69, 147
   see also Treatise on probability
      (Keynes)
Problems of philosophy (Russell) 56
proceeds
   term used ambiguously in *General
      theory* 179
propensity to consume 219
propensity to spend 137
Protagoras 124
protestant ethic 54, 203–6, 221–2
psychoanalysis
   and economics of Keynes 7, 10,
      11, 51, 60–68, 70, 71, 232–6
   language used in 62–3
   as a science 64–5, 71
   truth of 125, 232–3
psychology of society 10, 54, 71,
   202–7, 221
public opinion
   Keynes and 24–5, 98–9, 100–101
purchasing power parity theory 148
puritanism
   and protestant ethic 54, 203–6,
      221–2
   rhetoric of 22–3
Putnam, H. 145, 149

quality
   defined 123–4
   principle of 172, 174
quantity
   principle of 173

railways 203, 221

DATE DUE

MAY 1 0 1995			
MAY 0 8 1996			
DEC 2 0 1996			